Oxfordshire

Within Living

Memory

Compiled by the Oxfordshire Federation
of Women's Institutes from notes sent by
Institutes in the County

Published jointly by
Countryside Books, Newbury
and the OFWI, Oxford

First Published 1994
© Oxfordshire Federation of Women's Institutes 1994

COUNTRYSIDE BOOKS
3 Catherine Road
Newbury, Berkshire

ISBN 1 85306 303 7

Cover photograph courtesy
of Bucknell W I

Designed by Mon Mohan
Produced through MRM Associates Ltd, Reading
Printed in England by J.W. Arrowsmith Ltd, Bristol.

Contents

Acknowledgements

Oxfordshire Federation of Women's Institutes would like to thank all WI members who supplied material and photographs for this project through their local Institutes.

Unfortunately we were not able to include extracts from every submission; to do so would have meant considerable duplication of content, and of course we had to take into account the total amount of space available in the book.

But all the contributions, without exception, were of value in deciding the shape and content of the book. We are grateful for them all, especially the beautiful line drawings supplied by Mrs Howard of Wendlebury WI.

Sheila Westall
Co-ordinator

List of Contributing Institutes

Appleton & Besselsleigh, Ardington & Lockinge, Ascott-under-Wychwood, Asthall & Swinbrook, Bampton, Beckley, Begbroke, Benson, Bix & Assendon, Bledington, Blewbury, Bloxham, Bodicote, Brightwell-cum-Sotwell, Brize Norton, Buckland, Bucknell, Burford & Fulbrook, Cassington, Chadlington, Charlton, Cholsey & Moulsford, Cleeve-by-Goring, Cogges, Combe, Cowley, Crowmarsh, Cumnor, Deddington, Didcot Evening, Dorchester, Drayton, Enstone, Eynsham, Farmoor, Filkins & Broughton, Finmere & Mixbury, Finstock, Fitzharry's, Frilford St Peter's, Fritwell, Garsington, Goring, Great Coxwell, Great Rollright, Grove, Grove Morning, Hailey, Hanney, Hardwick & Ducklington, Harpsden, Holton & Waterperry, Horton-cum-Studley, Iffley, Ipsden & North Stoke, Islip, Kennington Link, Kiddington, Kidmore End, Kingham, Kirtlington, Littlemore, Marcham, Marston, Milton-under-Wychwood, Minster Lovell, North Leigh, North Oxford, Old Headington, Otmoor, Peachcroft, Peppard, Salford, Shilton, Shiplake, Shipton-under-Wychwood, Somerton, Sonning Common, South & North Moreton, South Leigh, Spelsbury, Stanton Harcourt, Steeple Aston, Stonesfield, Sunningwell & Bayworth, Sutton Courtenay, Tadmarton, Thame, The Bartons, The Heyfords, Uffington, Baulking & Woolstone, Warborough & Shillingford, Waterstock & Tiddington, Watlington, Wendlebury, Weston-on-the-Green, Wheatley, Wigginton, Witney, Wittenham, Wolvercote, Woodstock, Yarnton.

Foreword

Most people enjoy listening to others reminisce on times past. How much better to have these memories recorded, thus allowing the reader to select short passages at will, or to read the book from beginning to end. As an 'incomer' to the County I have enjoyed sharing the memories of so many WI members; their contributions will allow some readers a glimpse of life in Oxfordshire in times gone by and prompt others to recall memories of their earlier years.

The task of collecting the stories and memories has been willingly undertaken by members from all around our County and we hope that the finished book will give them, and everyone who reads it, much pleasure.

My thanks go to every member who has made this book possible and to Sheila Westall for her 'labour of love' in collating and typing all the entries.

Sheila West - County Chairman

TOWN & COUNTRY LIFE

G.HOWARD

SOME TOWNS AND VILLAGES REMEMBERED

Manually pumped fire engines, errand boys whistling through the streets, the lamplighter at dusk – memories that seem so distant now but which are in fact easily within living memory. Here are just a few reminders of what life was like in Oxfordshire's towns and villages a few decades ago.

KIDDINGTON: ESTATE VILLAGE

'My home was Kiddington – which is much the same size now as it was at Domesday. It is an estate village, with only four "new" houses built since 1856 when the school was built by Harry Lomas Gaskell.

I was born May 1915. My father was stud groom to the Gaskell family who lived at Kiddington Hall.

Also employed at the Hall were a butler, footman, cook, kitchen maid, two housemaids, head gardener and two under gardeners. The whole of the gardens, laid out by "Capability" Brown, were kept in good order by these latter three men, including all mowing by hand mower. The walled kitchen garden had every kind of vegetable and soft fruit including strawberries, raspberries, black, red and white currants. Around the walls were wonderfully flavoured plums, peaches and nectarines. In the greenhouses were a splendid vine, tomatoes and cucumbers. There was a potting shed, tool shed and fruit room, where all the fruit when harvested was laid out on racks and always gave off a wonderful smell. There were also walnuts, filbert nuts and an apple orchard.

Our cottage was joined to the head gardener's and that at one time had been all one house – the Priest House. We had a large "built on" kitchen with shallow stone sink, and a large sitting room with an open fire with ovens on either side which mostly burnt very large logs which my father and I sawed with a cross-cut saw on Saturdays. Two large bedrooms were reached by a very narrow, twisted staircase. Only very small furniture could be taken up there, all the remainder had to be put through the large sash window, by means of ladders and ropes. The only food storage was a very big cupboard under the stairs, in which everything was stored, food on the shelf and pots, pans, jam jars etc on the floor. There were also large cupboards either side of the fireplace and a big walk-in cupboard made when the house was divided. The toilet was at the end of the garden, next to the coal shed and consisted of a long wooden seat with a large and small hole. There was a wired-in run for chickens, and a large garden with a mulberry tree in the middle.

One of the highlights of the year was the Flower Show when the lawn outside our house was covered with the best of our crop of potatoes, onions, carrots and beetroot, awaiting selection of the best six of each. The night before the show, "the committee" erected all the tables for the exhibits and the side shows of hoop-la, fishing for bottles, coconut shies, treasure hunt etc. When all was ready "the committee" gathered in the bothy for a meal of cold ham, beetroot and salad prepared by the head gardener's wife. On the day there was great excitement – and a few complaints – as to who had got the prizes, which were presented by well known local people – friends of the Gaskell family such as Lord Tweedsmuir.

At five years of age I started at the village school, when there was a head teacher, an infants teacher and about 36 pupils. Up to the outbreak of war in 1914 there had always been a headmaster but after he went to war he was replaced by a woman. The teacher lived in the house adjoining the school.

In the village at this time there was a stonemason who kept all the stone walls round the estate in order. He quarried the stones from one of the estate fields, pushed them in a barrow to the wall needing repair and then cut each one to the required size. He also dealt with the estate houses, doing decorating, roofing, cleaning blocked drains and mending leaking roofs. In the evenings after work he taught his daughter and me to play tennis on the Gaskells' tennis courts, which the village tennis club was allowed to rent for one shilling a year. It was a nominal rent so that after a number of years we could not claim the court.

Also in the village, living in The Chequers, an old coaching inn, was the wheelwright who made farm waggons and carts and did agricultural repairs. The wheelwright's shop was made into a very nice village hall, on a lease given by Mr Gaskell, but unfortunately this folded when the estate was sold in 1953. The wheelwright had a son who did carpentry and cabinet making and played the church organ. They also dealt with local funerals. There was a village post office and separate shop with an off-licence.

The village water supply was two taps on the road where all the village people fetched their water in buckets. They also supplied the people living in the council houses built about 1921. A well was sunk

11

for those houses but the water was never fit to drink. The wheel still remains.

Almost everyone in the village was employed in agricultural work on the estate, though an AA man did live in one of the council houses.

At this time we had our own rector who lived in the rectory – we did not share with Glympton and Wootton. All Kiddington Hall staff were expected to go to church morning or evening and children went to Sunday school in the afternooon. Mr Gaskell and his family sat in the "chapel". His family gave the very attractive screen in the church, also some stained glass windows. The gardeners decorated the church for all festivities, Harvest, Christmas, Easter etc. Mrs Gaskell always gave the children a Christmas party, where we took our own mugs and received an orange and some sweets.'

WOODSTOCK

'When there was a fire in Woodstock a bell was rung at the town hall, to call the local firemen who worked in the town. Two of the men would then run or go on their bikes down Oxford Road, to a field where the two horses were kept, catch them, bring them back to the town hall where the wooden fire engine was kept, put the horses in the shafts and then drive the horses to the fire. My brother was one of the firemen.

Many people remember the Welsh miners walking through Woodstock, on their way to lobby MPs at London. They had about one hour's rest sitting on the pavement in High Street, about 200 of them. Mrs Brown, who had a cafe in Oxford Street, gave them tea and sandwiches.

Sir Frank Gray MP also stopped the night in Woodstock workhouse, after he had tramped England, to see how tramps lived. After chopping wood in the morning he walked down Hensington Road, where his car was waiting, to be driven home to Shipton Manor, Shipton on Cherwell, Oxon. A few of us waved to him as he drove off. Afterwards he wrote a book about his travels.

In the school building, classes for the boys and girls were separate, but later the classes were mixed. The girls wore starched white pinafores, trimmed with lace embroidery, and laced black boots.

The Sunday school outings were the highlight of the summer. The children travelled on farm waggons, lined with clean straw, to the grounds of nearby big houses, where they picnicked and played games and had a sing-song on the journey home. Another event took place on the lawn of Fletchers House, where they performed in plays. At night the Guides and Scouts did fancy marching, carrying lighted night-lights in coloured glasses, and made quite a spectacle.

There was a fortnightly market in the street where farm animals and horses were sold. These were then driven down to the station yard to board the train *Fair Rosamund* to Oxford. This train took people to work and school in Oxford doing about five or six trips a day. On its return journey to Woodstock it would carry coal and parcels. The coal would be bagged and sold at two shillings and sixpence a cwt. The big event of the week was the sixpenny return "Woolworths" train on Saturday, taking folk to the shops and the cinema in Oxford. This was much favoured by courting couples. Woodstock also had its own little cinema and shops of every description.

The main occupation for men and women was glovemaking, carried on in several factories, and also "out working". The skins drying in the fields was a well known sight. Gloves made in Woodstock were presented to both Elizabeth I and Elizabeth II when each in turn visited Woodstock.

The curfew bell rang every evening at 8 pm to guide walkers back to Woodstock. This was started when a man was lost in the fog in the park, and was continued until the outbreak of war in 1939. There was also a town crier, wearing a tricorn hat and long black coat. He would ring his bell and announce any public notices and news.'

GROVE

'We came to Grove in 1955, when my husband took over as manager of Grove Bridge Farm, a small farm of 60 acres, which belonged to Mr Hiskins. It was a small dairy farm with a mixed herd of milking cows and some arable. The milk was taken in churns to the dairy just along the road, owned by the Smith family.

When we came to Grove there was only the Main Street leading down to the village, Cane Lane which went over the brook, left from Main Street, and St Ives Road on the right (pre-fabs) from Main Street. Main Street was a gravel road running from Grove Bridge down to the centre of the village, with grass edges – no pavement just the grass worn away where people walked. It was lined with houses, cottages and bungalows, but apart from that and a couple of small farms (Mr Priddles in Cane Lane and Bob Cottrells off Main Street) the rest of Grove was open fields. There were council houses in the village in Oxford Lane.

There were no shops or garage in the village – shopping was done in Wantage apart from a little shop in the Denchworth Road.

In the centre of the village was a large field (owned by Smiths) where an annual show was held, then the field was sold for housing and the show later went to the recreation ground. In 1955 there were still the remains of the old canal at Grove Bridge. The arches could be seen from the farm, under the road, and there were two lots of lock gates still to be seen on the farm. Then the canal (what was left of it) was filled in from Grove Bridge to Gipsy Lane. When we first came there was still water in the canal at Grove Bridge and moorhens lived in the area, also frogs.

The Wantage tramway came in front of the house in the old days, running from Wantage Wharf to the railway station at Grove, and although it had stopped running some time before we came, there were still sleepers outside the front wall.

Mr Bob Cottrell had a few cows which he used to drive up the village towards Wantage to a small field for grazing and also to Palmers Field near Grove Bridge. He would drive them up the Main Street and then up the A338 to this side of Wantage (Chandlers Field) – impossible now.

The Victorian church was still standing when we came to Grove but was unsafe and not used very often for services. Mr and Mrs Bourne were the vicar and his wife then, and they worked very hard to get the new church built. The old school (now gone) was used for meetings.

Charlton-on-Otmoor

A peaceful scene at Charlton-on-Otmoor in the early 1900s.

14

Bread was delivered each day from Wantage, Mr Smith's baker (Mr Dawson who lived in the village) came three days a week and Mr Cane, a baker from Mill Street, came on the other three days. As well as the bakers most of the other shops in Wantage delivered in Grove.

Mr Jack Stevens was still working his mill (near Cane Lane) and using water from the brook as well as electricity, and he regularly ground oats for this farm.

When we came to Grove Bridge, Wantage Road station was still open and we would go from there to London for the occasional "day out". Mr Powell was stationmaster and had a very resplendent uniform! Many people took the train from Wantage Road to Swindon on Saturday for shopping.'

BENSON

'The airfield, for which Benson is probably now best known, was opened in 1937 and has since been enlarged twice. The arrival of the airfield brought in many folk from outside the village and there was some excitement among the ladies of the village at the thought of lots of young men coming!

The old village hall was built in 1923 for the men returned from the war. Concerts and dances were held to raise funds and a loan was taken out. Sadly this hall was demolished five years ago and the land sold to raise money for a larger new hall to cope with a population which had increased from about 1,200 in 1937 to four times that now.

The doctor held an open surgery in a house in Castle Square each morning and he returned in the evening with any medicines which were needed. A Miss Bird, an ex-matron from a London hospital, lived in the village; she owned a car which was rare in those days and she was always taking people with a broken arm or leg to hospital in Oxford.

Before the war there were eleven farms in the village but now only two large farms remain. Every house had a large garden or an allotment and people grew lots of vegetables. They also kept chickens and sometimes pigs. They caught rabbits for the pot! There were two dairies in the village and the milk churns were carried on bicycles round the streets and the milk was ladled into your jug at the door. Fish was sold from a high-sided cart pulled by a pony. There were three grocer's shops, a draper's shop which sold everything, a sweet shop and a fruit shop. The muffin man came with his bell on Saturday afternoons. There was a hairdresser and a shoemender.

15

Paraffin was delivered by horse and cart. There was also a carrier who went daily to Wallingford undertaking all sorts of jobs.

In addition to the Oxford–Reading bus route which is still with us there were four buses from Oxford to Henley, the Black and White coaches from London and Cheltenham and the South Midland coach between London and Oxford – all stopped in the centre of the village. People went to Oxford for big purchases. One villager remembers trips to Reading on the train from Wallingford, having cycled from Benson and left bicycles at Mr Napp's shop by the station. The fare was one shilling after 4 pm and they would do their shopping and then go to St Mary's Butts and have fish and chips for one shilling and arrive back at Wallingford about 8.30 in the evening.

Coal was brought in barges pulled by horses along the towpath to the coal yard by the river where the Cruiser station now is. The old ferry stopped in the First World War and the lock ferry operated after that.

Most children in the village went to Benson C of E school in Oxford Road. From age four to 14 each class had two standards and one teacher taught both in all subjects. Older pupils were taken in Mr Aldridge's bus to Dorchester for cookery and woodwork lessons. They all learned to swim in the river in summer. The boys also learned gardening.

Most people went to a place of worship and there was a chapel and a mission hall in the village in addition to the Free church and St Helen's.

There were eight pubs, but now only four. Everyone walked a lot. There was a lovely walk to Ewelme to buy a fourpenny bunch of watercress – the beds have now gone. Small, very pretty cottages and tall trees where the rooks nested along that road were pulled down for the airfield. There were meadows of kingcups and cowslips down towards the river and walks to Ewelme down to see the Hunt leave. Much merriment was had at the river in summer where all the village congregated. On Sundays the band played near the boathouse. In winter there was skating when the river and fields froze over. There were marvellous concerts in the village and several carnivals each year.'

HOLIDAYS IN THE 1930s

'I have lived in Oxfordshire since 1938, but before then I have memories of holidays spent in Oxford with relatives.

I cycled there one year with my father from Northamptonshire, and another time the whole family walked there, spending a night at Banbury on the way. I remember trudging up the long hill out of

16

Banbury, then turning into the meadows and following the towpath by the canal. It was one of our really hot summers, there were wild flowers everywhere. Occasionally we saw a barge with the horse plodding patiently along, and it was a great thrill to help open the lock gates.

My aunt and uncle lived in Hayfield Road, and we used to watch the barges unloading at the coal wharf there. We went for long walks across Port Meadow, up to Jarn Mound, to Shotover – quite a lovely road then with only a few buildings – and by Mesopotamia near Magdalen College. We toured the colleges, the Radcliffe Camera, the museums, and were deafened by Old Tom striking the hour just as we were in the tower at Christ Church.

Dad was born in Kidlington and told us how he used to drive the sheep and cattle to Oxford market. At one time they lived at the mill, and the children had to be lifted on to the table because of floods.

Springtime in Oxfordshire to me means primroses, anemones and bluebells in the woods. In the meadows by the river there are cowslips, lady's smocks and fritillaries. Then comes May morning, the crowds gather on Magdalen Bridge and in punts on the river. After I was married we came to the May morning celebrations several times. Six o'clock boomed out by the church bells, a sudden hush, then the clear sound of the choristers singing the May morning hymn, rising, falling, as the wayward breeze carried the sound over the crowds below.

It was a moment of magic I shall always remember. We had left home early that morning, furnished with flasks of coffee and sandwiches ready for a later breakfast. Driving towards Oxford, the mist was rising over the fresh green hedgerows promising a warm day. The birds were singing and we felt a tingle of excitement.

We seemed to be the only ones about and agreed we must be mad to have left our warm beds so early, but as we parked the car, people appeared, all approaching Magdalen Bridge. We put on our straw hats, relics of seaside trips, and now decorated with fresh spring flowers, and joined the crowds. On the river below were punts filled with picnickers dressed in jeans, shorts, and others in full evening dress who had spent the previous night on the river.

The white-robed choristers disappeared from the tower above, as with accordion, pipe and tabor the musicians led the Morris dancers up the High. One, two, three, hop, one, two, three, hop we all followed on across the road, factory workers, shop assistants, undergrads, and young and old. Behind us the traffic began to move again to resume the business of the day. We branched off, some along Longwall Street, some by the Radcliffe Camera towards the Bodleian Library. There the Morris teams danced in turn all the old favourites,

17

with bells jingling and handkerchiefs waving. Jack o' the Green, the fool with his bladder, and another carrying the cake on his sword, pranced among the crowds. The old heads on the Sheldonian Theatre railings stared in stony silence.

Then it was time to leave and return to the work-a-day world. Years ago lads and lassies would have made their way to the meadows and woods to pick bluebells and cowslips and spend the day enjoying the countryside. In the villages round about the May Queens would be holding court, children would parade with their garlands, and dance round the maypole. Some village schools have revived the old customs, and children are taught the art of plaiting the gay ribbons round the high pole.

Continuing our holidays, I can recall watching Eights Weeks on the river, and the parties on the College house boats. There was a little grocer's shop in Walton Street where they sold a special rich fruit slab cake, only made for Eights Week – I think it was called Togger cake.

When I first lived in Tiddington during the war we used to help on the farm during harvest time, stooking the corn. We picnicked in the fields and swam in the river, and watched my friend and his father cutting rushes, which they used to dry before sewing them up into mats and shopping baskets. Then came blackberry time and our precious sugar was used to make jam and crab apple jelly. Later it grew colder and we would wheel our prams round the hedges to collect wood to supplement the coal ration, with the older children helping with their loads.'

WATERSTOCK & TIDDINGTON

'Most Waterstock and Tiddington villagers lived in cottages before the war, with open fires for all heating, cooking and washing purposes. At one cottage, the fire wouldn't draw unless the man of the house climbed on to the roof once a week to push brushes down the chimney to clear it. Toilet facilities were basic, for instance a bucket in the garden shed which was emptied once a week during the night. Some were even double seaters, which led to disaster if a child tried to use the adult one and fell in!

Usually a tin bath hung on the wall outside, to be filled in front of the fire for baths once a week. Water was either pulled up from a well by buckets or was pumped; sometimes more than water came up in the bucket. There were no refrigerators to keep food fresh. Meat was kept in a safe with perforated sides to let air circulate. In most cases the children slept all together in one bedroom.

When electric light was finally brought in, one old lady was discovered sitting with her hat on; she was afraid of getting sunstroke from the bright light. One farmer bitterly opposed the proposal for electricity in the school, he said paraffin lamps had been good enough for him!

Most of the men worked on local farms until just before the Second World War, and girls went into domestic service, but as the car factories at Cowley were developed, so the trek to the towns started. Milk was taken to the station at Tiddington in churns, and cattle were driven to the market at Thame. There was a blacksmith's forge at Tiddington.

Most Waterstock villagers worked for Squire Ashhurst, lived in his cottages and were ruled by him. Church attendance was compulsory. When a doctor was needed, someone had to walk across the fields to Wheatley to summon him. The squire was succeeded by Miss Ashhurst, and then by his nephew. After the war, the house was sold and eventually pulled down. The estate was developed as riding stables where several top show jumpers have been trained.

When war broke out evacuees were billeted in both villages and some cottages were commandeered. Some evacuees stayed and spent the rest of their lives in the villages.

Food rationing was introduced. In some ways it was easier in the country with home-grown vegetables and fruit, supplemented by such things as wild mushrooms, crab apples, blackberries, with rabbits and poultry for extra meat. On the other hand, any special extras in short supply were snapped up in the towns, where women could get to the shops quickly to queue up.

The car factories were changed to producing munitions, aeroplanes and other military items to build up the stocks lost at Dunkirk, so more manpower was diverted from the farms to the towns, in spite of the necessity to produce more food.

The Home Guard was formed, fire-watching rotas arranged and air raid wardens appointed. One local warden cycled round the village to raise the alarm, only to be met by his wife on foot when the all clear was sounded.

Dances were held in the village school, and sometimes in the schoolroom at Tiddington House to raise funds for Wings for Victory. Prizes were usually in the form of savings stamps and certificates.

Till well after the war a butcher from the next town delivered meat by pony and trap. Greengrocers and bakers made their rounds, milk came from the local farm, all sorts of commodities like coal, paraffin and kitchen utensils were brought round, so there was no need to visit the town except for such things as clothing. There was a village shop and post office at Tiddington which sold everything

19

from aspirins to elastic, and cheese to paraffin. Waterstock had a post office and shop with a smaller range of goods.

There was a primary school in each village, after which the children attended schools in Great Milton or Haseley, unless they won scholarships to grammar schools.

The school at Tiddington was governed by the Church of England, so had regular visits by the rector, and on special days like Ascension the pupils walked up to Albury church. At the Candlemas service they all held lighted candles, not very steadily, to the dismay of the mothers who accompanied them.

During Advent the Sunday school children helped the rector to construct a crib in the church, and afterwards he let one child drive the car back to Tiddington. He obviously had a special guardian angel watching over him, because one very bad foggy night he got lost, and was discovered in the middle of the road sitting in his car reading his prayer-book and waiting for someone to rescue him.

During the weeks before Christmas the children were led round the village singing carols. At the big houses like Major Case's and the rectory, they were regaled with lemonade and mince pies, with sherry for the adults. On Christmas Eve they finished in the Fox Inn, and on Boxing Day the Headington Quarry men performed their Mummers play at The Fox with St George, the Turk and the Doctor.

On Good Fridays it was the custom to pick primroses in Fernhill Wood to decorate the church for Easter. On Bonfire Night a bonfire was built on the village green, which now has a slip road across it, and singing and dancing was accompanied by an accordion player.

For a time whist drives, wedding breakfasts and other social events were held in the Cadet hut behind The Fox. There has always been a thriving cricket team at Tiddington, using a lovely field behind the railway line, and of course darts and dominoes were played in The Fox.

When the villagers decided they needed a proper village hall, funds were raised and it was built by voluntary labour in time for the Coronation in 1953.

Ickford village challenged Tiddington to a tug-of-war across the river Thame, as that was the county boundary between Buckinghamshire and Oxfordshire. Tea was being prepared in the hall when the victorious team of stalwarts from Waterstock and Tiddington drove up noisily. They were very wet (inside and out!) not because they had lost but because they had joined the losers in the river afterwards. This event has been held annually ever since.

The Coronation celebrations finished with fireworks in the playing field, viewed from the hall windows because of the rain, but enjoyed none the less.'

WENDLEBURY

'Wendlebury was in the news when flooding occurred as a result of heavy rain which caused the brook to rise and flood the road, the pub and some houses. During the war, due to the lack of manpower, the brook was never cleaned out and so all sorts of rubbish collected – villagers' rubbish and also weeds and reeds. The water level rose from a few inches to several feet and there was often flooding in the village. I can remember water running down Church Lane and people living in the cottages at the bottom used to open their back doors and their front doors to let the water run through.

The brook has always featured largely in the village and there used to be a saying, "You weren't a Wendlebury person until you had fallen in the brook!" Most of the time it was children paddling in the brook and over they would go, but my experience was different. In my childhood they used to use a barge to clean out the brook and at nights and at weekends they would moor it up somewhere. Well of course, the youngsters of the village would play around with the barge and pole (it was a bit like a punt) and what did I do – I pushed myself off the barge and straight into the water!

The village school closed about 1959. It never had any proper toilets, only buckets outside, and George was the person who had the unpleasant task of emptying the buckets. They used to send one of the children down to put a note through his door and he would go up and empty the buckets.

In those days, of course, there was very little transport. Most people had bicycles and the men would cycle to work on the farms and buildings, but if the women needed to go shopping they had to walk to Bicester. You would often see them with a pram and young children walking to Bicester and then walking home again later in the day.

My father was a farmer and in the late 1940s a law came in that all the dairy cattle had got to drink proper mains water. We had a well on our land and someone from the Ministry of Agriculture came and tested the water. He came back with the sample a few weeks later and said the water wasn't fit for the cattle to drink, but we as a family were allowed to drink it, so my father had to pipe the mains water into the fields for the cattle. He was a struggling farmer and always short of land and come the spring and summer time when he was keeping some of his fields shut up to make hay for the winter, we used to turn the cattle out on the side of the Bicester–Oxford road.

21

White Road, Woodcote in the early 1930s when roads were playgrounds for the children and a car was a rare sight.

We used to go up there from six o'clock to eight o'clock every night to graze the cattle, and that was worth an extra two or three fields to my father that he would have otherwise not been able to use for hay. That was every night, seven days a week, regular as clockwork.

In the days before there was a parish council the Brigadier at the manor house was looked upon as the "squire" of the village. For example, he used to go up to the school two or three times a year. He would sit there and have a talk to the teacher and want to know how everyone was getting on. If there were any fêtes in the village they would be held at the back of the manor house, and if there were any village meetings the Brigadier would act as chairman. He would always help and encourage the villagers and they looked upon him as a leader.

I remember the days when the wife of one of the farmers had a dairy at one end of their house and she would do the churning and at about five o'clock every evening all the villagers would come and get their milk and she would ladle it out to them into a jug. A baker who had a bakehouse in Bicester used to come to Wendlebury after he had closed his shop in the evenings and sometimes it was as late as nine o'clock when he was delivering bread to the villages round about.

Many of the people in the village had a pigsty and they used to keep two pigs, one to kill at Christmas and the other to sell to pay the cost of the first one. People used to live quite well in those days – they didn't have the entertainment that we have nowadays but they grew their own food and had plenty to eat, and there was plenty of wood to supplement the coal so they could keep warm.

When we were children the schoolmistress used to take us out for a picnic on a nice day and we went to the field on the Bicester road which is on a Roman site and would collect quite sizeable amounts of Roman pottery, some of them quite big, and put them up in the school. We also used to find old coins. The village had a whist drive to raise money to buy a radio for the school so that they could listen to schools programmes. One day the teacher couldn't understand why all she was getting was music on the radio and then the lady who helped with the school dinners came in and said wasn't it sad – the King had died. That was how we learned the news and that was obviously why there was just music on the radio.

Of course there was a big celebration in 1953 for the Coronation. We cleaned up one of the farmer's barns and had a big party with fancy dress and dancing and a marvellous meal for all the village. There was so much food and drink left over that we had to have another go the next day to finish it all off! It was such a success that it was turned into like a feast day and celebrated for about 15 years after the Coronation.'

SOUTH LEIGH PUBS

'The Mason Arms was a meeting place for the men of the village. For 45 years it was run as a small farm and pub by Albert Hopkins, who took it over from his uncle. Villagers were able to buy their milk there as well as their beer.

Dylan Thomas lived in South Leigh from 1947 to 1948 and was a regular at the pub. He would have found it a very traditional pub with beer brought up in large jugs from the barrels in the cellar. He is remembered walking back home to the manor house, bottles clanking in his bag, and occasionally he would need a helping hand out of the ditch!

One lady, now in her sixties, remembers her mother telling her about the other pub in the village – The Sibthorpe Arms, where the men would gather to sit and eat their lunch on a bench outside and enjoy a pint. An elderly neighbour would frequently push her there in her pram, promising to bring her mother back a bottle of stout. (You had to take your own bottle or jug for beer or stout.) She would sit there enjoying her stout and chat with the men so long that she frequently had great difficulty in negotiating the stile over which she had to get herself, pram, baby and stout, to reach their homes.

South Leigh is remembered by the older villagers as a place of quiet country lanes with large elm trees everywhere and wide grass verges – the lanes so quiet, the verges so wide that Harry Moody would turn his cows out to graze freely on them after milking. Many of the fields were kept for pasture and grew wonderful mushrooms, and there were wild flowers everywhere – carpets of primroses, wild violets and daffodils, wood anemones and bluebells. Armfuls of wild daffodils could be picked to decorate the church at Easter.'

HENLEY

'I have very happy childhood memories of walking down Friday Street in Henley to the riverside where my father kept his punt moored to go fishing. We had a very long rake and rye peck which were tied to the side of the boat and we carried two weights for anchorage. We sat in the punt just below Marsh lock above the first island. The weights were lowered to the river bed and the rye peck put into it also to keep the punt steady. The rake was used backwards and forwards on the river bed to clear the ground so that gudgeon would come there which we caught for bait to catch pike.

The river was a very leisurely place in those days. The beautifully varnished boats belonging to Mr Jack Arlett were a picture in themselves. He was a boat proprietor and took a great pride in all of his boats.

My father used to talk about the baker's shop where Foster's Menswear is and how a cow saw its reflection in the plate glass and crashed into it. The owner Mr Webb made good advertisement out of it, saying that the cow did this because of seeing his delicious cream cakes. WH Smith had their shop on this same corner before they moved to Bell Street and in those days they had a lending library as well as selling many other items. Boots on the opposite corner also had a library besides being a chemist. The British Restaurant further along sold reasonably priced hot meals and soup on the ground floor and a selection of salads on the next floor.

The cattle market where they also sold day-old chicks etc was right next door to the GWR, along with Dees auction rooms which made it a very busy area on market days.

Mr Philip Pearce who was a dental surgeon told me that he and Mr Anchor Simmons were the first two people in Henley to own and drive a car. Certainly in those days Henley must have been a very different place. He also had a generator in the cellar for supplying electric to his household.'

FIRE!

'Long Wittenham had its own fire engine. At first this was kept in the church under the auspices of the churchwardens, then it had a shed of its own by the cross. The small building is still there.

It was manually operated. The ladies used to make a chain of buckets – they were leather buckets with "LW" on for Long Wittenham – and pass them down to the river empty. The men would pass them back up again full and the water was tipped into the sides of the fire engine, which was then pump-operated.'

'At our farm at Chadlington in 1931, the Dutch barn caught fire while they were threshing; it was thought a spark from the steam traction engine used to run the drum caused it. Chipping Norton was one of a number of fire engines which attended. It was a steam engine on wooden wheels (this was the last time it was used). Due to lack of water they had to lay hoses down to the brook, three quarters of a mile, but the hoses were not standard size which caused a problem. Charlbury fire engine (petrol driven) ran continuously for four days and nights pumping water up to the farm. Due to the combined efforts of all these fire brigades (all volunteers) the nearby houses and farm buildings were saved. My mother supplied meals for the firemen and her beefsteak and kidney puddings were much appreciated. The fire insurance company paid the various fire brigades to attend.'

'Islip had a manual fire engine dating back before 1920. It had wooden wheels with iron rims and was pulled by the firemen themselves. It had two handles either side which worked a pump. This went up and down and ejected water. The faster the men worked the stronger the jet. The fire station was very small and situated behind The Walk opposite River View, where at that time Mr Forest, the Chief Fireman lived. The old fire engine remained redundant for years and as far as is known it was kept in the fire station and then taken to Bicester when the shed was demolished. A Morris Commercial lorry and a Dennis petrol trailer pump was supplied in its place at the beginning of the Second World War.

Part time volunteers were then on duty two at a time during the night, using a room at the Manor Farm. Some Sundays they went on parade either at Bicester or Kidlington and practised releasing the pumps. When the war was over they each received a certificate of service.'

LIFE IN ABINGDON

'Abingdon has been a well known market town for many years: the cattle market stood where the Precinct now stands, tucked away behind the fire station and Corn Exchange. Farmers gathered with their cattle and livestock: they travelled many a mile to be there on a Monday. The only day the market didn't take place was Michaelmas Fair Monday. It was eventually moved to where the very new council offices now stand. The animals were auctioned: we would stand and listen to the auctioneers for a great length of time, fascinated by the quick banter.

The church hall was also demolished to make way for the council offices: it is sadly missed. The quaint little building was the home of WI markets, church youth clubs, blood donor clinics and many a church social evening. It had a stage which accommodated many a show.

Still in the same region of the town we had the railway station. My uncle was a GWR employee. In his time he looked after the horses that pulled the waggons that made the deliveries around the town. He remembers it vividly with great affection. In the school holidays we spent many an hour travelling to and from Abingdon and Radley on the "Abingdon Bunk". My husband didn't ride in the carriages if the right engine driver was on duty. He was in the cab stoking the engine and blowing the whistle! The MG cars were transported to all over the world from our little station.

In the late 1950s the Town Hall was renovated, and reopened by the Queen. The whole town came to a standstill. We lined the streets with our Union Jacks in our hands and waved at her passing. Bun Throwing is a very old Abingdon tradition and only takes place on rare occasions; in the evening of the day of the visit, this old ritual took place in her honour.

Sadly, there are not many of the original shops left now. How lovely it was to walk past grocer's shops and have the smell of sliced bacon or ground coffee wafting through the door. My favourite shop was the leather shop which stood on the corner of Bath Street and Broad Street. Anything made of leather could be bought there and anything made of leather could be mended there: the smell of leather filled the air.

My school was in Conduit Road, which I walked and later cycled to. My very first classroom was in the Trinity church room, and we walked across the road to the playground. School dinners arrived in large metal containers which were delivered from the only school kitchen in Abingdon. Here all the school dinners for Abingdon and the surrounding areas were cooked and distributed. For our games and swimming lessons we had to walk to the Abbey open air swimming pool and our sports ground was in Caldecott Road where two schools now stand. By the time we had walked there and walked back we didn't have much time for the lessons: always seemed a waste of time to me!

We, of course, had no telephone: people like us didn't have phones, that sort of thing was for the rich! When my Granny died, the local policeman knocked on the front door to inform my mother of her death. Gran lived in Stoke Row and the village policeman rang Abingdon police station to pass the message on: it was the only way in an emergency.

My parents kept chickens as most people did. Nothing was wasted: potato peelings were boiled and given to the chickens as feed, we had their eggs for tea, and when the hens were passed laying chicken was on the plate for dinner! We thought nothing of the pungent smell of a chicken being plucked or gutted on the kitchen table: it was our Sunday dinner being prepared. Veg from the allotment, chicken from the run, apples in the pie from the tree, or gooseberries and blackcurrants from the bushes at the bottom of the garden (just for a change). If they were not all needed they would be bottled and stand in the pantry until they were. One regular visitor to our road was the rag and bone man; this is where a lot of the chickens would come from. Old rags would be saved in exchange for chicks, and they would be kept in the hearth to keep warm until they were strong enough to live outside in the run.

We had many events to look forward to. One was the annual fête at Caldecott House, then Dr Barnado's Home. We always went along to help out with the Girl Guides to run a stall. Another was Beating the Bounds with the church youth club. Every Christmas we took part in a Nativity play at church: we practised hard, dressed in our angels' costume of white, gold and silver, and sang to our hearts' content. The year I enjoyed most was when the Co-op butcher let me take his model lamb from the window to place near the manger: I looked on with pride!

Michaelmas Fair was a big event for the town; still is in many ways. We always had two days off school: the roads were too busy for schoolchildren who attended school around the area. Fair rides were cheaper in the morning, only a penny on the helter skelter. The big horses didn't "go" until the afternoon but we always finished off the morning with two penn'orth of chips.

At dusk, a regular visitor was the man from the council on his bike with a ladder over his shoulder, keeping the gas lamps on the road alight.

Our back door was never locked, and our washing very rarely got wet: there were always willing hands to fetch it in if we were out.'

GROWING UP IN WANTAGE

'Wantage in the 1920s and early 1930s was a small market town governed by an Urban District Council and Berkshire County Council. The population probably numbered between 3,000 and 4,000. The UDC consisted of a mixture of tradespeople, the local mill owner, school teachers and retired professional men. They were all independent non-political men and women, unpaid for council meetings and all worked for the good of the town.

The majority of the population were "working class" but wages were very low and there was a lot of poverty, although the cost of living was relatively cheap.

There was a good selection of shops with about seven butchers, two saddlers, five drapers, three fresh fish shops, five grocers, four greengrocers, four bakers (cakes and bread baked on the premises), two ironmongers, two chemists, five shoe shops, three hairdressers, and numerous sweet shops, three china shops etc. Quite a few delivered the goods bought, especially the food shops and I remember the butcher's "boy" calling at our house in the morning for any orders which he would deliver the same morning. Most of the shops had blinds in the windows and they would always be drawn all day on Sundays.

If any of the tradespeople died, a flat board, the depth of the shop window and about a foot wide, painted black, would be nailed up outside the shop. On the day of the funeral the neighbouring shop blinds would be drawn in sympathy. In fact, when there was any funeral in the town neighbours in the same street would also draw their curtains or blinds as a mark of respect until the funeral was over.

There was no library in the town until about 1930 when the new council school was built and Berkshire County Library used a small room in the school as a branch library on just one day a week.

There was no resident dentist in the town but a dentist came one day a week and rented a room over a hairdresser's shop in the Market Place and I remember running there after school (when aged six or seven) to have two first teeth removed each week for about a month. Eventually, about 1930 a full time dentist opened a surgery in the Market Place over Lloyds Bank.

There were two doctors' surgeries in the town. The old cottage hospital was used until the present one was built by voluntary subscriptions and opened in 1927. There was one "Queens" district nurse in the town and some people having babies would employ a private nurse "living in" for about a month, if they could afford it.

Almost all the tradespeople lived over their shops and as it was a close knit community we knew everybody. All the children over the shops had parties in each other's homes and often used their shops and showrooms, when convenient, for party games such as Murder, and musical games like "My Friends Seat", "Musical Bumps" or "Simon Says".

All children played games on the pavements – we bowled hoops, skipped, whipped our tops and played hopscotch; later on we had roller skates. My parents once caught me playing marbles in the gutter outside our shop and I was promptly warned never to do it again. It was not ladylike!

There were very few cars in those days and we cycled or walked everywhere. We walked miles along the old canal paths, up to the Downs on the Hungerford Road and back down the Newbury Road. We walked to Lockinge House where they had an August Bank Holiday fête and walked home again. We walked up to the monument erected in memory of Lord Wantage, up on the Ridgeway and sometimes had birthday parties up there. The weather always seemed fine in those summers. Sometimes parents would accompany us but we could roam about the countryside quite safely in those days.

We were brought up in the Methodist church. Our father took us to the morning service and we also went to the Sunday school in the afternoon. We all enjoyed the annual Sunday school outing to White Horse Hill in the summer. We were taken by an ancient bus via Letcombe Bassett where Letcombe Sunday school scholars joined us. On the steepish hill out of Letcombe we had to get out and walk up the hill as the bus could only get up empty! On the top of White Horse Hill we played games and tobogganed down the sides of the "moat", walked to the eye of the White Horse and "wished", then later walked down through the woods to Britchcombe Farm for a good tea and afterwards the teachers would throw lots of sweets in the air for the children to scramble and catch or pick up as many as they could. As some of them came from very poor homes they loved it and almost fought for the sweets.

My father and his brother were partners in a draper's shop in Wantage, just a short walk from the Market Place. They came here from North Wales and Liverpool shortly before the Great War started in 1914. I was born in 1916 and both brothers were called up into the Army and RFC for the remainder of the war. A manageress looked after the shop with the assistants and my mother helped from time to time. I have been told that as a toddler I was tied by a piece of string to the shop door so that I could not run off into the road! When I was six the grocer next door offered his premises – house and shop – for sale to us as he was bankrupt. The brothers bought the property and my uncle stayed in the flat over one end of the shop and we moved to the house the other end. We had three ground floor rooms at the side of the shop and four bedrooms and attics at the side and over the shop. There was no bathroom, no electricity, no hot water system and the only toilet was in a brick building outside near the back door. There was a deal box seat with one large and one small hole which opened directly down to the open sewer which ran under the lane at the side of the house. There were quite a few outhouses at the back of the house. One was the brewhouse with two coppers, old stone sink and flagged floor, where beer had been made. Apparently most households made their own beer in the last century. There were sheds with raised brick "beds" and drains where pigs had been killed and salted.

Behind the shop was a cobbled yard, stable and slaughterhouse belonging to one of the local butchers. The horse and trap used for deliveries were kept there and cattle, pigs and sheep were killed in the slaughterhouse. An old drover called Mooney Joe would drive six to ten cattle there, leave one or two or however many needed for slaughter and drive the remainder either to another slaughterhouse or back to their field. Huge blocks of ice used to be delivered there in hot weather to keep the meat cool. The blocks were cut by band-saw in sizes to fit the butcher's refrigerator.

Along the side of our house and garden wall ran the old Rope Walk which divided our property from the neighbours. There had been rope works there in the 19th century and numbers were incised in some of our bricks where they measured the ropes.

There were no milk bottles until about 1930 I think, and milk was delivered by horse and milk float. The milk in a large churn was measured out into our own jug. There was also a dairy shop fairly near where we took our jug to be filled when necessary. Bread also was delivered daily by horse and van. Opposite our shop and house were four cottages and when the horse left anything on the road the people opposite rushed out with their buckets and spades for the good of their gardens!

There was a cinema near us – rather a basic building, an old barn probably. Programmes were changed on Mondays and Thursdays – closed on Sundays of course. It was very popular and some people were regulars. I remember seeing the old silent films, serials which left Pearl White tied to railway lines in front of an oncoming train, until the following week. Meanwhile a local man played the piano with appropriate music for each film.

If we wanted to go to Oxford we caught the famous Wantage Tram from the town to the station (Wantage Road) two and a half miles away, train to Didcot and change there for Oxford. The passenger tram stopped running about 1926 but the goods carried on until the war.

The fire brigade was run by volunteers – mostly self-employed men as they were available to attend fires when needed. My father was a volunteer until after the war. I cannot remember how they were called out in the early days but about 1930, when we had electricity connected to our house, a private system of bells was installed in each fireman's house. All the fire practices and maintenance work was unpaid but I think they were paid ten shillings for "turning out" and five shillings an hour while actually attending a fire.

Most people joined the "Radcliffe Scheme" at twopence per person per week so that we would be given treatment or taken as patients at the Radcliffe Infirmary. If anyone had scarlet fever or diphtheria they were taken to Abingdon Fever Hospital.'

CHURCH AND CHAPEL

At the heart of the community was the church and the chapel, in the days when many families attended services twice or even three times on a Sunday. For children, Sunday school was part of life – and the annual outing was eagerly anticipated when treats were few and far between.

WE ALL WENT TO CHURCH

'As a child in the 1930s at Kingham, Harvest Festival (or Thanksgiving) seemed the most important time. We had a service on the Friday evening before the Sunday of the festival. The church was always well filled; all the farming families came. Sheaves of corn were in the porch and huge marrows that had been specially nurtured were a feature. Flowers and produce were everywhere.

Sunday school was at 2.15 pm every week. We sang hymns from the *Golden Bells* hymn book and choruses such as *Will your anchor hold in the storms of life?* and *Build on the Rock*.

We had no outings from Sunday school but there was a Christmas party in the village hall. The teachers had their tea first and then waited on the children. We played games – musical chairs, twos and threes, oranges and lemons. We always had a "potato" race using small blocks of wood provided by a local engineering firm. Five or six children would compete at a time. Each stood by a box at the head of a line of "potatoes" spaced down the hall and the object was to see who could collect all their potatoes the quickest by picking them up one at a time and returning them to the box. There was great excitement as we urged on our favourite runner and shouted to "go for the farthest first."

Each child received a bag of sweets and an orange to take home. Some of the older boys were crafty and went back into the hall by another door and joined the queue again to get a further supply but the teachers always spotted them.

All women and girls wore hats to church. We had our own hymn and prayer books. None were provided in our church until the late 1930s, which was hardly encouraging to people unused to the service. People expected to sit in the same seat each week and did not take kindly to finding it occupied by an unsuspecting visitor.'

'Our village church was well attended and nearly all had their places, families sitting together. The organist would play for the choir to move forward to take their seats at the top. Their surplices, so white, shone in the sunlight as they stood singing the usual three hymns set out for that particular Sunday. The choir assembled in their special pews were a delight to listen to. The churchwarden in those days, I remember, always said "Amen" a long while after the rest of the congregation and very often slept during the vicar's address from the pulpit.'

SPECIAL DAYS

'The church at Waterperry is very old with high boxed pews and, until things became more up-to-date, each pew had a lighted candle just above the book rest. Only tall people could be seen over the pew! Miss Henley played the small organ for the services.

We children went to Sunday school, then on to church, home for dinner – then I was given a penny for pocket money – and went again to afternoon service. Usually only a very short service, owing to only having candlelight.

Good Friday was a very special day. After morning service we were given baskets and made our way to Waterperry Woods, about a mile away, to pick primroses for the decorating of the church ready for Easter Sunday. We took sandwiches, and near the wood we were met by the wood keeper and taken to where the flowers were largest. We worked in pairs – two to pick and two to bunch. I remember this as a very special day.

Whit Sunday was special too, as we always had a new frock and a new hat trimmed with a band of poppies.'

A TIGHT VILLAGE

'When I came to Wigginton in 1958 most people had been born within a few miles of it and I was only the third "outsider" to move in. It was a tight village, never having had a squire or lord of the manor in the village; there was a wonderful feel of one community with the old rector at the head (regardless of whether folk were church-going or not). He served the parish for 50 years and was greatly respected and loved. He always wore his black suit and clerical hat – even when riding his motorbike, which was his favourite form of transport!'

THE CENTRE OF THE VILLAGE

'The church was the centre of the village at Finmere. A group of men loved to ring the bells and kept the churchyard tidy. In 1935 the curfew bell was still being rung daily at eight o'clock.'

THE RECTOR'S FAMILY

'My father was rector of Peppard and I was two years old in 1916 when, quite unexpectedly, twin boys were born to my parents. Although they were christened Cyril and Basil they were always called Tweedledum and Tweedledee (Dum and Dee for short) in the family. My sister was born two years later in 1918. Sadly, one of the twins died at the age of four in 1920 and near to the rectory garden wall is a small tombstone with the name "Dum" on it.

I used to pump the old organ to enable my mother, who was organist, to play for church services. I'm afraid I was not always as attentive as I should have been and often allowed the lead weight to fall below the minimum required, and it ran out of puff and all sound ceased. My Sunday dinner suffered accordingly!

On Christmas Day 1921 my father sang "Hither page and stand by me" and I obediently left my place in the choir to sing the answering lines. I liked helping round the church, especially being allowed to help ring the bells. I remember getting a clip round the ear on one occasion for running round the base of the new war memorial just before it was dedicated.'

33

EVERY SUNDAY

'My family were strict Baptists. Each Sunday the whole family took a waggonette to the Baptist chapel (now converted to a house) in Alvescot. We went for the whole day, taking our food with us.'

SEGREGATED!

'The church of St Barnabas at Studley was well attended in the days when we had four services every Sunday. Certain seats in the church were allotted to certain households. For instance, the Studley Priory seat next to the war memorial; the vicarage seat was opposite, and behind them came seats for Manor Farm, Studley Farm, West Hill and Ventfield Farms. If you did not live in one of these houses, you were afforded a greater degree of freedom – you could sit where you liked.

There was a full choir of twelve boys, who walked in dignified procession to their seats in the stalls, but when the girls asked to join

A charabanc outing from Horton-cum-Studley in 1925. The top could be folded back in dry weather, but they look well wrapped up for their trip!

34

and be allowed to do the same thing the answer was an emphatic no. They were, however, allowed to sit in the first three seats on the right-hand side of the aisle, to help with the singing. The thinking behind this was similar to that which kept the playgrounds separate at the school. Boys and girls were not encouraged to mix – but usually found a way to do so.'

THE SUNDAY WALK

'We always attended Sunday school on Sunday afternoons and afterwards Father insisted the whole family go out for a walk. We would always meet other families we knew, out walking too. It was quite a social occasion.'

SUNDAY SCHOOL TREATS

'My memories are of Sunday school Anniversaries at the Primitive Methodist chapel in the hamlet of Moreton, near Thame. These were always held on the first Sunday in June, the chapel having been springcleaned beforehand by my aunts. Floors were scrubbed, windows cleaned and cobwebs dispelled. The large coke stove standing in the middle of the chapel would be burnished ready to receive a special flower arrangement on top, usually of dark red peonies from a cottage garden. The children would bring along jam jars of wild flowers to adorn the windowsills, and bunches of garden flowers would be brought along by chapel members and friends to make the chapel look beautiful. The girls usually had new straw hats for the occasion and possibly a new dress as well.

It was always a lovely warm sunny day – it *never* rained! The children sat on a raised part at the front of the chapel facing the congregation and each, in turn, had a recitation which they had rehearsed for weeks. What agony, waiting to be called to stand up and say your piece, rushing through it and sitting down as quickly as possible. My father played the organ and if the summer was very dry a large bucket of water was placed nearby to create a moist atmosphere so that it didn't wheeze.

Sometimes the services were taken by a visiting preacher and I well remember an uncle doing this one year and trying his best to persuade me to read the lesson for him with the promise of a sixpence. I couldn't be tempted, the recitation was quite enough for one day. Many relations would come for the Anniversary, we would have large family gatherings for lunch and many more for tea. There were always three services to attend, Sunday school in the morning and afternoon service at 3 pm followed by an evening service at 6 pm, the little chapel being packed to capacity. Everyone getting rather warm and the ladies' dresses sticking to the backs of the seats, I remember. On the Monday following, we were rewarded for all our efforts with a tea party in the chapel followed by games in the meadow behind it. And it still didn't rain!

A Sunday school outing was another exciting event of the year. We would catch the 9 am train from Thame station to West Wycombe and walk to the hill. We were able to hire for one penny a wooden chair-back which we used as a sledge on the side of the hill; hours of fun were had sliding down and climbing back up to the top again. We also purchased candles in cardboard holders and were able to wander in the Hell Fire caves at our will, it was very spooky and we were always scared of getting lost. I also remember that we climbed to the top of the church tower and actually into the golden ball on the top. We were always sure that it swayed in the wind!

Sometimes we went to the Rye at High Wycombe which was a large play area for children, and many happy hours were spent on the swings and climbing frames. The paddling pools were a great attraction, the girls who hadn't bathing costumes would tuck their dresses in their knickers and nearly always got them wet. I remember that there was a gentleman who looked elderly to us children but most likely he wasn't at all, who was in charge of this part of the Rye. He sat in a sentry box all day long keeping an eye on us. We all loved him very much.'

GETTING ABOUT

At the beginning of the century we either relied on real horse-power or on Shanks's pony – we walked! Then came the bicycle and gradually cars became more common on our roads, with country bus services proving a boon to isolated communities and steam trains a well loved part of our lives.

IT WAS DIFFERENT THEN

'We came to live in Finstock in 1910. The village was very different then. There was no public transport, bicycles had not come into use. The nearest railway station was at Charlbury, three and a half miles away, and very few had their own transport, pony and trap or such like. Mr Harris had a waggonette and horse for hire. The vicar Cary Elwes was the first to own a car. He also ran coal and clothing clubs for householders, investing the money which he handed out to members each year.

Farmers had farm carts and waggons, as did three or four smallholders. Mrs Edwards had a carrier's cart and horse and went to Woodstock on Thursdays and Saturdays and to Witney, chiefly to take and return finished gloving.

Roads were not metalled or tarred for some years, they were dusty in summer and muddy in winter. In stormy weather water ran down the sides of the roads, though there were some drains, and we could, except in wet weather, walk halfway down High Street on the grass bank, and in summer there grew many wild flowers. That bank has been so much eroded by widening and tarring and draining that one cannot walk (in comfort) along it today.'

'I am 90 years of age and was born in what was then Stanton St John parish, but is now Forest Hill. To go to Oxford before I was four years old we went by pony and cart to Wheatley station where the pony was stabled at the Railway Inn. We then travelled by train to Oxford station and from there went by tram drawn by two horses up to High Street.'

'At the turn of the century a carrier's cart went into Oxford from Appleton on a Saturday, in which a few people could travel, but unless you were fortunate to have some form of horse-drawn vehicle, or later a bicycle, there was no means of getting into Oxford or Abingdon except by walking. A carrier from a neighbouring village called twice a week to take orders for goods in Oxford and would bring these back in the evening.

The Oxford Bus Company started to run a limited service in the late 1920s. The fare for many years was a shilling return and ninepence single.'

'In the 1920s there was no dole for agricultural workers, so if they were laid off they applied to the council to be employed breaking stones in council stone quarries, which were found every few miles along each road. The broken stone was used for repairing the road surface, which was then rolled-in chippings. In the early 1920s the top road at Chadlington (the main A361 Burford to Chipping Norton road) was tarred. Everyone predicted horses would slip on this surface and cause bad accidents. Of course, the motor car was soon to take over from horse-drawn transport.'

WE JOGGED ALONG FOR HOURS

'The railway had arrived at Yarnton in 1854 so trains were available for the occasional trip to Oxford or Witney, but there were no buses until comparatively recent times so we walked everywhere. Most farmers and larger households kept ponies and used traps or governess carts for visits further afield.

I remember how lovely it was to drive to Kidlington to visit friends. We jogged along for what seemed like hours, enjoying the peaceful scene.

I spent many happy holidays at Mead Farm in Church Lane. Visitors were always collected from the station by farm cart as the track across the field was too rough for a pony trap.'

BIKES, CARS AND TRAINS

'We had no car, few people did. Buses ran most days to Chipping Norton for shopping but were not convenient for workers because the last one left the town at 4.10 pm except on Saturdays when there was one at 8.30 pm to take people home from the cinema.

I travelled by train to work in Oxford which was 25 miles away and the journey took about 50 minutes, stopping at all the stations and halts. I cycled to the station, just over a mile away. There was always a good fire in the waiting room in winter. The journey was friendly and one shared a carriage with the same people every day – the one who boarded first "bagged" it for those getting on farther up the line. In the winter of 1947 the trains home were often late and without heat and light but as a mixed company of teenagers that worried us not at all!

We cycled to neighbouring villages to visit friends and relations and to local places of interest eg Rollright Stones and Chastleton House.

Unless one was lucky enough to have a dynamo on one's bicycle, lights were a flashlight in front and a small rear light. To make the latter contact better, one put an old penny under the battery, thus forcing it nearer the bulb to improve the light.

Cycling in school days, we fixed a thin piece of card to the brake-shoe so that it flapped in the spokes of the wheel and made a wonderfully loud humming sound. I am told the boys did this to pretend they were riding a motorbike, but girls did it too, for fun.'

'Our cycles did not have dynamos so we had oil lamps which had a nasty habit of blowing out on a windy night and we always had to carry matches to relight them. Later we had acetylene lamps but they had to be lit, of course, though they did not blow out quite so easily.'

'Mr Pancott's hire car at Cassington was famous for being overloaded – we were told to sing up, then we wouldn't hear the wheels rubbing!'

'My mother's brother and sister each had cars and lived in London. When they came to visit us we were the envy of our schoolfriends to be able to go out in a car, even if it was in the dicky seat at the back – always in our best clothes.'

'There were so few cars about you would know them all. You could sit at the end of Queens Road and take the car numbers and it would only take about an hour to take all the numbers in Thame.'

RELYING ON ONE-HORSE POWER

'In 1927 I became an apprentice motor mechanic at Colletts garage in Wheatley. At that time, Dr McCausland who was a keen horseman owned a bright yellow Morris Cowley. Batteries were unreliable and if his car wouldn't start he would seek my help, no matter what time of day.

One night, he was called out to a lady at Charlton-on-Otmoor who was having a baby and we couldn't get the car started so he called to his housekeeper to saddle his horse and off he rode into the night!'

ROOM FOR EVERYONE

'During the Second World War public transport was always difficult, because of shortages of manpower and fuel. By the middle of the war, most of the buses were old and kept running with secondhand spare parts, whilst women were in great demand as conductors to collect the money and issue the tickets. In country areas, where the local bus was often the only means of travel, passengers were piled onto the bus with little regard for safety. As a child, I can remember waiting for the bus to travel to Oxford to visit the Christmas pantomime, which was performed at the New Theatre in George Street (now the Apollo). I was disappointed as the bus pulled up, already filled to capacity. But the resourceful driver shouted, "Double up inside", and we were all able to climb aboard, with passengers sitting four to a seat and standing all down the aisles.

In our village, during the war, it was rumoured that one 54-seater bus had arrived at its destination carrying 110 passengers; this was considered a local record.

At this time, many of the local farmers and their wives travelled to Banbury every Thursday, which was market day. The service from Enstone was provided by Worth's, and some weeks three or four buses trundled round the hilly country lanes between Enstone, Great Tew and Banbury. Once, as the buses were being loaded up for the return journey as usual, the drivers were shouting "Double up, double up." One local wag, who had probably visited several of Banbury's public houses, besides the market, was heard to remark, "These buses are like heaven. There's room for everybody!" '

CATCHING THE TRAIN

'When I wanted to visit Oxford I would use the train from Bampton station. I would go to the cinema there with my fiancé who lived at Cassington. After the show we would catch the last train home. He would get off at Cassington where, because it was the last train, he would turn out the station gas lamps and see that the station gate was shut. The fare to Oxford was a shilling return.'

Islip railway station in 1957. Steam trains were a familiar and friendly way to travel and many a child spent time down at the station train-spotting.

THE WORST THING TO HAPPEN

'The worst thing that ever happened was when the trains went. In 1962 the last regular train ran between Oxford and Witney.

Until then South Leigh had been well served by the "Witney Flyer", the nickname given to the regular train which ran seven times a day. It was well used, mainly for short shopping trips to Witney and also by villagers going to Oxford on business and pleasure. A popular train was the Saturday night special which ran to Oxford at 5 pm returning at 10 pm; a return ticket cost sixpence. There were day excursions to the seaside and day trips to London.

The station was well-kept with neat, beautifully tended flower beds. The station-master Mr Gunn and later the porters, Bill Mitchell and Ern Wickson were familiar and well loved characters in the village. They would keep an eye out for regular travellers and were always willing to deliver parcels and run errands. Jean and her niece Sue used the train daily to go to school in Oxford and, if they came running along late, could always rely on Bill or Ern to be there holding a carriage door open for them as they scrambled aboard. "We were never late when the wind was in the right direction," said Jean. "We could hear the train chuffing its way out of Witney, three miles away."

The sound of the trains, steam to the end, is remembered fondly by many of the villagers. It was a good time check for the men working out in the fields too.

The station was very important to the local farmers who used it daily for transporting their milk to either Oxford or London. Older villagers remember, pre-war, the little horse-drawn carts loaded with clanking churns rattling through the village from the farms to catch the 7 am milk train. Farmers also used it for deliveries of animal feed and fertiliser and sometimes for transporting cattle and agricultural machinery.

The station and its trains are remembered with affection for more than their utilitarian functions however – it was a meeting place for the villagers, where they could chat and catch up on the news. Hazel said that when her son Martin was little she'd push him down to the station as the train came in and there was always someone getting off to walk back with and chat to.

Now, for the elderly and those without a car, although only three miles from Witney, South Leigh is more isolated than it ever was, with only two buses a *week*!'

41

HOUSE & HOME

G. HOWARD

THE HOUSES WE LIVED IN

Picturesque thatched cottages, roses round the door – if that is your picture of the good old days, think again. Those cottages were often cold and damp, overcrowded and hard to keep clean. Odd, isn't it, how we still think of our old homes with affection and nostalgia!

MOVING HOUSE

'In 1908 we moved to Stanton St John and there were no furniture removers in those days. Everything went by farm waggons drawn by two horses. There was also a cattle truck, like a present-day trailer, with two horses, one in the shafts and a leader.

My mother and two maids had to pack up all the china and small items in packing cases (wrapped in newspaper). My brother, aged about five weeks, and I went with our Nanny in a brougham, which was a closed carriage drawn by two horses and driven by a coachman, who sat up in the front. My father's barometer went with us. I suppose we were his most treasured possessions!'

NO ROSES ROUND THE DOOR

'I was born in Kennington in 1925. There was a steep slope down to our row of cottages – we were three in a row and we were in the middle one. "Cottages" conjures up a very rural "roses round the door" picture, but they were nothing like that. They were stone cottages, tiled, and with very thick walls and small windows. We only had one small window. There was one large room downstairs, with a piece partitioned off for what we used to call a scullery, which was the kitchen really. Upstairs there were two bedrooms, one of which you had to go through to get to the other one.

The cottages were quite cramped. The other two were a little bigger because they had a little bit built on for a kitchen, but we couldn't because we were in the middle.

We all had a piece of front garden but there was just a wire fence. We couldn't partition it off altogether because we had to go up to either end to get out. We had no separate entrance to our house.

They were not as warm as people think, those old cottages. Though, it was nice and warm around the old stove. There was a big open fire and ovens at the side, which we didn't use very often, and you had to sit in front of the fire if you wanted to be warm. But the bedrooms were very cold – very cold. And towards the later years we lived there, when they were condemned, they were very damp too. I couldn't sleep in my bedroom, and all the wallpaper you tried to put up, I remember, used to come down because the plaster behind it all fell down. It wasn't idyllic, really, like they think. And the floors were stone, so that the lino became dented with the shape of the stones. And it was difficult to keep clean.'

THEY LOOKED PICTURESQUE

'There were more thatched cottages in South Leigh before the war; they looked picturesque but many of them were in poor condition and although small, housed large families. Rain poured in through the roof of our little cottage behind the Manor so that it was condemned and we were very glad to move to Wayside Cottage which had just been left to the National Trust.

This had previously been a smallholding and was a spacious thatched house with four bedrooms. The weekly rent was ten shillings, but my husband, who worked for the council, only earned 30 shillings a week, leaving £1 on which to keep our family. The house, although roomy, lacked all modern conveniences, with no bathroom and an outside privy; in fact there was no water or electricity until 1959. Water had to be drawn from the well and many buckets were dropped down it until the National Trust fitted a pump.

The house, as most in the village, was lit by oil lamps and these entailed a lot of work, first washing the lamp glasses, then trimming the wick carefully before filling the lamps with paraffin. Candles were used to light people to bed and before going out in the evenings my husband Ernie would always leave a candlestick with the candle ready on the table and say to me and the children, when we returned home in the dark, "Now all stand there while I light the candle."'

LIFE IN WATLINGTON

'Lavinia was born in the Forest of Dean in 1911 and came to Watlington around 1938 with a baby son. She had lived in a cottage in Britwell for two years since her marriage and had just got used to having electricity when she moved to Watlington. The cottage, which was convenient for her husband's work, had two bedrooms so there was more room with a baby but there was no electricity or water supply.

In her part of Watlington water was collected from the stream with a bucket and as much rainwater as possible was saved. This was very soft for washing in. There being no electricity, out came the oil lamps again. It was, of course, necessary to spend time cleaning them and looking after them.

The day was busy, with lots of callers – the grocer came and collected her order on Wednesday for delivery on Friday. The fruiterer came round on Saturday with horse and cart. He lived in another village. On Wednesday a man came on a bicycle from Cuxham and she remembers particularly him selling bananas. Lavinia gave her little boy a penny so he could buy a banana himself and the man was known as the 'nana man. They used to enjoy looking out for him. Coal was delivered one cwt at a time and they still bought it in the summer so as to keep stocks up ready for winter. Sometimes they would buy from the log man as they had an open fire in the living room.

In the kitchen there was a range which had to be blacked and as the chimney did not go much above the roof, there was often smoke coming back into the room and ashes were sometimes blown back through the grid in the range. At these times they had to give up using the range but there was an alternative means to heating the kettle etc – the primus. In fact, the kettle was usually heated on the primus for the early morning cup of tea!

In Watlington it was necessary to collect paraffin from the local garage, candles too. Also, the wireless accumulator needed to be re-charged at the garage and one had to be very careful carrying it on the way home if it had been topped up with distilled water, not to burn a hole in one's clothes if some acid was spilt from it. Not a job to be given to children.

Her mother, still living in Forest of Dean, would sometimes send Lavinia a chicken tightly wrapped up. It would come by post and always arrive the next day. She would find her mother had put two eggs inside! Also she might receive some butter wrapped in rhubarb leaves.

The milkman called with his urn and they had to take out a jug so the milk could be ladled into it. They changed to bottles of course at some point. The dairy was in Watlington and they could see the cows going in to be milked by hand.

Lavinia used to have a baking day – Saturday evening in fact. She would bake a cake and usually a fruit tart for Sunday so as to leave the oven in the range free for the roast. She would work as she listened to the radio and her husband would go to one of the 13 pubs in Watlington that night, although lots of the men spent more evenings that way. On Sunday she would cook plenty of vegetables so as to have "bubble and squeak" on Monday, which was washday.

After a short while electricity came to Lavinia's part of Watlington (other parts were already connected) and three lights and a plug socket were put in free, more were added when funds were available. Before this the iron was heated on the primus stove and so it cooled down by the time you had done a bit of ironing. Lavinia admitted to doing a bit of "bruising", ie ironing only the bit of clothes which would show when worn!

It was some time before the first cooker was installed – Baby Belling first before a full cooker – and this was thought to be wonderful. Lavinia and her husband bought their first cooker through the Electricity Board, paying some money with each electricity bill.

A few days after it was installed a lady arrived unannounced and said that as Lavinia had bought a new cooker, she had come to show her how to use it properly and give a few tips. One tip was to put water in the tin which had been used for roasting the meat and then place it in the oven during the cooling period. This would help to ease the grease burnt on the oven walls during cooking.

Neighbours were friendly and Lavinia helped an elderly lady next door. She used to help her to get coal and wood for her fire but as the lady got older she became more mistrusting and accused Lavinia of stealing! She would also tell her not to put too much coal or wood on the fire. Before main drainage and indoor toilets, they all had toilets – buckets – in their sheds and when the elderly neighbour became too old to go to the shed, she had her bucket in the kitchen.

Lavinia's cottage had been the home of a "DIY" enthusiast previously and he had tried to modernise it by making the toilet flush. A pump he had installed had to be taken out and his actions may have caused the well to become contaminated, thus necessitating the continued used of the stream for collecting water. Varying numbers of cottages used a well – five to one well and two to another. When the nearby watercress was replanted, Lavinia would find the water in the stream very muddy when she went to collect it.

There was a cinema in Watlington which showed films Thursday to Saturday. The back three rows of seats were plush and raised up. The other chairs were movable and the front area was used for whist drives and dancing. There was a balcony with a few plush seats for courting couples but in the early days the balcony was screened off with two or three buckets for ladies' toilets. It was also the cloakroom for coats and hats and as ladies would cycle in to Watlington from other villages, they would wear their everyday clothes for the journey and then change at the cinema.'

ON THE EDGE OF THE BEECHWOOD

'I was born in Peppard in 1934 and grew up in a tiny beamed cottage on the edge of a beechwood. There was only one entrance door, one tap (and that was quite a refinement added later, as my father reminds me he had to fetch water from the village well when I was a mere toddler), a shiny blackleaded grate for warmth and cooking, twisty stairs, an oil lamp in the living room and candles elsewhere, a huge well down which a suspended pail kept the meat and butter cool, and a privy situated behind the cottage, under the edge of the beechwood. Here, at dead of night, all the evil spirits met, according to our childish imaginations! All waste water had to be carried out through the house, from the scullery, to a ditch.

I have such romantic memories of this Hansel and Gretel cottage, but it must have been very hard work for Mum, especially when evacuees arrived from London at the outbreak of the Second World War.'

COTTAGE IN THE ROW

'As a child of about eight or nine, I often went to stay with my grandmother who lived in a cottage in a row of ten or twelve cottages. It was a cottage with two rooms, one up and one down,

A typical thatched cottage at Horton-cum-Studley in 1920. Picturesque looks did not always compensate for a lack of amenities.

48

the only door opened into the downstairs room and the stairs went out of that room straight into the bedroom. There was a pocket handkerchief-size garden and across the other side of that was the washhouse. Water had to be carried from a shared tap outside, and the loo was at the end of the cottages, again shared. Also at the end of the cottages was a bigger piece of garden with shared washing lines, and each family had their day to hang out the washing. If it rained on your washday, too bad, there was no hanging it out the next day as it was someone else's turn.

The cottage I thought was very cosy; there was a kitchen range and all the cooking was done in the oven at the side. The scrubbed table was covered by a chenille cloth when the work was finished as on this table everything had to be done – meals prepared, a bowl of water for washing up (there was no sink, all the water had to be carried outside and emptied down a drain), the ironing – and of course we sat to this same table for our meals. On a winter evening the oil lamp would be lit, and the fire would be burning in the kitchen range, and that was when I thought it was really cosy. I don't remember what my grandmother thought of it, she had lived there a good many years, and I don't remember the number, but the address was Bakehouse Cottages, Ock Street, Abingdon, aptly named I suppose, because they were built behind a baker's shop and bakehouse, but of course after all these years they are no longer there.'

ALL BORN THERE

'Like my two elder sisters and brother, I was born in the cottage at Combe where we lived. About the bottom three feet of the wall all round the living room was painted wood and the top part was wallpaper. The ceiling was low. The only door of the cottage opened straight into this room. There was an old dresser, a chest of drawers and a large deal kitchen table taking up most of the room. This table was scrubbed every week and on Sunday afternoons it always had a cover put over it. On the floor was coconut matting which was taken up once a week to reveal a dusty pattern on the flagstones.

In front of an open fire in a black grate was a rag rug that my mother had made with old clothes cut up and pegged into what was a sack bag. All the cooking was done by the heat of this fire; and the oven at the side and saucepans on the fire. A black kettle was used for all the hot water: to drink, to wash up, cleaning, or to have a wash. To light this fire was my mother's first job every day of the year.

Saucepans were often mended with "pot-menders" when they had a hole in them. When the vegetables were cooked the saucepans were taken outside to strain the water out as we had no sink.

Branches from fallen trees were brought home and sawn into blocks on a sawing horse with a crosscut. These blocks were burned on the fire in the evenings. I have vivid memories of the sap sizzling out of these damp blocks as they burned.

All our water came from a well which was in our washhouse, but we did have a pump to get it out. On Saturday nights I was given a bath in a tin washing tray in front of the fire. On the table was an oil lamp as we had no electricity until I was six or seven years old. I went up to bed by the light of a candle.

There was no flush toilet – just a chamber pot under the bed. The lavatory was a little house at the bottom of the garden with a bucket in and a wooden seat. No toilet roll, just newspaper cut up and hung up with string.

In the winter it was so cold upstairs as there was no heat. I used to have a stone hot-water bottle. On frosty mornings the windows were covered with leafy patterns – they did look pretty.'

MY GRANDMOTHER'S HOUSE

'I was born at my grandparents' home in Windmill Road, Headington in 1926. The house was built around 1900 and was semi-detached with a narrow sideway. It had a passage leading to the front room, the staircase and the living room which you passed through to get to the kitchen and scullery. The WC was outside, although joined on to the back of the house. It had a long wooden seat with a flush toilet underneath it. At night we had to take a candle in a jam jar and my mother would sit on the seat beside me and read me a story by candlelight.

Upstairs there was a landing leading to the front bedroom and second bedroom and another landing which led to a small boxroom and the back bedroom. My parents and I had the two front rooms until they could afford a place of our own and we moved to a "modern" bungalow when I was nine years old. It cost my father around £600 which he borrowed, I believe, from The Oddfellows Society. It has recently been sold for £110,000!

My grandmother's kitchen was warm and cosy. She had a black kitchen range, which she did all her cooking in, and boiled kettles and saucepans on top. Two flat irons were heated on top of it when she did her ironing and a line was strung across the length of the kitchen to air the clothes or dry them on wet days.

In the corner of the scullery was a stone copper which we filled with water and heated up by burning all our paper, rubbish and bits of wood and coal in a fireplace beneath it. Washing day was quite a major operation and the quarry-stoned scullery floor would be flooded by the time the washing was finished. It then had to be scrubbed with water saved from the washing, and on our hands and knees we scrubbed through the kitchen as that also had red quarry stone floors. We usually finished up by scrubbing the "front" from the door to the front gate and "whitening" the door steps with a stone used for that purpose. I use the term "we" as I went to live with my grandmother when I was first married so all these chores then fell upon my shoulders. The only difference then was an old grey gas stove but I still preferred the food cooked in the kitchen range.

When I was a child we had gas lights in the three downstairs rooms. There was one either side of the fireplaces and one in the centre of the ceiling. They had flimsy white mantles which were always having to be replaced. We used candles upstairs.

We didn't have a bathroom at Windmill Road so when we wanted a bath the water had to be heated in the stone copper and emptied by jug and pail into a long zinc bath which had been placed in front of the kitchen fire. The back door was always locked so too bad if anyone needed to go outside to the toilet while bathing was in progress! The worst part was having to bale all the water out again when you had finished so it was quite usual for all the family to use the same water.

We didn't have carpets on the floor although in the kitchen I believe there was coconut matting. My mother used to make peg rugs using pieces of material from old clothes and they lasted for years and were quite cosy to lie on in front of the fire. Of course we had coal fires in those days, even in the bedrooms if one was confined to bed. The floors were generally covered in linoleum or else the floorboards were varnished. Lino-covered floors had to be polished every week and "mopped" each day with a cotton mop to remove the dust.

Milk was delivered by handcart in large churns and was ladled out into the housewives' own jugs with a measure. Bread and cakes were delivered by horse and cart and the coalman also had a horse. We would go out with a bucket and shovel after they had gone to see if they had left us something for the garden. We had quite a long garden and my grandfather grew flowers, fruit and vegetables. He had a greenhouse where he grew tomatoes and chrysanthemums and he also had an allotment and grew enough potatoes and greens, onions and carrots for all our needs.

Families used to visit their relatives in those days as in spite of all the everyday chores they always found time to keep in touch with

51

each other and help out in times of trouble. Clothes were handed down and never thrown away. Most of my clothes were "hand me downs". A lot of women made their own bread, jams and pickles and some made wine. I have followed in my grandparents' footsteps and still do all those things although my wine making is not quite so primitive. I use demi-johns whereas I can remember seeing wine in big red earthenware basins with mouldy bread floating on top and covered with muslin.'

ALMOST LUXURY

'I was born at Woodcote in the early 1920s. There were very few houses in my early days which had bathrooms, and the toilets were "up the garden" – a cold errand in winter! Street lights were unheard of in Woodcote. When my parents moved to Goring in the 1930s, life seemed almost luxurious. We moved to a new bungalow with a bathroom. There was gas laid on so we had a gas stove to cook on, though the washing was still done in the copper. There were street lights – even though they were gas ones – and it made a great difference.'

COOK AND HEAT?

'At Long Wittenham in the 1920s we used to cook on a stove called a "Cook and Heat". The family always said that it didn't cook and it didn't heat either. Before that there was the coal-fired range and out in the scullery was a Beatrice oil stove which had two rings. With that and the oil lamps, there was always a smell of oil there.'

MAKING RUGS

'Our house in North Leigh was cold in the winter except for the one room where there was an open fire. We spent many an evening during the war years cutting up old clothes to make rag rugs. We worked out the pattern first on sacking, and the rugs were very pretty and wore well.'

ANTIMACASSARS AND WARMING PANS

'I can remember my mother always having antimacassars – covers over the backs and arms of chairs to protect them from wear. When I was small there was always a "frill" round the mantelpiece and an elaborate overmantel. A neighbour, who was born before the turn of the century, used a warming pan.'

ON THE EDGE OF THE VILLAGE

'My memories of Swalcliffe begin on 1st April 1938, when I moved with my husband and nine month old baby into 3 Brick Row, on the edge of the village.

On the flagstoned ground floor was a living room with a small black range and the door to an old baking oven in the inglenook, and a small pantry, with a spiral staircase leading up to a landing and bedroom and from thence up to an attic divided into two by a wall, not quite reaching the ceiling, and a tiny window. The upper floors were of wide elm boards, with many crannies, some polished, and the attic stairs and floors were scrubbed white. The casement windows were small, one of metal with leaded panes and the other, woody, which had to be removed to get the bedroom furniture in! The light came from an oil lamp on the table, and candles for upstairs. Water was piped from springs to a standpipe out in the lane. If it failed unexpectedly it meant a walk along the village, and the tap had to be lagged well in winter. The toilet was a bucket arrangement at the top end of the row, emptied into a hole in the garden at dead of night. Three doors down in the opposite direction was a large dry stone hovel as high as a house, with a wash boiler, and space to store fuel, cycle, etc.

Much to my surprise, the landlord called with his bailiff after a few days and suggested we might need something, wallpaper for living room and bedroom, walpamur for attic and stairs. The pantry floor was worn hollow after a few hundred years of wear and I asked if he could do anything? I received a pattern book (with pages marked) for wallpaper, paint and whitewash – and cement and sand for my husband to level up the floor. The wallpaper only cost fourpence halfpenny per roll but at least it was fresh and clean. Our rent was three shillings and sixpence a week!

Most cooking was done on the living room range, no problem in winter when the oven was usually hot. In summer the fire might be lit in time to cook the evening meal, bringing a lovely smell of woodsmoke round the village. A primus stove was very useful, especially for early mornings.

Food storage was a problem in summer, when without a proper cool larder meat and fish really needed to be bought and cooked on the same day. A good food safe was necessary, and tins and jars etc with well fitting lids, because of insects and cockroaches – finally eradicated with Borax and removal of flagstones for a concrete floor.'

MARRYING AFTER THE WAR

'I married just after the end of the war. As food was still rationed we had to give the baker some fruit for the wedding cake. Coupons had to be saved for my wedding dress material and the bridesmaids also gave up their coupons for their dress material.

One of the best presents I had on my wedding day was a book of petrol coupons, pressed into my hand by my uncle, just as we were leaving on our honeymoon. We were going up to the Lake District so the coupons meant we could do a bit of extra touring. When we returned we lived with my mother for twelve months (my father had died two years previously).

After twelve months we rented a cottage in the wilds, outside a village and were able to spend our ration of dockets. As newly-weds we were allowed three sheets, three blankets and I can't remember how many towels. But everything, including furniture and floor coverings was on dockets. I don't think carpet was available, only linoleum.'

SUNDAY TO SATURDAY

'In my childhood Sunday was special. We went to church twice or perhaps three times; there was not much else to do. All outdoor games were forbidden, work was kept to the minimum except for school homework. We were encouraged to read, but not to play cards, nor were we allowed to invite other children to play, but my parents often entertained and massive meals were eaten.

Breakfast was always a cooked meal of rasher, eggs, sausage and tomatoes in season, followed by toast and marmalade. Sunday dinner at 1 pm was always a roast. (Villagers who had no ovens took their meat to the village baker who baked it while they attended matins. He charged one penny for this service.) Home-grown vegetables in season were served liberally, followed by fruit tart and custard, jelly or trifle.

Four o'clock tea provided plates of bread and butter, sandwiches or scones, cakes and pastries. We usually had relations to tea, and they might stay on for supper at 8 pm. This was always a cold meal of meat and salad and home-made pickles, with cheese or a cold sweet to follow. Cocoa was the favourite drink – to keep out the cold for those who had to take a long walk home on cold nights. Home-made wine was favoured in the summer, especially if we had been for a walk. Those Sunday walks were often quite lengthy and our family would often meet other Brightwell-cum-Sotwell families some miles from home, thus we grew up knowing all the local foot-paths –

well-worn in those days – and we learned the habitats and names of many wild flowers, and knew where to look for birds' nests.

The clothes' copper in the scullery would have been filled with water pumped from the kitchen sink on Sunday morning ready for Monday's wash. By 7 am the copper fire would be alight so that there was plenty of hot water by the time the washer-woman arrived at 8 am. It took her all the morning to do the family wash, although she always had a break for her bread and cheese and stout – the only alcohol regularly consumed in the house. Later, she scrubbed the stone floors in scullery and pantry. We dreaded wet Mondays, because then the clothes had to be dried on a clothes' horse placed around the kitchener. Wet floors, a steamy kitchen and a cold meal of Sunday left-overs, have left a poor impression on me!

Tuesday was Ironing Day. A big wicker basket held a pile of neatly folded clothes, damped down if necessary, so that the starched garments would come up crisp under the iron. There might be six or eight sheets, pillowcases, linen towels, tablecloths as well as shirts, blouses, pinafores etc. Five flat irons were heated on the well-stoked kitchener and the two to three-hour session started. A shield was used over the base of the iron for fine linen, and a goffering iron was needed for frilly dresses and blouses. Casseroles and baked puddings were served on Tuesdays because the well-stoked fire provided a hot oven.

Wednesday was Bedroom Day. Every mattress had to be turned, dust in the bedsprings had to be blown away with bellows, beds had to be made tidy and slops emptied. Then damp tea-leaves, saved from the week's tea brewings, were liberally scattered over the carpets to absorb the dust before a stiff handbrush and dustpan were used to take up the combined tea-leaves and fluff. While the dust settled the wash stands, often marble-topped, were scoured, and the basin, soap box, toothbrush holder, glass and chamber-pot were all given a thorough cleansing with a weak solution of Jeyes Fluid. Dusting and polishing of furniture and floor surrounds completed the task.

On Thursdays the sitting room and dining room were given the tea-leaf treatment; there was more polishing and dusting, and either the silver or the brass was cleaned.

Friday was Window-cleaning Day, but all had to be finished by noon, ready for an early meal (usually fish) so that an early start could be made to do the shopping. I can remember being pushed in my perambulator the two miles to the nearest town. A carefully prepared list would be presented at the International Stores where delivery of goods was promised for the following day. We liked to linger there, choosing our weekly allowance of sweets – 4oz only, and our favourite biscuits – always displayed at a child's eye level in glass-topped boxes, and we were fascinated by the huge blocks of butter from which our pound would be skilfully cut, weighed and patted into shape.

The town baker was another favourite shop because it was here we bought the weekly treat of doughnuts or Chelsea buns. Now on to the draper's where high chairs were provided for the customers and a man stood ready to open the door to bow us in. Here the great amusement was to watch the little round wooden boxes, into which money and bill were put and which sped across the shop over our heads to the counting house; back it came with a receipted bill and the correct change.

Often repairs had to be taken to the cobbler, the tinker or the umbrella man, or perhaps the sweep had to be ordered to come to sweep a smoky chimney. Always there seemed to be a requirement from the sweet-smelling chemist's shop, perhaps the ingredients for home-made cough or digestive mixture. As Friday was market day one always met acquaintances, perhaps from distant villages, thus the afternoon passed all too quickly and we arrived home with an appetite for a late tea.

Saturdays when I was young meant relaxation, a late breakfast and chance to play with friends, but from the age of eleven there was Saturday morning school and afternoons were often occupied with games. If it were an "away" match we would travel by charabanc up to 20 miles, taking our supporters along to fill the seats and perhaps to cheer us to victory. Meanwhile, Mother would have spent the morning baking scones and cakes and making pastry. In the afternoon she usually cycled to visit her sister who lived two miles away, while Father, who only had Saturday afternoon off, would have been catching up with jobs in the garden, perhaps picking apples, lifting potatoes or just mowing the lawn. In the evening shoes and boots had to be polished ready for us when we donned our Sunday best.

Saturday night was bath night, with an enormous hip-bath brought into the kitchen and the fire well stoked to provide endless kettles of hot water, and a nice cosy atmosphere in which, starting with the youngest, all bathed, washed hair, cut nails and generally prepared for the Sabbath.

On reflection, childhood was a happy carefree time. Our simple pleasures were mostly found within the family, visiting or being visited by our large extended family, most of whom lived within walking distance, although my grandfather lived eight miles away. To visit him we required the services of John Batten and his "Victoria" at a cost of two shillings and sixpence for the day.'

DOING THE ROUGH WORK

'If you had a larger house there were always people to employ for help in the house. We had a lady who came in to do the rough work – she had to scrub the red tiles outside up to the front door, all through the mosaic-tiled passage through to the scullery which also had a red brick floor and a large scrubbed table. She once told me she loved scrubbing, and always talked about "her" floors and woe betide any child who stepped on one which she had just cleaned. She always wore a black coat and a black hat well screwed on with hatpins, and underneath a Norah Batty-type apron.'

WATER, WASHDAY AND LIGHTS

Most of us had to collect every drop of water from wells or pumps until after the Second World War – and no piped water meant no indoor sanitation and a walk down the garden path. Washday was a chore to be dreaded each week, and so was the regular emptying of the 'facilities' – our vegetables grew well, though! How pleased we were to see mains water, mains sewerage and electricity.

WELLS AND PUMPS

'We had quite an extensive property at Islip in the 1930s, as we ran the general store. There were many facilities for collecting rainwater for washing and bathing, but water for drinking and cooking had to be drawn up in a bucket from a 60 foot well. My neighbour with whom we shared the well was lucky enough to have a landlord who provided her with an electric pump. Of course, in dry weather rainwater became scarce and more had to be drawn from the well. Mains water did not arrive in Islip until 1952. Main drains had been brought here in 1936 but without water they were little use to us!'

'There were only six or seven houses of any size in Finstock in 1910; many of these cottages were built of stone, some with thatched roofs, picturesque maybe and looking cosy, but expensive to be re-thatched and no use for collecting rainwater.

There was no public water supply, only a public draw well with bucket and chain in School Road, a tap (public) and a horse well in The Bottom, and Gadden Well at the bottom of Gadden Hill – left in the village when the forest was enclosed. Some people had draw wells in their garden but most had to carry water in buckets hung on chains from a yoke fitting on the shoulders (or not!). Water came to the village in 1936 along with the supply of electricity. People with guttering on sheds or houses carefully saved rainwater from gutters under eaves. Finstock House, the vicarage and Manor Farm had a supply of water from Cornbury estate. Thatched roofs could not be used for storing water, obviously.

1936 was a date to celebrate – electricity supply available *and* water!

In the very hot long summer of 1936, Mr Jimmy Lane, with a man helping, took his horse with his large water barrel down to the river where he could, from the springs, get clean drinking water, and sold it round the village at twopence a bucket. One barrel was not sufficient for those who thankfully paid for buckets of drinking water!'

'Every house at Kidmore End had a rainwater tank for general use and a small filter for drinking water; or the menfolk went with yokes and two large buckets to the village wells at Gallowstree Common or Kidmore End to wind up clear water for drinking. It was a hard and time consuming job when the buckets were full.'

'We had to fetch water from a well at the bottom of our yard in Cogges in the 1920s. It served five houses. You had a yoke on your shoulders and two buckets. Very often the bucket came off the rope down the well and it had to be hooked up. The water was lovely to drink. We didn't have tapped water and water toilets until after the war. We had to go out the back to the toilet and when it was dark my mum and dad used to come and stand outside if I wanted to go.'

'Some cottages at Bampton had well water. One of these was Sandford Cottage, who also allowed their neighbour at Brook Cottage to come each morning at six to collect two buckets of water. The buckets were lowered by means of a clip-hook on a long pole. The cottagers also used the well as a fridge, keeping milk and butter in a basket just above the water level. The well never ran dry. Tested annually, it was decreed the "best water in Bampton". Sadly, three years ago it was found to be polluted.'

'At our house in Kennington there was a well in the grounds. It was shared between two houses and there was an oscillating pump – the sort you pump from side to side. It was pumped into a tank at the back of the small bedroom upstairs and that supplied water to the lavatory system and to the taps, well, to the bath anyway. If you wanted water from the kitchen tap, you had to turn on the water and pump at the same time. You got used to it after a time.'

BATH NIGHT

'I was born during the First World War and we lived in a terraced house in East Oxford. Saturday night was bath night. The kitchen range was stoked up with a lovely fire and the bath was brought in and put in front of it. I was bathed, my hair was washed and then I was dried in warm towels. But the best bit was to come. Earlier Mother had scrubbed potatoes and put them in the oven so when bathing was over we could have supper of jacket potatoes with a little bit of salt and lots of butter. I can taste them now.'

'Thursday nights were bath nights in our house in Oxford. My brother, being the eldest, bathed first, my sister having carried upstairs for him several buckets of hot water from the kitchen copper. My sister then bathed, after taking up another bucket of hot water to add to the same bathwater. I was last, with the addition of yet another bucket of hot water! How my mother and grandmother bathed I do not know; this was a closely guarded secret.'

'Bathing took place in a tin bath, in front of the range, once a week. The whole family used the same water. It was not the cleanest or indeed the dirtiest, who went in first. The youngest went first and the oldest last; in this way the tinies could be put to bed immediately after washing. Water had to be carried from the nearest standpipe and then heated in a kettle on the range.

I remember one day one Uffington lady who was expecting a baby, decided to get into the copper for a relaxing bath at the end of washing. After a lovely refreshing soak the time came to get out. It was impossible. She could get no grip with her feet and the bump was a definite handicap. The water began to get cold and so did she. However, help was at hand – the baker came to make his delivery and came to her assistance. It might have been more difficult if it had been the coal merchant!'

WASHDAY

'By tradition, washday was always Monday. After breakfast, the copper was filled with cold water and the fire below it lit with paper, sticks and small knobs of coal. It took about 20 minutes to heat the water, during which time the beds were made and the bedrooms tidied. The water was then transferred to the washing machine. This was one of the first types – hand-operated. It was a square metal container on four legs. The capacity was enough for one double sheet or the equivalent. The top was a hinged lid; on the underside was a sort of paddle, which was moved backwards and forwards, when the lid was shut, by a rotary arm. It took two or three minutes for each load. The articles were then put through the mangle. This was attached to the back of the machine by clamps. The rollers were of rubber with a side handle to turn. The cleaning agent was grated Sunlight soap and soda. Any articles with stains or very dirty, eg shirt cuffs or collars, were rubbed with soap. Shirt collars were separate in those days. The articles were then rinsed in clear water and mangled again ready for hanging out.

All white articles were put through a blue rinse, made by swishing a blue bag in the water. Table linen and some other articles such as shirt collars were then starched. The starch was made by mixing a paste with Robin's starch, either powder or lumps, with cold water. Boiling water was then poured on, stirring all the time to prevent lumps, until the liquid turned transparent. The consistency was varied according to the required stiffness of the articles. The washing was then taken into the garden and hung on the line, using either gipsy pegs or wooden doll pegs. If wet, the washing was dried indoors. There was a rack, attached to the kitchen ceiling, which consisted of four seven-foot long slats, supported by a metal framework each end, which could be pulled up and down with a pulley.

When the articles were dry, those for ironing were "damped down". This meant sprinkling them with clear water and then rolling them tightly to spread the moisture evenly. These were then left for ironing the following day. We were still using flat irons then, but soon after there were gas irons, with a trailing flex and later on electric ones, much less refined than today's.

The process of washing took the whole morning, so dinner would consist of cold meat from the Sunday joint and a fried mixture of potato and cabbage, which was called "bubble and squeak".

There was a great deal of satisfaction in seeing a line full of freshly washed clothes, table linen and bed linen, blowing on the line and being bleached by the sun.'

'I suppose washday in our house in the 1940s and 1950s began on a Saturday when all the family had baths and the beds were changed.

I hated washdays as a child. My mother was so particular everything had to be cleaned to a degree of being washed away. We didn't have mains water but had a well in the garden (as did many Fritwell gardens). The well had a pump which had to be primed enabling the water to be drawn. We had an outhouse which housed a copper and an enamel bath; all the clothes and bed linen used to be put to soak in the bath prior to washing, usually on a Sunday last thing at night. Monday morning dawned with the job of filling the copper with water, this alone took ages, then the fire underneath the copper was lit. Washday took *all* day in our household, not only consisting of the actual washing but there was all the cleaning afterwards. Mother retained the soapy water for this. I would return from school to usually find her on her hands and knees scrubbing the stone flags outside the front door, having worked her way through the kitchen and front hall which were also flags. Also any grime on doors and walls was subjected to the wash cloth. Finally the outside loo was scrubbed out.

If it had been or was raining, the floors were covered with newspaper and the smell of wet washing filled the house (to this day I will not have wet washing in doors).

Candles and oil lamps were a terrible fire risk. This was Islip's fire brigade in the early 1900s, with the hand-pumped engine behind them.

Tuesday was ironing day (if the washing was dry). However, that wasn't the end – it had to be aired. This took place around the fire on a large clothes horse. This went on into Thursday. Mother was very particular about her clothes being aired completely.

However, I still think there is nothing nicer than a pile of freshly laundered washing.'

'The day after washday there was the mending to be done – socks to be darned, elastics to be renewed, buttons and tapes sewn on, sheets patched and turned sides to middle when thin, little boys' trousers patched, which were usually made of flannel and an endless task.'

'My mother had an old lady called Topsy Gray to help her. Topsy stood on a box to reach the zinc bath. Wearing a coarse apron made out of a sack, with her arms engulfed in suds up to the elbows, she scrubbed and rubbed on the old washboard, using bar soap and soda. I can remember her red and roughened arms and hands. When all the washing was finished, the suds that were left were put aside ready for our bath in front of the fire that night.

Our lunch on Monday consisted of bubble and squeak, cold meat left from the joint on Sunday, and pickled onions. It fascinated me to watch Topsy spear those pickled onions with her remaining two up and two down teeth at the front. She never missed!'

DOWN THE GARDEN PATH

'We lived in Oxford and our toilet was at the bottom of the garden and called the privy, with climbing plants growing over it, and a large bush growing in front to give added privacy. There was a hole in the door so if necessary it could be seen if all was well inside. The privy stood on a soil floor, with a covered wooden seat with two round holes – a large one for adults and a little one placed lower down for children. Underneath were two buckets which were always emptied on a Sunday before anyone else was up. This was Dad's job as a rule, and the contents were dug into the garden. It helped to produce large cabbages. Some places just had a large hole underneath the toilet and a little man with a horse and cart came and emptied it in the night. No one ever saw him, and to us children he was a phantom who came when there was no moon!'

'The cesspits at Kennington had to be emptied with the bucket when they got to overflowing, and it was general practice for the children to be sent to knock the windows of the neighbours to warn them it was about to be done so they could close all their windows, because obviously it was rather smelly. Then the head of the house used to go down there with the bucket and just dip it out and tip it on the garden.

Ours was actually much more organised than that. My father had one of those old-type pumps that you used to get in farmyards, and installed it at the top of the cesspit. He had a friend who was in the fire brigade in Oxford, and he could get hold of lengths of fire hose which was "life expired" – he paid him a shilling or two. He used this to connect up to his pump and then he could put the end of the hose in various parts of the garden to, er, sort of lubricate the garden in the right places. So every so often he would have to pump away for about a quarter of an hour or 20 minutes – and the amazing thing was that wherever the outlet of this pipe was, the potatoes and everything else used to grow about three times as big as anywhere else.'

'The lavatories in Bampton used to be outside. Each Tuesday and Friday buckets of sewage were put out into the road to wait for a man with his horse and cart to come and empty the slops. Some of the buckets were covered with ashes, some with newspaper, but some were left uncovered! Sometimes they would be there all day. Often the man would eat his sandwiches as he collected them.

One day Miss Marjorie Pollard came to Bampton to view a house. She thought Bampton would be a friendly place and bought the Deanery. However, she soon became horrified at the sewage collection and as a county councillor she threatened to borrow the horse and cart and follow the Lord Mayor's coach in London if there was no improvement. Fortunately this was not necessary as the new sewerage system was put in during 1949.'

'Many at Great Rollright can remember the "night walk", when the buckets were emptied into big pits at the bottom of the garden covered by wooden planks and called "The Vaults". These were emptied annually, using a ladle! One lady can remember sitting in the privy and watching through a hole in the wall as the trains passed by, while another remembers her husband dropping the bucket on the way to the allotment and having to spend the rest of the night swilling the road!'

'Most people at Chadlington grew their own vegetables, either in the garden or allotment or both. Access to a reasonable amount of land was needed not only for the vegetables but also for emptying the buckets. The bucket was put on a high-sided wheelbarrow, a heavy sack over the top and pushed to the required place. It was not until the mid 1950s that there was a sewerage system, although by that time some people had septic tanks.'

LIGHTING UP TIME

'There was great excitement in Enstone village. The rumours had been confirmed – electricity was definitely coming. This was in the latter half of the 1930s when the rural electrification programme was part of the plan to get things moving again after the depression of the early 1930s.

So at last we would be "on the electric" – we would catch up with our cousins in town. We too would be part of the modern world. Not that there were many appliances in those days – freezers and microwaves were for the future. People were mainly concerned with the convenience of light at the flick of a switch after a lifetime of the autumn and winter ritual of trimming and filling oil lamps and laying in stocks of paraffin and candles.

Then came the gossip – who was going to have what. Some people, of course, weren't going to have any truck with such new-fangled things. We were well ahead here though, we were not only going to have electric light in the dairy as well as in the house, we were also to have an electric pump over the well to pump water across the farmyard to save the twice-daily chore of watering the stock. Grampy had been going to have electricity in his cottage, but one of his contemporaries on hearing the news exclaimed, "Electric in a thatched cottage – set the place afire!" That did it – he changed his mind and nothing Dad said could budge him, much to the chagrin of his housekeeper. Another householder who took in lodgers said she would have electricity only downstairs – if it was installed upstairs people would only read in bed at her expense.

Many meetings and consultations took place as to whether it should be installed in the church or the village hall. All this chatter was an anticipatory surge similar to that of electricity itself.

Finally though, all was agreed, contracts were signed, and a team of workmen arrived, first of all to put up poles and then to do the work of actual installation in our houses. Piles of cable drums three feet across with thick lead-covered wire appeared and the wire was uncoiled from the drums on to the equally thick walls of our ancient dwellings. Short offcuts were everywhere and we kids had great fun melting down the lead in cocoa tins over bonfires – no medieval army ever prepared molten lead with such enthusiasm as us!

At last everything was ready for "switch on". The whole village would be connected on the same day. Mum and Dad were pledged not to light up before we arrived home from school, but as their excitement was as great as ours I suspect they did. Anyway, home we pelted and conducted them round while we tried out all the lights – they worked! We were really in the 20th century.

Of course, there were adjustments to be made. How different our rooms looked in the bright glare compared to the mellowness of the old oil lamps. How sybaritic to put on a light at the foot of the stairs and turn it off at the top. How much would it cost to run? No doubt more than the paraffin and candles. Jimmy Draper, who had blown the church organ manually twice each Sunday for years, and who had been insistent on an electric motor being installed so he could have an occasional lie-in, still appeared regularly at matins and evensong - the habits of a lifetime were not so easily broken, even though he could now sit among the congregation.

Then there were some changes, possibly also disadvantages. Village social events no longer had to be planned for the nights when the moon would be full. Surely also the stars weren't so brilliant – the constellations we so confidently named seemed somehow to dim as though the wattage had been reduced. Shadowy corners disappeared and I lost one of my great pleasures. How cosy it had been to dive down under the bedclothes, smuggle in a torch and a book and read: just must find out what happened next, just one more page. Now alas, torches were withdrawn from bedrooms and Mum could tell when I had the light on.

Possibly, though, the biggest loss was the lingering autumn dusk, when we sat in the firelight watching the sudden flaring of the logs or a shower of sparks shoot down on to the hearth before it was quite dark enough to light the lamp. Now it was just too easy to go from daylight to artificial light with one swift movement.

How fortunate too, that we couldn't look just a few years ahead and see the blacking-out and dimming of our smart new lights. And what would those people who embraced the supply of electricity so thankfully have thought if they could return and wander round our antique shops and see the oil lamps and flat irons that they so joyfully threw away now for sale at what to them would seem such ridiculous prices!'

HOW OUR LIVES CHANGED!

'I could never have imagined how our lives would change. At the time I was upset at being told I must give up my playhouse. This had the name "the coach-house" – looking back the grandest vehicle likely to have been kept in it was a pony trap. It was a wonderful playhouse for most of the girls from our end of Weston; we made cakes from sawdust collected from under the saw benches, and "iced" them with a mixture of whiting (powdered chalk) which we took from the paint shop when no one was looking. Our treasures were turned out and in no time at all our playhouse became the store for the Wessex Electricity Co (the name was painted over the door in red).

Electricity was coming to Weston to those who had been persuaded to have three lights and a plug at £1 1s 0d per point.

The coach-house was soon full of wire, brackets, screws and bolts. Poles were left in the fields and alongside roads. The Electricity Company paid a rent of two shillings and sixpence a week which was recorded in a ledger beginning in May 1930 and ending in February 1933, as well as payment for odd items such as nails, screws and timber.

I can still remember how excited we all were, waiting for the power to be switched on for the first time. What a shock when we could see into corners that only candles had previously lighted but dimly.

A year or so passed before we had lights installed upstairs, and several more before my father thought it was safe for his workshops. The joy of the first electric cooker installed at the beginning of the war, and the pleasure of ironing with an electric one after the smuts from the flat-irons!

I was too old for the playhouse when it was empty again. The sign stayed up for many years, until at last through age it was pulled down.'

THREE LIGHTS AND A PLUG

'When we first moved to our farmhouse at Wittenham in the 1930s there was no electricity, it was all lit by oil lamps. Soon after, we had electricity put in. You could have three lights and a plug put in free to encourage you to have it done.'

'In 1930 the Wessex Electricity (as it was called) offered every house in Woodcote three lights and one wall plug free. What a transformation!'

SHOPPING AND CALLERS TO THE DOOR

Shops had their own distinct characters in the past, reflecting their owners, and a trip to town was a real treat. Tradesmen delivered most of the essentials direct to our doors, and became part of the family.

OXFORD DELIGHTS

'Approaching Cornmarket Street from St Giles in 1923, we call in at Elliston and Cavell, "the centre of fashionable shopping for ladies", where the black-gowned assistants give their full attention to their clients, determined to send them back into the world satisfied, with emphasis on their best features.

Next door, we come to Taphouses Music Rooms, where we take our pianoforte exams at the appropriate times. Adjacent is the Penny Bazaar.

We now cross Cornmarket Street. On the corner of Ship Street, occupying a lovely old Tudor building, is the shop of Zacharias. They sell all varieties of rainwear and we stop fascinated by their window display, a fountain playing on a base of waterproof material.

Next door is Fullers with their mouth-watering walnut cakes covered with a thick layer of walnut icing. A little further we pass Buols – their chocolates, hand-made, are packed in crepe paper vanity bags in pastel shades lined with white and drawn up at the necks leaving inviting frills.

Opposite is the Cadena Cafe with its balcony, much favoured in the morning for coffee or in the afternoon for tea, with its trio of musical ladies playing popular excerpts from the *Mikado*, *Maid of the Mountains* and *The Merry Widow*.

Continuing towards Carfax we pass Grimbly and Hughes, the family grocer exuding delicious aromas of "sugar and spice and all things nice". Very courteous service and your orders promptly delivered.

Turning into Queens Street we admire Badcocks elegant display of ladies fashions according to the seasons.

Had we turned up the High at Carfax we should have perhaps

visited Webbers, a drapery store with a small lift upholstered in green velvet.

Our last call today will be Dolbear and Goodall, on the corner of King Edward Street, a popular chemist recognised by magnificent pear-shaped glass flasks filled with gallons of coloured liquids.'

'I well remember in the 1940s, my brother going off on his bike to St Ebbe's with an earthenware bowl to collect "faggots 'n peas" – I think it was from Del Nevo's shop. On Saturdays he would cycle up to Summertown to the Cadena bakery and with luck would return with a cake.

As children we would collect old clothes and rags to take to Warburton's, the rag and bone man in the St Ebbe's area (now all gone) for a few pence – "Mind you tell him there's some wool in there – it's worth more than cotton!"

There was a wonderful shop in George Street called Grubbs. The smells were gorgeous. On the one side was sold animal feeds, sacks of grain, etc, and on the other cakes! Never be allowed nowadays! They had pastry tarts filled with soft date mixture and topped with chocolate also a battenburg type with pink and chocolate squares and covered, not with marzipan, but with chocolate.

Who can forget the cakes in Fullers or the tea-rooms above; the grandeur of Grimbly and Hughes – high class grocer, or the attentive service at Capes, where a gentleman stood at the entrance to direct you to the right department and where there were *seats* at the counter and dotted about the store!'

THE CORNER SHOP

'My childhood memories go back to the corner shop in Windmill Road, Headington, in the 1930s. It sold everything from bundles of wood and paraffin to groceries, sweets and cigarettes. The bundles of wood were called faggots and consisted of small lengths sufficient to light two fires, they cost about twopence.

When I was quite small, I was allowed to cross the road and go to buy sweets. My penny would buy a sherbet dab, a bar of toffee and a stick of liquorice. A stool was placed in front of the counter so that small children could climb on it to choose their sweets from a display.

Mrs Wilkins who owned the shop was a tall lady with her hair worn in a bun with combs to hold it in place. She always wore a long black dress with a pin-tucked bodice and a frilly "front". Around her neck dangled her pince-nez spectacles on a gold chain. When she put them on to read they perched on the end of her nose and she had to look over the top of them when she spoke to anyone.

I was always fascinated when she used the bacon slicer. "How thick do you want it?", she would ask the customers, and by moving a knob and turning a handle, the machine would cut it to the thickness required. I think I expected to see sliced fingers as she removed the rashers and piled them on to greaseproof paper on the scale at the side.

The cheese was cut into wedges with a strong wire and butter was taken from a block and patted into shape with two wooden spatulas, weighed and wrapped in greaseproof paper. It was very difficult to stop it melting before refrigerators were invented and polythene bags and wrappers were unheard of at that time.

Sugar came in bulk and was weighed and put into strong blue paper bags, as was dried fruit and tea. Flour was also weighed according to requirements and was delivered in strong hessian sacks.

Mrs Wilkins had a large wooden desk in the window of the shop with an ornate till on the top of it. It had large keys like that of a giant typewriter with amounts in £.s.d. stamped upon them. If your bill came to one and sixpence, she would press down the keys with one shilling (1/-) and sixpence (6d) on them and the till would make a jingling sound and the money drawer would shoot out at the bottom. She would then place the coins in little individual trays and give change when needed.

The corner shop was the place where you could hear all the local gossip, meet your neighbours for a friendly chat and have personal attention for all your needs. You didn't need to "dress" to go to buy the odds and ends, in fact the housewives usually came in wearing their "pinnies" and slippers and with their hair in curlers.'

'My grandfather started the village store in Bampton, then known as Eeles' Store. He sold groceries, hardware, even tin trunks which were used by girls who went into service. It was a magical place for me and my cousins as we were allowed to help fill blue paper bags with various sugars and currants from drawers behind the shop counter.

The shop assistants wore stiff white starched aprons with fringes. Below the shop was an enormous cellar and that was where the sausages were made.

Behind the counter on one of the shelves there were glass-lidded tins containing biscuits of various brands. Broken biscuits were never sold but kept for the children along with sweets.

My grandfather lived in Folly View, overlooking the Square. He was later crippled with rheumatoid arthritis and bedridden. In his bedroom there was a huge mirror, placed so he could see the whole of Bampton Square.'

VILLAGE SHOPPING

'I still live in Sonning Common in South Oxfordshire, the village I was born in nearly 70 years ago. I remember it before the war as a quiet, friendly village, grass roadside verges bright in spring with buttercups and dandelions, the houses with large gardens, many with fruit trees and a hen run and some with a pig in a sty at the end of the plot. In between were some quite large orchards with many cherry trees, a picture at blossom time.

In the late 1920s/early 1930s, the village had a post office and two grocers who called for orders (daily if asked) and these were then delivered, usually by a boy on a trade bike. There was a butcher, two drapers, two garages, a cycle shop, a shop selling newspapers, a coal merchant who also sold animal feed stuffs, and at one time delivered by mule cart. Three bakers came round every day and four dairymen delivered twice daily, including Sundays. Mr Nash pushed his milk round in a handcart; he had a white beard and I was convinced he was Father Christmas when I saw him speaking to my father very early one morning in mid December.

Two fishmongers brought fresh fish round, one coming on Tuesdays and Thursdays, and the other on Wednesdays and Fridays; they also carried fruit, but I don't remember many vegetables on board, nearly everyone grew their own. In spite of all these people vying for custom, there were still things that could not be bought locally. If my mother could not make the bus trip to Reading, our nearest large town, over the border in Berkshire, she called on the carrier.

There were three carriers serving the village, but our regular was Mr Clarke. I loved the days the large white card with CLARKE on it in black was hung in the window and sometimes I was lifted up to hang it on the window catch myself. We watched and waited until his van chugged into view and stopped at the gate. This Model T Ford was unusual as it had been used as a missionary van in Africa, and had ventilators along the ridge of the roof; it also at times would run backwards when on a slope. If this was at a road junction or other vehicles were about, the passenger, usually a boy, had to jump out and stand behind, until Mr Clarke was in control again.

I remember Mr Clarke wearing a warehouse coat, gaiters, having a General Kitchener moustache and being rather glum. Mother always had the list ready. Fennings Cooling Powders and Tussiloc (a cherry flavoured cough linctus) were often needed from Dysons the chemist

70

in the Market Place, and sometimes Aspro, iodine, Health Salts or syrup of figs would be ordered.

Another call would be to Alice Baker's in the Arcade, a little shop which was bombed and destroyed completely during the war. This order would include liberty bodices, Chilprufe vests and knickers and socks in varying sizes, the list was always handed to Mr Clarke with the mysterious words "on appro". I don't know why I did not ask what it meant, but it puzzled me for a long time.

At tea time Mr Clarke would arrive with the goods. He always seemed more talkative, in fact sometimes quite jolly at the end of the day; I thought he must enjoy shopping (I certainly did not) and I didn't know then that the carriers' yard was at The Boar's Head in Friar Street, and refreshment was consumed in quantity on the premises.

At bath time the brown paper parcel was opened, the paper and string being carefully saved, and the clothes were tried on. Sometimes my mother would say, "No, I think you need the next size, they can go back tomorrow, they are 'on appro'," and tomorrow the card would be put in the window again.

Today we have a variety of shops, including a chemist, in a village that has grown out of all recognition since the war, but some things still have to be fetched from town. When I have been shopping,

The village store at Uffington in the 1940s. Such shops were an essential part of village life.

71

sometimes with a grandchild "to help", and I have queued in the traffic, queued at the car park, have done my shopping and queued to pay for it, have carried it back to the car and then unloaded it at home, I sit with a welcome cup of tea and my feet up and I think of Mr Clarke's card hanging in the window and the goods "on appro", not a phrase used much when shopping today!'

'It was not necessary to go out of Fritwell village for anything in the 1930s.

Dew's shop sold groceries, fruit, hardware, clothes, shoes, millinery, haberdashery, paraffin, corn for chickens, meal for pigs, etc. If required, someone came to get the order and then it was delivered to the house the next day. The post office was combined with a small shop, too.

Milk was delivered from the farms, or you could take a jug or milkcan and collect your own. Most people had skimmed as this was cheaper than full cream. Bakers brought bread to the village daily, plus dough cakes, lardy cakes etc. The coalman came every week, or if you had space you could buy in the summer when coal was cheaper. My family had three tons tipped in the barn, to last the year. All cooking was done with coal ovens, of course. Wrighton's the butcher had their own slaughterhouse (as they do now) and sold quality meat and poultry of every kind.

The carrier, Mr Isaac White, went to Banbury several times a week, with his motor van and for a small fee would do your shopping, delivering it on his return in the evening.

There were three public houses in the village. The landlords ran Slate Clubs (to help when the family breadwinner was ill) and Thrift Clubs (money paid in throughout the year was paid out plus interest at Christmas).'

FROM THE DAY WE MOVED IN

'On the day my family moved to Peppard, 6th June 1934, we found two lots of milk and butter each with a card from local dairymen. My mother who was such a gentle person, didn't want to upset one by asking the other to deliver, so, typical of her, she asked them both, and so it was that we had two milkmen, one in the morning and the other in the afternoon.

I well remember one incident that took place with our morning milkman – a Mr Taylor of Colmore Dairy, Kingwood Common. He was a perfect gentleman, but not too good with figures. My mother was planning on giving us a treat – boiled eggs for tea – and so asked him for four eggs. At that time I believe they were about one shilling and elevenpence a dozen. She had already worked the amount out, but Mr Taylor would not listen and after much counting on fingers and scratching of head, he asked my mother if she would mind having half a dozen because he knew the price for that.

Our village bakery at Peppard was owned by the Kew family and they not only baked bread and cakes, but also sold a limited supply of groceries. They would also bake cakes for people – special fruit cakes which were put in the oven after the bread had been removed. They knew just how long to leave them in and the cakes were always cooked just right. Of course in the years just before, during and immediately after the war, families found it a little difficult to cook a large turkey or goose at Christmas. I well remember my father taking our Christmas bird down to the bakehouse while my mother managed to cook the vegetables on a kitchen range or oil stove. There was quite a procession down to the bakehouse on Christmas morning. We didn't have an electric cooker until 1947.'

CALLERS TO THE DOOR

'The baker at Bampton called three times a week. Just above our house in Church View there was a dairy where I used to fetch the milk in a can. Mr Busby owned the dairy and each morning he walked the cows from Church View through the village to a lane turning off Buckland Road, putting them in a field. Each evening he would bring them back. Mr Busby also had a bakery where villagers could bring their Sunday joints to be cooked in the bakery oven. The charge was sixpence to a shilling. Another bakery called Constable's in the centre of the village had the same facility. We also had a carrier called Mr Green. He lived in Buckland Road and delivered letters and parcels to Oxford, Swindon and Faringdon. He charged sixpence for a letter.'

'There were just two shops in Woodcote, both selling groceries and both bakers delivering bread every day. Milk was also delivered daily by horse-drawn float and dished out into your own jug at the door. Much later on another milkman started coming and bringing it in bottles. Butchers from Pangbourne and Goring brought meat three times a week and a greengrocer and a fishman came twice a week. Baylis from Reading came for an order fortnightly on a Monday and delivered on a Wednesday, so we were well catered for. Newspapers were delivered daily, and as everyone had coal fires the coalman came every week. I still have a coal fire and the grandson of my mother's coalman delivers to me.'

'In Oxford in the 1920s, a muffin man came round ringing his bell and carrying his tray on his head. From another man you could buy a rabbit for ninepence and the rag and bone man gave you threepence for the skin.

All the shops had delivery boys on bikes and in vans. They came for orders in the morning and delivered the same day. No one had phones in those days.'

'We collected our milk from Well Place Farm at Ipsden, or if the cow had gone dry, from Garson's Farm. There were no coal deliveries: when farm waggons went to Goring station they would bring back coal for Farm Cottages (before 1916 it came from the wharf at Benson). Bread was delivered three times a week, and meat and groceries once a week. When we went shopping at Wallingford we went by pony and trap or walked or push-biked. If you had young children, you took the pram and a picnic and made a day of it.'

'Shops at Abingdon used to deliver to Long Wittenham, and there was also a carrier's cart. You had to put a card in your window and he knew then to call for your order, which he would get in town and deliver to you. This was especially useful on market days.'

'Three bakers delivered to South Leigh and competed for customers – Baker Swingburn, Baker Harris and Baker Berry, so that at least one baker delivered every weekday, two on Wednesdays and Saturdays. Fishman Keen also delivered fresh fish and fruit. Milk could be bought from the shop or from Mr Hopkins at the pub and Harry Moody kept cows and delivered milk round the village, knocking on the windows of his neighbours who found it difficult to get up for work in the mornings! If you needed scissors or knives sharpened, you could take them to Mr Pickett who would grind them for you on his machine at home.'

'Frank Didcock had a coal tip in his yard at Appleton Road, Cumnor, where he kept the coal carted from the Oxford wharves. He put it into sacks and lifted them with his metal hook arm to make his weekly deliveries. In the shed nearby his son did shoe repairs. For Pat Fowler, who ran the shop, nothing was too much trouble. "I remember Pat slicing bacon rashers with a knife from a long side of bacon," one resident recalls. Sugar was weighed out and put into bags, lard was cut to order and you took your own bottle for vinegar. "You'd ask for five Woodbines and she'd wrap them in a piece of newspaper."

There was no baker in the village. Bread was delivered from

Appleton in a covered horse van by Mr Hicks. He turned round at the bottom of Leys Road and some people would wait for him there. Sometimes it was a long wait because Mr Hicks liked to stop at The Vine for a game of dominoes. In Botley, deliveries were made by Surman. Then there was "Cakey" Harper who pushed his handcart all the way from Abingdon, wearing a top hat, to sell cakes.'

'Traders at the door were daily visitors up to the 1950s. The baker came six days a week with a pony and cart. The bread was baked in the village and, before the war, several Farmoor people would take their Sunday dinners to be cooked in his ovens.

At least five butchers came to the village; most of them coming two or three times a week. Some would sell from the van but others only took orders. A greengrocer came once a week with a horse and trolley. Oranges were seven for sixpence then.

A fishmonger came with his pony and smart black trap. He had the fish in the back and made several stops around the village, usually followed by the cats.

In the 1930s ice creams were strictly a summer treat. Walls' Stop Me and Buy One man came on a bicycle with a big container in front and rang a bell. The penny ices were really lollies encased in cardboard. I did not like them much; they always tasted of the wrapping. Another ice cream seller was the local chimney sweep! He came from a neighbouring village with a motor-bike and sidecar and no sign of his sooty labours. He was very popular and always smiling. On Saturday nights another seller came with a van and stopped by the post office. He blew a whistle and there was soon a crowd. Sometimes my mother would fetch a cornet costing a penny or halfpenny for me and I usually had this sitting in the tin bath in the kitchen.

Travelling shops came round with all kinds of hardware, paraffin etc. A shopkeeper from Chipping Norton used to take cases of clothes from door to door and the Co-op in that town would always send out garments by the baker "on appro".

Other callers included tramps, seen frequently travelling between the various workhouses in the 1930s. One would bring rashers of bacon and ask my mother to fry them for him. She would add eggs and bread and he would sit on a seat by our back door with the food in the frying pan, mopping it up. No one was ever turned away from a door in those days. There was no fear.

People who were regarded as rather a nuisance were those who tried to persuade one to change to another newspaper or take a magazine. Incentives were given such as a tea set if one collected so many coupons from a number of issues.

75

One man collected rabbit skins, giving a copper or two for them. They must have been rather "high" if they had been hanging in the shed for several weeks.

Occasionally gipsies would wait outside the village school and promise to give us a goldfish if we brought some rags when we came back from lunch. Gipsies also called at the door frequently, selling the usual wooden pegs and flowers.'

FOOD – AND THE PIG

Our food was seasonal and filling, yet how delicious. Perhaps some delicacies are best left to the past, such as lambs tails, and few of us would nowadays want to face killing the pig, but in those times when most country families kept a pig at the bottom of the garden the resulting bacons, hams and other titbits were surely tempting.

SELF-SUFFICIENT

'Our diet was quite stodgy, based mainly on suet puddings (butcher's suet), which were sweet or savoury. A suet crust was made with 4oz suet and 8oz plain flour (most people now use self-raising flour); this was mixed with water to a pliable rolling dough. With this basic dough the well loved bacon clanger was made. The dough was covered with chopped bacon and onion, and grated potato could be added to give a moist clanger. This was rolled like a Swiss roll, placed on a cotton cloth, tied with string, put in boiling water and simmered for one to two hours. Steaming or rolling in foil will *never* give the same flavour. The clanger was served hot and left-overs were often warmed in the frying pan next day.

Every household was fairly self-sufficient – hens in the back garden and vegetables and fruit home-grown or from the allotment. Potatoes were in clamps of earth and straw but if the winter was very severe it was impossible to open the clamps. Runner beans were salted and eggs preserved in isinglass (I did not much enjoy these). Most families kept a pig and many kept two, one for themselves and one to sell. They would go round taking orders for the various parts, and when the time for killing came it was surprising how many "friends" the family seemed to have!

My grandfather was the baker at The Bartons who, as well as baking bread, also used the oven to cook the Sunday Yorkshire puddings and joints. It was the men who went to collect the dinners, and they used the occasion as a great opportunity for the exchange of news. They carried the dinners home under a white cloth – and no Yorkshire pudding today ever tastes as good. The batter was made from skimmed farm milk (which cost fourpence for a four pint can). Pies and tarts were also cooked and these provisions lasted over the next two days to feed the family while the ritual of washing and ironing was carried out.

My mother cooked by oil stove and also had an oven by the fireplace. I can remember her browning the top of a shepherd's pie by holding a red-hot shovel near it. We didn't have a grill in those days, and one of our pleasures was sitting by the fire on the (home-made) hearth rug toasting bread. It tasted delicious.

We had no piped water and no flush toilets. The contents of the privy were spread over allotments, a practice that was said to produce exceptionally good rhubarb! Most of the men worked on farms and many walked great distances to work. I can remember

The ladies of Kingham Women's Institute in 1925. The WI gave many countrywomen their first opportunity to broaden their horizons.

them in wet weather wearing sacks cut to form a hood and hanging down at the back.'

LAMBS TAILS

'As the lambs grew, their tails were cut off, as it was easier then to keep the lambs clean. The wool was plucked from the tails and we had lamb-tail pie for dinner.

Rabbits, hares, pheasants, partridge or pigeon were also regularly served for dinner. We lived mainly on what we could get from the farm. The grocer delivered to isolated farms about once a month in the 1920s.

Looking through a farm account book for 1921, a few items were sold – twelve rabbits at one shilling and fourpence each, five pheasants at a guinea, three partridges at three shillings and sixpence, 15 lbs butter at one shilling and sixpence a pound.'

'My aunt, aged 96, remembers her father bringing in bundles of lambs tails, which were skinned and then fried.'

HAYBOX COOKING

'The haybox method of cooking and saving fuel was a technique used by my mother. A casserole was brought to the boil on the hob and transferred to the haybox where it simmered for many hours in the well insulated container. Rice puddings and beetroots cooked well by this method too.'

ALL IN TOGETHER

'When I was young I was sent down Mill Road at Marcham to leave a message for an old lady we called Granny Lawrence. She was cooking out in her garden, which lots of people did in those days, on a fireplace made of two piles of bricks with two iron bars across the top to stand a large oval saucepan. As I was there, it started to bubble over and she lifted the lid. To my amazement, it was a bright purple colour. I asked what it was and was told, "Cabbage and taters and a blackberry and apple pudden." Of course, the pudding was one with a suet crust wrapped in a pudding cloth and all was cooked together in the one pot. A purple barbecue!'

THE CIDER PRESS

'I lived on a farm near Churchill and one thing I remember happening was the cider press coming from Bledlington.

My brothers and sisters and I had collected up all the cider apples from the orchard and placed them in sacks. They were then taken to the cider press in the yard and cider was made. It was put into barrels and into our cellar for use throughout the year.

A hot toddy was made on very cold days – the cider was put into a pan with sugar and ground ginger and heated, and very much enjoyed. It was quite potent, too!'

WHAT IT COST IN THE 1950s

'Rationing was still in operation in the early 1950s and below is a week's order for two adults and three children. The items on the end of the list varied according to what the Oddington grocer could offer.

	£	s	d
10 oz butter		1	10½
1½ lb bacon		6	0
¾ lb tea		3	6
Biscuits		1	10
Rice Crispies		1	3½
Shredded Wheat		1	0
Quart vinegar		0	10
1 lb 14 oz sultanas		2	6
Large tin salmon		3	6
Tin fruit		3	3
Margarine		1	2
1 lb 2 oz cheese		2	6
Sausages		2	8
6 matches		1	
Total	£1	12s	11d

RABBITS, PIGS AND THE BAKEHOUSE

'Rabbits were used whenever possible for a good wholesome meal for the family. When they were in season, on a Saturday morning several children met at the Drive corner to walk to Kytes Lodge on the Heythrop estate. Mr Kyte the keeper sold rabbits, one shilling and sixpence for two. They were tied together by the hind legs. We put them on a walking stick and carried them on our shoulder. Cooking was done on a blackleaded fireplace with an oven at the side. We grew all our own vegetables and it was usual to have a large boiler (or pot) with a piece of bacon or ham, with cabbage and potatoes in a net, and a boiled suet pudding, either a spotted dick or plain which was eaten with golden syrup.

When we had pigs the pot was filled with potatoes and cabbage stems and boiled up for pig feed. They were given this with toppings (I think it's now known as bran). When they were large enough they were given barley meal to fatten them up.

It was quite a day when the pig was killed. We had a butcher who did this. The neighbours came to help. One stood by to catch the blood to make hog pudding; every part was used. It was cut up. Flitches of bacon and hams were covered in salt brine, saltpetre was rubbed into the part with bone in to keep the flies away. We had backbone pie, liver and fry, faggots and tongue. Chitterlings were cleaned and plaited for frying. Small joints were given to neighbours for their help.

We had two bakers here, one Taplins, mostly cottage loaves. They would cook our Sunday joint of beef on a wire stand under which would be a Yorkshire pudding. You took it there and collected it: it cost twopence per joint. You could buy a quarter of dough, take it home to have lard, sugar and fruit mixed in and take it back to be baked, result a delicious dough cake! The mill had an oven for baking bread – it was used for several years. We used to think nothing was more enjoyable than the crusty top of loaf with a piece of cheese and an onion.'

PIG KILLING DAY

'Pig killing day arrived and I was glad to go to school. I did not like the squealing and the gore. The butcher came on the 7.15 am bus from Chipping Norton. The straw for the fire was put into the middle of the yard and the pig, who seemed to know what was to happen, was fetched from the sty, killed and the bristles were burnt off. The carcase was cut down the belly and the innards removed. The liver ensured a good and tasty fry. The lights (lungs) were cooked in a large iron pot (I have it still) to make faggots. The leaf (fat surrounding the kidneys) was rendered down into lard. Rosemary would be added and seasonings and it was delicious spread on bread. Brawn was made from the head and odd bits of meat. Someone always wanted the intestines to make into chitterlings. I never ate those; I had seen them in their raw state!

The carcase would be propped open with sticks and placed upright in the barn until the next day when the butcher would return to cut it up. Joints were given to people who had given meat to us when they had killed a pig.

The two sides of bacon were salted in a lead trough for several weeks and then placed either on a rack on the kitchen ceiling or hung in cloths on the walls. This bacon was very fat with only a thin layer of lean left on and was boiled and eaten cold for breakfast or for supper with pickles and chutney. The hams were put into large earthenware bowls and basted daily with vinegar and various spices. They would be put beside the bacon – all in a warm kitchen. There were no fridges but it did not seem to go bad.'

'We kept three pigs, one for home and two for market. Father used to go to the farms around Bampton and buy small "pig potatoes", cook them in a large cauldron, mash them, fill the cauldron with water, add some toppings (meal) and that fed the pigs. Mr Townsend from Church View collected the pigs to take to market. Charlie Ponder was the village pig-killer. Word would get around that a pig was to be killed and children would congregate in a yard in Slaughter House Lane to watch the procedure. The pig was held over a bench and its throat cut, letting the blood pour out amidst much squealing. Then the animal was hung up in the slaughterhouse to drain. Charlie killed for the butcher.

Most people kept their pigs for salting down. A gipsy called Jack Smith gave the recipe for curing pork and many of the cottagers had a side of salted bacon hanging up. Because of this there existed something called "salt bacon rot". This was where the salt from the bacon had over the years soaked into the stone fabric of the building, causing the stone to crumble.'

'All we cottagers at Peppard kept a pig, every part of which was used when it came to its timely end. Mum stripped hazel twigs to turn the chitterlings (pigs' smaller intestines) inside out for cleaning, plaiting the smallest before boiling. Delicious cold! The main part of the pig was cured into two sides of bacon, one kept by the family in the 1940s, the other purchased by the Ministry of Food.'

'Most households in Cassington kept two pigs; one for home consumption and one to sell to the bacon factory. The carrier who took them to the factory said it was difficult because the pig was usually fed by the lady of the household so they disliked being handled by a man. His routine was a bucket with some food, then grab the pig by the tail and drag it up the ramp, but if you missed the ramp then it was most likely you had to chase the pig round the village.'

FROM THE CRADLE TO THE GRAVE

We were more likely to be born, to suffer our illnesses and to die in our own homes in the past, in the days before the National Health Service when the doctor and the nurse had to be paid for and many villages had their own sick clubs. No wonder we relied so much on home cures – odd though some sound today!

BORN AT HOME

'There was no National Health Service or Social Services in those days between the wars and if we were ill we relied upon each other for help, and especially upon an excellent nurse who lived at Studley. When she walked, she used very small steps and appeared to be running, so she was nicknamed "Dame Trot". Confinements usually took place in the home and were overseen by the nurse, who only called the doctor if necessary. When my younger sister was born, I had been told she would be brought by the doctor in his black bag, so I waited by his car until he was ready to go and then asked him please would he bring another one when he came next. He said that he couldn't promise anything but would do his best. This satisfied me because I hated being the baby in the family.'

'Babies were christened at about six weeks old. This was the age when traditionally all babies went out of long gowns and into short clothes.'

'A local story relates why Baby Alley in Kingham got its name. A childless woman longed for a child, but her husband didn't. Unknown to him she sought medical advice and was given a potion to cure her infertility. On finding the medicine and discovering what it was for, the husband became enraged and hurled the bottle into the well which served the daily needs of all the cottages in the alley. Sure enough, nine months later a number of babies were born to the families living there. Hence the name.'

'TRUE MORALITY'

'James Holmes lived in East Hanney for most of his long life. His local activities are well remembered, but he was a man of many parts, not all of which were easily observable.

As a landlord of his 15 or so cottages he could regularly be seen on his Monday rent-collecting round. He did much to enhance the appearance of the village. Parish council minutes record his efforts to get trees planted, seats provided and amenities maintained. He is fondly remembered for setting up the bathing place on the Letcombe Brook. Erected in 1896, it provided enjoyment for young men and boys for nearly 50 years.

Just downstream from the remains of the bathing place is Lower Mill which Holmes purchased in 1903. Here he stored apples from his orchards.

Apart from the mill and cottages, he also owned two fine houses in the village, The Mulberries and Hazelwood, the former his gracious home, the latter his base for carrying on his surprising business of supplying contraceptive aids and literature to places as far away as India from 1890 to the 1930s.

Well respected he may have been; well understood he probably was not, certainly in his early adult years. The basic nature of his business was known, for he employed a few local people. His regular journeys down to the post office on his bicycle, carrying his little packets was a familiar sight. Few, however, would have known the strength of his commitment to the cause of population control. Among those with an inkling of his hidden depths were the few able to recognise G. B. Shaw and H. G. Wells among his occasional visitors.

These eminent men may well have been giving Holmes moral support in the legal trouble he was involved in through the circulation of his little book, *True Morality*. This crusading compilation advocating family limitation was selling in tens of thousands shortly after its publication in 1891. Its fervent, tract-like nature seems merely strange to a modern reader, but its advocacy of birth control was repugnant to Church and State at that time. It was deemed "obscene" literature, and a bookseller in the north of England was imprisoned. Shortly after this, in 1912, Holmes himself was prosecuted for sending out one of his catalogues, also reckoned as "obscene". (His fearlessness and integrity at the time of the court case would have caused no surprise to those who may have witnessed his behaviour twelve years earlier when, after advertising his pro-Boer views in the press locally, a mob attacked The Mulberries.) One can understand how his subsequent good works in the village enabled him to live down his early unpopularity.

He died at The Mulberries in 1938 on his 79th birthday. Hanney people, young and old, gathered around the little memorial garden that he gave to the parish, to witness the placing of his ashes under "Holmes's Oak".'

THE MIDWIFE

'I came to Oxford in 1958 to complete my midwifery training. I had spent most of my nursing career in south east London, and Oxford was a complete change.

The eight pupil midwives lived in a hostel in Abingdon Road under the iron rule of Miss Needham. We were each allocated to a District Midwife and to a part of Oxford City. My area included Iffley, Cowley, Rosehill and the just emerging Blackbird Leys, and Miss Viner was my excellent supervisor.

Many babies were born at home then, and District Midwives provided a professional and highly organised service. Mothers were visited for ante-natal care, and to leave the necessary equipment. We were called by the mother or father when labour began and usually stayed throughout the labour, drinking strong tea made by the nervous father and getting to know other members of the family. After the delivery we tidied up, had some more tea, or sometimes something stronger to wet the baby's head, and cycled off, only to return after a short while to make sure that all was well. Visiting each day for a fortnight afterwards completed the feeling that we had played a small part in the new family's life.

We used our own bikes and set off each morning in navy uniforms, with a blue bag strapped behind the saddle. I usually had some left over toast to feed the swans as well. At night we took it in turns to sleep by the only phone and to call other pupils if necessary. We had no fears about cycling around Oxford at night, although I didn't cycle along the tow-path in the dark. Coming home over the weirs to Abingdon Road in the misty early morning is one of my happy memories of this time.

I stayed on in Oxford after my course was over, though not as a midwife. In time I married and had three children of my own – one in Oxford, one in Woodstock and one in Eynsham. All born at home, of course!'

HOME CURES

'Goose grease was a popular remedy for chesty coughs in the winter months. If you had a cold, mustard baths and being fed with onions and milk were common. If children had whooping cough they were sent to the gasworks to breathe in the fumes.

A treat if you were ill was to be allowed a fire in the bedroom. Paraffin stoves are remembered with a certain fondness as they made patterns on the ceiling and also very blobby toast with a distinct flavour of paraffin.'

'When a young lad at Combe cut his finger badly with a penknife, his grandfather wrapped the wound in a large cobweb and told him it would be better. Today he has no scar there.

His grandmother's favourite remedy for an ailing child was to go to the cheese dish and slice off a piece of mouldy cheese and pop it in their mouth.

Everyone seemed to have chilblains years ago – was it from toasting our feet before the open fire or was it inadequate footwear in very cold winters? One remedy was Snowfire, a block of green balm to rub on our cracked feet.'

'I have vivid memories of nights sitting by the bedroom fire holding to my aching ear a flannel bag about the size of an envelope, filled with hot salt. It was very comforting. For aching tummies, my mother gave us mild doses of salt in water, for bruises home-made ointment, for septic sores bread poultices (a small cotton bag filled with bread soaked in hot water and well squeezed out), for chesty coughs goose grease or camphorated oil. In fact, all sores, bruises, cuts and sprains were treated with home-made remedies. When my young brother ate some arum berries he found under the nut tree, we hustled him into the kitchen where Mother gave him salt water to make him vomit. Up came the berries, followed by a ticking off for us for not watching him. Stinging nettle rashes were painful but eased by crushed dock leaves rubbed well in.'

'A cure for earache was to warm an onion, remove the core and put it on the ear. An onion cut in half and rubbed over a wasp sting helped to relieve the pain.'

DOCTORS AND HOSPITALS

'There was no resident doctor in Appleton, as is still the case. The nearest doctor was about four miles away or at Abingdon. Later we had a village nurse, and a local Nursing Association was organised. It was run by a committee of village ladies, under the auspices of the County. The Nursing Association also ran a weekly baby clinic. People paid about sixpence a week towards the cost of this service.

"Nurse", as she was affectionately known, brought nearly all the village babies into the world, dealt with illnesses, wounds and the laying out of the dead. There was also a kind old woman who would perform this sad service.

The Radcliffe Infirmary at Oxford and the Abingdon cottage hospital were the two main hospitals to which you went if you were seriously ill. The isolation hospital at Abingdon dealt with cases of scarlet fever, diphtheria, and TB.

In the late 1930s the doctor's surgery was held at the Plough Inn. Two collectors made a regular weekly round of the village for contributions towards the hospitals, sixpence or a shilling a week being the average payment.'

'There was the time that a farm labourer of Salford fell off a straw rick, breaking both of his legs, and he had to lay on the farmhouse kitchen table from eight in the morning till four o'clock in the afternoon before they took him to hospital. He returned home with steel pins through his legs with corks on each side to hold them in place. In spite of this he was up and about within a year, and with the aid of two sticks went off to Choice Hill to go hoeing up swedes and turnips. They couldn't afford to sit around for long in those days.'

'Almost in Bix parish, right on the edge of the town, was an isolation hospital, the Smith hospital, where people (usually children) with infectious fevers were sent. I was lucky not to go there, but I was treated four times at Henley War Memorial Hospital which, sadly, is no more. There were men's and women's wards, each with about eight beds, and two or three small private wards. Run of the mill operations such as hernias, tonsils, removal of cysts etc were done there.'

'I had a great uncle who was a doctor. He lived to be 100 and at one time was the oldest doctor in the country. When he was 89 he decided he would like to take a cruise so he applied to be taken on as a ship's doctor. When he was asked how old he was he said, "Well, I'm getting on a bit." He was taken on and did his cruise!'

SIT ON THE PATIENT!

'One day Derek got tangled up on some railings and cut his throat. His mother was out so Auntie Lily put him on the back of her bike and they rode round the village to look for her. Eventually they found her and got home. It so happened that the doctor was nearby seeing someone who was in bed with pneumonia, so Derek's mother fetched him to look at his throat, which the doctor decided needed stitches. Derek immediately dived under the table and hung on to the legs, but his mother dragged him out. Dr Cruikshank got the equipment out, and Derek's mother held his head and his aunt sat on him.

Another boy, Roy, remembers he was running round behind a fence where he should not have been when he stepped on a bit of wood with a rusty nail, which went right through his sandal and into his foot. The nail was pulled out and he was taken over to the district nurse who lived in the end almshouse at Cassington. She said, "You'll have to sit on him while I pour this iodine on," and he was held down, his foot held up and the nurse poured the iodine on. This particular nurse was a large lady! It was usual for the nurse to live in the almshouse beside the church.'

TAKING OUR MEDICINE

'Early this century, a flu epidemic hit Kingham. Sir Henry Curynghame and his wife were living in Kingham Lodge at the time and obtained quantities of quinine to give to the children of the village. They had to proceed to the Lodge to receive it.

Such was the deference of those days, that Lady Curynghame – a Queen Mary-style person in appearance and dress – insisted that the girls curtsey and the boys bow to her before and after receiving their medicine.'

THE CLUB

'Weston had a very good Friendly Society. Each member paid a little each month while they were working. When they were ill they were paid a few shillings each week, just enough to keep them going. When the National Health came in, the Club finished, but it was very important until then. They held a Club Day on Whit Tuesday – a gathering at the school with a dinner. A band was engaged to play and they had a most beautiful flag. The band went round to play at the farms and the manor, where we could all go and dance on the lawn. The last Club Day when they were closing down was rather sad.'

SCARLET FEVER

'I had scarlet fever when I was five years old and was taken to the isolation hospital at Abingdon. No visitors were allowed inside the hospital but communication was by notes held up to the windows or french doors. I was too young to write but other patients did so for me. Adults and children were in one ward. I was there for eight weeks and any presents of fruit etc brought in had to be shared. I did not like carrots but was taken into the bathroom by a nurse and made to eat them. I do not think she liked the task much but the matron insisted.

At home my bedroom had to be fumigated and my toys and clothing burned. My parents, who had a small farm, were not allowed to sell milk, butter or eggs for two weeks. This meant a loss of income and there was no government help in the early 1930s.

Measles, mumps, chickenpox and whooping cough all necessitated a visit from the doctor and a certificate to say one was unable to go to school. At the beginning of each term at grammar school we had to take a form signed by our parents to say that we had not been in contact with infectious diseases during the preceding two weeks.'

THE LAST JOURNEY

'When someone died at Farmoor the body was kept in the house until the funeral – this must have been a problem in the two up, two down cottages. The body would be laid out by two of the village women, who regarded this as a service. The local carpenter made the coffin and carried out undertaker's duties. The coffin was taken to the church on the bier, pushed along the street by the bearers and the family walked behind in strict order of precedence. Most wore black or had black armbands or a black diamond-shaped patch sewn onto their coat sleeves.'

'After the First World War there was a real need for a bier at Weston on the Green, as nothing suitable was available and the cost of hiring one for carrying coffins to the church was out of the question for the majority of the villagers.

If a bier was requested, one was hired from Middleton Stoney or Chesterton at a cost of five shillings. It then had to be collected and returned which, with attending the funeral as well, took up much of a working day.

The parish council organised a collection and requested my father (Mr R. Boddington, the village wheelwright and carpenter) to prepare drawings and an estimate. Eventually the bier was ordered and made with seasoned oak, the wheels being made of ash. A shed was also erected to house the bier, the total cost of £24 in 1938. Our lives were simple then, before the last war. Then came motor transport. Our way of life changed and the bier was needed no longer. It still exists and is kept in the church to preserve it.'

'Bampton had a brilliant carpenter named Jack Joyce who made all the coffins and was also undertaker to the village. The coffins were put on "the wheels", a trolley universally used and the use of which had no stigma. The undertaker followed it to the church, wearing a tall black hat.

When my friend's mother died in the 1950s, her children, aged between 17 and 21 years, had to arrange her funeral. They envisaged a sort of Thomas Hardy-type scene – a rather dramatic, melancholy procession, with the children dressed in black or grey traversing Sandford Field with the coffin on "the wheels", but their grandmother was shocked, thinking only paupers used such things.'

'There were always local ladies at Combe who would lay out bodies when a death had occurred. One villager remembers her mother was called at any time of day or night and always responded immediately. She took her daughter to show her how it was done and she remembers the legs being tied together, the false teeth put in place and a scarf tied tightly round the face under the chin.'

'When a teacher named Mrs Chapman lived next door to the church at Ipsden, she would stand outside when funerals took place and would always make up the number of mourners to an even number. Apparently it was not done to have an odd number of mourners.'

'In my young days at Thame, when a funeral hearse was due to pass any houses the curtains would be drawn until it had gone by. Anyone standing in the street would stand still as the hearse went by, the men taking off their hats as a mark of respect, and any workmen stopping whatever they were doing. The undertaker wearing mourning suit and top hat would walk in front of the car. Often the mourners would walk behind if they could not afford to hire cars. Generally the only ladies present would be the next of kin as it was usually an occasion attended by men only. How different it was then, and how much more respect was shown.'

CHILDHOOD & SCHOOLDAYS

G. HOWARD

A VILLAGE CHILD

Growing up in the close community of an Oxfordshire village had its own pleasures and delights.

'As in most villages the school at Bucknell was a church school. The Rev Read lived in the rectory and came into school two or three mornings a week to take the scripture lesson. He was chairman of the governors and was consulted about everything, so ties between church and school were strong.

When I started school in the 1920s at the age of five, Miss Letch was headmistress and took the "big room". Miss Malins was in charge of the "little room", into which I went. In all there were about 20 children in the school. Miss Letch was an elderly, kindly soul, who lived alone in the first cottage opposite the village hall. She was nearing retirement age and was not always well. She often fell asleep during afternoon lessons, then we were artful enough to be quiet. She rode a large tricycle and kept a big golden setter dog.

Miss Malins was much younger but equally kind and walked or rode her bicycle from Lord's Lane farm each day. During my six years at Bucknell school, numbers gradually fell, so for the last year or so only Miss Letch was employed.

It was a happy easy going school holding none of the strictness and terror often associated with the period. Miss Letch took it easy and so did we. The worst I remember was having to stay back ten minutes to re-write spelling I had got wrong that afternoon.

The classroom clock often mysteriously stopped, then a big boy was sent out on to the crossroads to see the time on the church clock. If it said half-past eleven, Miss Letch was told ten to twelve and out we went 20 minutes early, being careful to dawdle home so as not to arouse suspicion.

In spite of everything, Miss Letch was liked and respected by children and parents. She was an educated lady who had come into teaching to help support herself and her mother who was a rector's widow and lived with her until her death. Our academic attainments may not have been high but I think we all benefited from her influence.

The year took a definite pattern governed by seasons and customs. In spring and summer we roamed the fields and woods in complete freedom without a care in the world, our aim only to find the first violet or to see if the primroses were out, or in their season where the biggest blackberries grew or the sweetest crab apples.

The boys looked for birds' nests (and there were plenty about). They often took an egg to add to their collection. They would climb trees like monkeys, bringing an egg down either in the peak of their cap or in their mouths.

Of course there were a few rules to keep, like be home before dark, not to leave a gate open (most gates were too heavy to open, so we climbed over, carefully handing down to each other our baskets or bunches of flowers) and not to go into a field where there was a bull. Our sex education started early and in the general run of things.

We often met the farmer or farm workers. They would chat to us while we watched them work. They knew us by name and we looked upon them as friends. We knew of course if we did anything wrong, our parents would hear of it and we would get a lecture.

The limit of our wandering was Trough Pool. We didn't go there often, when we did it was an adventure. We rode on the crossbars of the boys' bicycles, often after a certain amount of persuasion. Halfway down Trough Pool Lane is the big stone water tower, and about six feet up is a ledge. We bumped one another up to sit on this ledge where owl pellets could be found. This feat was seldom completed without skinned knees.

The stream at the bottom of the lane was great for catching sticklebacks and amused us for hours. In the boggy places, yellow iris and king-cups grew. To pick a few often meant a wet foot.

Near the stream stood a small stone-built engine house. This engine pumped water up into the tower to supply the village and for some reason was the responsibility of Mr Thorne, the head cowman at the Manor. Bucknell was ahead of its time having piped water to standpipes outside each group of cottages. The previous owner of the Manor, a Captain Hurlock had arranged all this. He gave my grandfather (who was a master shepherd by trade) a five pound note to plan and supervise the laying of the pipes in about 1911–1912. The note was framed and hung on the wall until needed.

One day each week Mr Philips the blacksmith cycled from Stratton Audley and opened up his blacksmith's shop near the crossroads. As soon as we could get out of school we ran to watch what was going on. We were allowed in only if we stood still and kept quiet. This we did, only too pleased to watch the blacksmith in his leather apron filing and cutting the hoof, ready for the red-hot shoe to be bedded in for a good fit. This was the part that we enjoyed, when clouds of smoke came from the scorched hoof. We could never understand how the horses remained so calm. Mostly carthorses were shod, but sometimes a hunter needed new shoes or a loose one replaced. We then kept a safe distance, as these animals were more spirited and nervous. I remember so well the smell of the blacksmith's, the warmth of the forge and the clanging of the hammer on the iron anvil.

Saturday night was bath night. The big tin bath was brought in and placed on the mat in front of the open fire. Water was heated in a smaller tin bath placed on the oil stove. There were four of us, so starting with the youngest, Mother bathed us, Dad dried us, put our night clothes on, then carried us up to bed on his back. He brought us up cocoa and one slice of hot lardy cake, cooked at the bake-house after the last bread had been brought out of the large brick oven. I don't think toothbrushes had been invented.

Children between the wars, like this likely pair from Bucknell, grew up in a safe and friendly environment.

Next morning we put on clothes only worn on Sunday, and went to the eleven o'clock service in church. After dinner we went to Sunday school at two o'clock, and often to the evening service as well. This we enjoyed. In winter the oil lamps gave a warm yellow light and flickered in the draught when the door was opened. By evening the church felt warm and inviting, the fire in the stoke hole having been lit on Saturday and stoked at regular intervals by Mr Bobby Rolfe the church verger. Often bats would dart around causing great amusement for us children.

In summer after church Mother and Dad (with his walking stick) would take us for a walk. They were both knowledgeable country lovers and would point out interesting things as we went along. In winter Mother played the piano and we sang again any hymn we had especially liked at church, then each chose a favourite hymn.

On Easter Sunday after Sunday school we went to the rectory garden for an Easter egg hunt. Brightly wrapped chocolate eggs had been hidden around the garden for us to find. This was a great treat.

To start the May Day preparations a King and Queen had to be voted for by the schoolchildren. The runners-up were made maids-of-honour and page. Maypole dancing was practised after school, nothing was allowed to interfere with the school time. Four children sat on the bottom of the pole to keep it steady, while the rest practised double plait, spider's web, gipsy tent and other traditional dances.

May Day was a holiday, starting with the King and Queen and attendants leading an orderly procession to church for a short service with hymns such as *All things bright and beautiful* being sung. Next we went to the Manor where Mrs Babington presented the Queen with a necklace and matching brooch, King and page with tie-pins, and necklaces for the maids-of-honour. Singing May songs we toured the village, boys taking turns to carry the May garland on the pole. The garland was made the evening before by mothers using flowers picked by the children in the fields. Primroses and cowslips were mostly used with greenery added. Other children rattled money-boxes. By dinner time we were tired and glad to go home for a rest, before gathering in the rectory garden for the afternoon programme.

The Queen was crowned by some important person, perhaps the rector's wife or local lady, before dancing started. I don't remember having any music, we sang as loudly as we could, helped and conducted by Miss Letch. Tea followed on the lawn, before a brief speech or two closed the proceedings. A social was held in the evening in the school or later in the hall to which the whole village went, mothers bringing children home early as the day had been long. We always started wearing short white socks on May Day. I remember very hot May Days and also a few cold ones.

Money collected on May Day went towards a school outing, always a local trip but a journey anywhere was a treat. One year we went to Wicksteed Park, where a boy fell off a swing and broke his leg. That caused quite a stir.

Another big event in May was Empire Day. Mrs Babington gave book prizes for essays written about countries of the Empire. First, second and third prizes for two classes were given. Essays were taken to the Manor for judging. We waited eagerly for the results, when Mrs Babington would come to school to present the prizes. One year we dressed in costumes of various countries.

Games were played in their season. We ran miles bowling hoops, mainly wooden ones, but a few boys felt very superior with their noisy iron ones. Tufts of grass grew in the middle of the Middleton Road, also the road down to the Turnpike. Ardley Road was deemed not suitable because of the hill (which seemed much steeper in those days) and the Bicester Road was "dangerous" because of the "pub corner", so we kept mostly to the village street, crossroads and triangle, the triangle being up the Middleton Road, round by Home Farm, then back to the crossroads. We often timed one another on this run, not very scientifically, I fear, as timing was done by counting. You counted fast or slow according to how you felt or who was running.

Opposite Home Farm rickyard was a row of seven or eight rather snug little cottages, which had wood sheds with earth toilets in them on the opposite side of the road. I am sorry to say this lane was often referred to by disrespectful children as "Pigsty Alley".

Top spinning took much the same pattern. If you had a good top it was a prized possession. Hopscotch was played by marking squares and numbers with chalk on the road, often the crossroads where we could sit on the wooden bench while waiting our turn. What traffic there was came slowly and could be heard a long way off.

We skipped, either with a short rope on our own or with a long rope, held at each end and twirled by two children; others ran in and out, skipping so many each time. What all this did to our leather-soled shoes I dread to imagine.

Hard on our shoes, too, was the game of Fox and Hounds, usually played at dusk when the days were drawing in. Two children started off, calling at intervals, to be followed by the "pack" trying to catch them before they could return to the seat on the crossroads. The summers seemed long and hot, although the school holidays were only four or five weeks long.

A large herd of pedigree Jersey cows were kept at the Manor to provide milk and butter for the house and staff. Mr Thorne was head cowman, helped by a young man named George Hanks who cycled each day from Chesterton and sadly was killed in France soon after D-Day. To provide food for the cows, the park and most of the Manor fields were cut for hay, which meant haymaking was quite a lengthy and important operation, with most of the gardeners and outside staff brought in to help. Three or four good carthorses, kept under the care of Carter Frank White were used throughout, the only exception being a temperamental, noisy engine which was brought in to replace the horse that usually turned the creaking elevator, taking the hay to the top of the rick. If the engine stopped, as it often did, panic set in, tempers frayed and we knew to keep out the way whilst my father wrestled with the "new fangled thing".

Mr Babington, a tall distinguished gentleman, would sometimes take us through into the walled kitchen garden and gave us strawberries on a cabbage leaf.

By contrast Mr Nicholson's farm was mostly arable with bullocks and sheep. Harvest here was an exciting time, coming later in the year than it does now. The weather was still good, crops had to stand in the fields in stooks to dry, until (as the saying goes) the church bells rang three times.

We were back in school by harvest, but couldn't get out quick enough to join the activity in the fields. As soon as the dew had gone, the binder would start cutting round the outside of the corn. The excitement mounted as the patch in the middle became smaller and frightened rabbits ran out, sometimes even a fox. Quite a crowd would gather, not to miss the fun. Children and grown-ups chased the rabbits with big sticks. I saw a rabbit crawl under a sheaf so I sat on the sheaf and screamed for my brother, while the poor thing wriggled underneath. I am glad to say our combined efforts failed to catch it and it made it safely to the hedge. It was often dusk and the big harvest moon coming up before the field was finished. We played in the stooks, being careful not to knock them down. The sharp stubble scratched our legs, making them quite sore. We were still wearing our short white ankle socks.

The carthorses were massive, beautiful creatures. We knew them all by name, and if Carter Frank Powell lifted you up to ride back to the farm on one of their broad backs, your day was truly made.

During the summer the men played quoits in Bert the baker's field. Heavy iron rings were aimed at a peg standing in a marked-off bed about a yard square. The player whose quoits landed nearest to the peg or, better still, over it scored so many points. Over a number of games the points were added up to produce the evening's winner.

In the autumn we played conkers. Around the churchyard were

large horse-chestnut trees, so conkers were in plentiful supply. Later these trees were cut down because branches started to fall and break the tombstones. Conkers were treated in various ways to make them hard; some were baked in the oven, others were soaked in vinegar, and great was the disappointment if a fiver or sixer met its match.

Not much importance was placed on Hallowe'en. Perhaps an attempt would be made to hollow out a swede, but these were hard and often enthusiasm waned before the job was finished.

Bonfire Night, on the other hand, was looked forward to with great excitement. The village bonfire was held in Col. Blacker's or Bert the baker's field. We collected a few fireworks, bought in ones and twos from the shops or from Bicester if anyone went. Coloured matches and sparklers were favourites, the latter lit under strict supervision, having been the cause of a thatched house burning down. The boy holding the sparkler had thrown it in the air when it burnt his fingers, it caught in the wire and quickly set the thatch alight.

We all suffered from chilblains on toes and heels and the boys chapped ears. Damp shoes, warming your toes before an open fire and frosts, were all supposed to cause them and various remedies were tried. Rubbing with a raw onion was one, and wrapping toes in sheep's wool was another, but nothing seemed to help and they were jolly painful.

The Bicester hunt was often through our village, then we were allowed into the playground to watch. Out of school we ran to open gates for riders, often rewarded with a few coppers. Col. Blacker was a "red coater" and would give us sixpence. Great efforts were made to get a hand on the gate then you were entitled to a share.

Electricity came to Bucknell in the early 1930s. Three lights and a plug wired into every house. We eagerly awaited the big "switch-on", and when it came we marvelled at the bright light. The one drawback, it showed ceilings and walls to be very grubby! Mother and her friend, Mrs Randle, saved up and bought an electric iron between them. It cost sixteen shillings and eleven pence. Mother would use it, then it was wrapped in an old blanket, put in a basket and carried by one of the children to Mrs Randle. The iron must have been well made, because Mother lived to be 102 years old and she used it for the rest of her life. I still have it.

Being a church school, the school was examined once a year by a rector from another parish, and prizes awarded for scripture. A Bible was first prize. This was called the "Bishop's Prize", then two certificates for runners-up. The exam took place in the morning, lasting almost to dinner-time, then the rest of the day was a holiday. Holidays were few and far between, so we thought the slight effort of a so-called exam was well worth while. At about eight or nine years old we joined the church choir and sat in the choir stalls underneath the tower. The boys and men wore surplices but not the ladies and girls. Once a week was choir practice, which in the winter was a creepy affair. Only half the church was lit, but enough to upset any bat not hibernating. The church was cold, so hymns and psalms were hurriedly sung. We knew the hymns almost by heart and often the psalms as well. Mr Albert Reeve, known to all as "Alby", was the organist; his son John, quite a young boy, blew the organ using a long handle at the side. It was a lovely organ and Mr Reeve played it well. I would watch his feet find the large wooden notes and notice the stops change the sound as he used various ones. Even as a child I loved the rich grand sound the organ made. Walking up the church path we kept close to the grown-ups, it seemed dark and scary, with often an owl hooting in the trees, but once at the church gate we scattered in all directions, not stopping running until we reached home.

In July 1934 we had a choir outing to Southsea. Luckily it was a lovely day and in spite of most of us being sick on the journey, it was a day to remember. Another outing was a trip to Oxford one Christmas. We travelled in a bus with wooden seats, and again many of us were sick as we bounced around the villages.

As Christmas drew near we started practising for the school concert, given each year. No practice allowed in school time, so we came back about five o'clock for an evening rehearsal. This was possible as all the children lived in the village, most of them close to the school. We enjoyed these evening outings. The school looked so different with the swinging oil lamp hanging from the ceiling, casting moving shadows everywhere. Mothers and fathers would come to collect us, waiting in the cold porch.

At home, Christmas was a wonderful time. We had a tree cut from Gruntal copse which we dressed with home-made decorations, and real candles clipped to the tree with little tin holders. The candles were lit at tea-time on Christmas Day when we danced round the tree, while Mother and Dad stood ready to pinch out any that toppled over and started to scorch the tree. Parcels arrived at Christmas and cards came on Christmas morning, often posted the day before. On Boxing Day, if the frost had been hard we trooped down to the common to slide on the floods. Some people skated on the moat, but we were not allowed to go there, my father saying the water was too deep.

As we neared our eleventh birthday a feeble attempt was made at the eleven-plus exam. Nobody from Bucknell ever passed, which didn't seem to worry us unduly. Our main concern was, "When was the man coming to measure us for our bicycles?" These were issued to the four or five children moving on to Bicester school. On the appointed days, parents and children waited on the crossroads for the big green van to arrive with the bikes. When it came, each child was checked for size, and happily rode the bike home. My father fitted wooden blocks to my pedals for the first year, the idea being that it would last longer as I grew.

I was sad to leave Bucknell school. It was a phase of my childhood over, but in a way I was ready to widen my horizons (slightly).

If this sounds like an idyllic childhood, it was. Perhaps with the passing of time one tends to forget the not so good bits, but there were not many. I would like to think that my grandchildren will be able to look back on their childhood with the same pleasure.'

CHILDHOOD DAYS

They seemed to last forever, those long, sunny days of childhood, but how long ago they seem now – the freedom to wander the countryside for hours without fear, days spent far from grown ups in woods and fields that were our playground, towns and villages that we knew so well because we had spent our lives there.

STAYING WITH GRAN STYLES

'When I was a small child, the person I loved most in all the world was Gran Styles. She was actually no relation at all, just someone my mother left me with when she had to go and look after her old mother in Stratford-on-Avon. We lived in Oxford. Imagine a long row of terraced houses, and Gran Styles' house about in the middle, opposite the brewery.

She was a tough old dear, and at 75 years old had taken on the job of looking after her two little granddaughters. She could be so kind and gentle.

In winter, with only the flickering fire and the lamp, then the living room floor became a make-believe icy waste in the far Arctic North, a slipper became a sledge and a celluloid doll (threepence from Woolworths) a beautiful girl fleeing from the wolves. Through it all, Gran sat with her feet on a hassock, stitching away. She was a beautiful needlewoman. Her washing was snowy white. Around the beds she hung white valances. On the chairs we had antimacassars. But I think her outside toilet was one of my greatest joys. On the wooden seat was a little box filled with small pieces of newspaper, while on the walls were colourful pictures, one a young English soldier in India, on horseback with a long lance, in full charge. On the opposite wall a picture of a very stern Gladstone.

When our summer holiday from school came, we always spent one week picking dandelions for wine. Gran with her hat fixed firmly on her head with a big hatpin and wearing a sort of black hacking jacket and skirt, and good stout boots, we three girls in sun bonnets, cotton dresses and button boots set off for the fields. We always took a loaf of bread, a knife, some cheese, bottles of water and a large tin of pineapple. We picked the heads off the dandelions under the hot sun all day, but about midday we would sit in the shade and have our lunch, and it went down great out there in the fields. We started for home when Gran's large bag was filled and pressed down hard. The flower heads were scattered on newspaper on the little spare bedroom floor, and there they stayed till they were dried. Later they would be boiled with sugar and oranges and lemon peel in the old stone copper, and we children would sit and eat the orange and lemon peel after it came out from the juices. Her wine was the best I have ever tasted, then or since, and she always had a barrel on her cellar floor and I really believed it cured everything I ever suffered from as a small child.

Gran was a great believer in girls having nice skins. I think I was a bit of a let-down: I had lots of freckles and chestnut coloured hair that refused to go into rags at night like Nora's and Nancy's did. Anyway, because we had to have nice skin we always had for Sunday tea brimstone and treacle. I hated it. But once it had gone we could have home-made fatty cake, which I liked. We also ate dandelion leaves and nasturtium leaves, and rose petals in salad which were quite nice.'

LONG SUNNY DAYS

'Memories of childhood are of long sunny days spent on a daisy-pattern lawn listening to a cuckoo and making daisy chains, or in the farmyard watching piglets play, and feeding pet lambs in the orchard.

There were less pleasant things – cold bedrooms, chilblains on fingers and toes, days spent in bed with something that was called croup. You never hear of it now. The bedrooms seemed so far away from the bustle of the household – two flights of stairs – and when an occasional woodlouse (we called them "pigs") was found in a bed it was "yells" for Mother.

After thrashing of the wheat rick in the farmyard several mice always found their way into the house. My sister was horrified to find one in the folds of her towel.

We were lucky to have so many animals around; there were bantams and guinea pigs in runs in the garden, chickens and ducks in the farmyard. The ducks used to go out to the pond in the daytime, at night they were shut in a small house under the tallet steps.

Almost every house and cottage in Shilton was clad with ivy – early insulation? Sparrows used to roost in the ivy, there were so many of them young lads used nets, going round in the dark to catch them. I don't know what they did with them, but some were plucked and roasted before the fire and were a tasty snack. I expect some were fed to ferrets. Most of the young men had a ferret and rabbit catching was a weekend occupation. Many families almost lived on rabbit meat, when the family pig had been eaten.

I was born during the First World War and have a faint recollection of the excitement when a small aeroplane circled very low over the village celebrating victory. There was a difficult time soon after this when my father, uncle and sister fell victims of the very virulent influenza which swept the country. I believe more people died in the epidemic than were killed in the war.

When I was older I saw the airship R101 cruise slowly over Shilton – it was on a Saturday and our fête day, an amazing sight.

At the age of five I started walking over two miles – with my sister – to a small private school run by two retired teachers, the Misses Green, who lived on the right-hand side of Brize Norton Road, Carterton. It was a long walk and to while away the time we gave names to local features – a deep ditch which usually had flowing water was The Thames, a strong spring Niagara Falls etc. We knew most of the people who lived in Shilton Road so it wasn't a lonely walk.

A yearly excitement was the large bonfire built on School Bank over several weeks, helped to burn on the night with liberal applications of paraffin. A great cheer went up when the guy collapsed.

Great fun was had by the whole village when hard frost occurred; a water meadow, "Coneyger", flooded every winter and provided a large sheet of ice. The young lads with their hobnailed boots were very dexterous at sliding. Tobogganing was popular. Very few people owned a sledge but sheets of corrugated iron were used, one end being turned up for the front. These went very fast. Children used old trays and boxes as well. One winter we had the roof of an old van and six of us got on it. That went very fast, and far, and we had to roll off as it came to rest on the very edge of the stream. It was hard work pulling it back up the hill, but kept us warm.

Mr Gerald Porter who owned the meadow was very tolerant of all these activities, but there was never a stone touched in the walls or the gate climbed over or left open, or I guess it would have been stopped. Mr Porter lived at the manor and was quite strict. He passed by once when my sister had her toes in the wall, trying to look over at the stream at the back of the forge. He tapped the back of her legs with his stick, it did hurt her dignity.'

OUR PLAYGROUND

'Dry stone walls are surprisingly comfortable to rest against and they must be the most harmonious barrier man ever devised. The stone is cream and powdery when quarried, but over the centuries weather and lichens combine to blend it into the landscape.

The meadow slopes away from me as I lean against the wall. At my back the village houses with the squat Norman tower of the church rising through the surrounding lime trees, to my left the solid structure of the ancient tithe barn and, just beyond that, unseen but giving reassurance of home and security, is the farmhouse.

But in front is playground and adventure. At the bottom is the field in the dip where I first saw an adder, not threatening in any way, just basking on the slope facing the sun.

Then, beyond the hedge, the water meadow with a brook running each side. The brook will become the river Glyme, join the Thames, and eventually reach London and then the sea. But here it is just the brook, flowing seemingly for our pleasure and entertainment. Here in the water meadow grow myriad wild flowers. Kingcups, flag iris, ragged robin, meadowsweet, ladies' smocks – truly a meadow of delight.

But the brook could also be used by wellington-shod children for Pooh-stick races, building dams, for jumping across, for bizarre experiments of collecting freshwater creatures. We tried to keep them in home-made aquariums, but as we had no means of oxygenating the water, they invariably died. Caddis grubs were a particular favourite: the larva of the caddisfly builds a tubular covering of grit or pondweed – anything available in fact. We would collect and take them home, extract the grub from its shell and give it pieces of coloured glass and silver paper to construct new coverings. What beastly children we must have been, although in our favour, when we found and observed birds' nests, we left the eggs, unlike most country children. I suppose creepy crawlies aroused less compassion in us.

What a fortunate child I was to have such a playground. It's 50 years since I played there. I wonder; could I still jump the brook?'

IT WAS ALL COUNTRY

'Osney, also known as "Frogs Island", is where I was born in 1925. I have many memories of my childhood there.

The fun (at least we thought it was) of going to school walking up on planks to try and keep dry from the quite deep flood water overflowing from the river in East Street. I learned to ride my fairy cycle in the street as there was very little traffic – this was about the only time my sisters, brothers and I were allowed to play in the street – always in the back garden, but what wonderful concerts and other games we devised – I remember them well!

At nine years old doctor's orders were "move to higher ground or this child will not survive!", having had several bad bouts of bronchitis and pneumonia. So the next 20 years were spent at "The Great Headley Estate" which is just below where the John Radcliffe is now.

We had a brick kiln at the bottom of what is now Headley Way – all the bricks for the estate were made here – plenty of clay in this area. We "helped" with the making of bricks then made our way home through the woods. Headley Way was thick woods with lovely springs and very up and down – this was our only way to get to school other than Pullens Lane which was a private road and the occupants disliked our usage of their lane. Once each year a gate was closed across the road to show us that it was private! Jack Straws Lane was so rickety and very dark with lines of trees on either side. Very few houses were in this lane and they were the extra large ones right at the top.

Fields were all around and we camped and dug dens – stole potatoes from mother's larder and cooked them on a smoky fire. We ate them half cooked and very black – but what fun! Once the road had been made through the woods and down to the Old Road towards New Marston we would run along the grassy banks to school. This was all country, not a house anywhere and it seemed the sun always shone.'

'It was 1923, when I was three years old, that my mother and father, sister Muriel aged five and my baby brother of a few months, moved from the village of Brize Norton to a very lonely house called Colebrook Villa.

The house had been built for the stationmaster of Brize Norton and Bampton GWR station. It was one mile from Brize Norton and two from Bampton. Both places had objected to the station being any nearer, fearing it would take the trade away from the business people.

We were surrounded by fields which we were quite free to roam in, and that is just what we did.

All through the year we scoured the fields and hedgerows for flowers, nuts, mushrooms and anything else that we fancied. These we took home to Mother, who had become tied to the house because my little brother was a very bad spastic. Little Arthur as we called him never walked, talked or did anything for himself, he could not even feed himself. Mother loved all these fresh flowers, and the kitchen windowsill was always a clutter of jam jars filled to overflowing with them. About Easter time we would go to a big copse, about two fields away, where the ground would be carpeted with primroses. We would tie our bunches up with wool and carry them home in cane baskets. A little later there would be the bluebell copse to visit. These we would carry home in armfuls, dropping them here and there so loaded were we.

On a fine day Mother would send us out to pick the heads off dandelions, they had to be dry to make into wine. A quart of dandies to a gallon of boiling water, leave for a week or so, boil up with some sugar and lemon juice, then after a few days the yeast would be added to work it. When it had worked it was put into sparkling bottles and put away for Christmas.

Father was a baker and our bakehouse was up in the village. He was away for long hours, first helping my grandfather make the dough, then delivering the bread round the villages. We were sometimes in bed before he got home, so we did not see much of Father.

Wintertime could be fun when the fields flooded and then froze. The bigger children would come down from the village to have long slides, and I would slide with them.

Well – the RAF station came and took away our copses, the farmers used strong weedkillers in the fields, and the council did the same on the road verges, many of our wild flowers disappeared, and now children are not encouraged to pick them because they might disappear altogether.'

FAR OFF DAYS

'I came to live in a village not far from Oxford when I was about ten years of age and that would have been about 1920. I was obliged to go to the village school for more than two years and this I did not enjoy very much because I think my sister and I and my parents were regarded as foreigners. I have heard my father say more than once that people in the village were not at all helpful in the early days when we were there.

The speech in the village was quite different to anything I had heard before. So many sentences commenced "Be you a-going . . ?" and the children would say, "Be you coming out to play?" This all passed away a long time ago as it is much more of a floating population in villages nowadays, whereas in the past they often stayed in villages for generations, or when they married they might go a few miles away.

There was a tall elderly gentleman who rode a bicycle (I think he refused to have a car) and he seemed to be regarded as squire of the village although he lived some way away. He invariably spoke to us children and one day to my great astonishment, I saw my companion, a girl named Nellie, bob him a curtsey. I asked her why she did this but I received no reply. This is the only time that I have seen this done.

Soon after I started at the village school the children were constantly talking about "the feast" which was coming in the summer and this, together with the annual Sunday school treat seemed to be the great events in the year as far as the children were concerned. I was disappointed when I discovered that "the feast" was really a

Travelling by pony and trap was always a pleasure. The Forest family pose near the Old Rectory, Islip in 1920.

small fair with a roundabout, swingboats and side shows. I think that, in those far off days, most villages had their feasts and most of them declined during the next few years until they ceased altogether. When they were in their heyday everything was brought in by horse drawn vehicles and caravans.

One of my very earliest memories concerns taking a hoop to school; this was propelled by means of a small stick (I wonder how many years ago it is since I last saw a child playing with a hoop). There seemed to be seasons of the year for the games that prevailed in the village then and these were hopscotch, marbles and tops.

When I was about twelve years of age I went with other girls from the school to the cookery centre in Abingdon and we travelled in the covered carrier's cart (horse-drawn, of course). We spent the time on the journey comparing notes as to how much money we had been given by our parents to spend on sweets. We had a break during the afternoon and we used this time in order to dash out to a sweet shop which was situated very conveniently close to the cookery centre. The sums of money each girl had, as far as I can remember, varied from a halfpenny to sixpence but I think the average sum was twopence or threepence and you would be surprised how much you could get for the latter sums. Sixpence, of course, was great wealth.

At that time very few people had the telephone and it was a momentous occasion when one was installed in the village post office. This building was just a small, attractive cottage where, besides selling stamps they also sold sweets and a limited amount of groceries, but everything was kept well out of sight and I think this was because the old lady who lived there was very house-proud. One day, a young man from London was staying with friends in the village and he went to the post office to use the telephone; after ringing the front door bell he walked in and was about to grab the telephone when the old lady rushed out and said, "Don't touch it, wait until I fetch my daughter who will start it up for you." I wonder how many times that story was told in London.'

BORN ON THE FARM

'I was born at Widford Mill Farm, where my grandparents had lived and kept a dairy farm for a number of years. Dad took over the farm when I was eight and my sister six and our baby brother just arrived. It was a very busy household with Edna cycling in each day to help Mother, and Chris, who lived in, doing most of the outside jobs, while Bert and Frank came daily.

Mother had lots of cooking to do on the kitchen range to feed all these folk, besides Mrs Smith who came from Burford on Tuesday to do the washing and on Friday to do the cleaning. Mother usually turned out the kitchen on Saturday, after dispatching Edna with the baby in the pram and we two to Swinbrook to visit Mrs Butler, Edna's mum. We all greatly enjoyed this: we could play by the stream, bowl our hoops or skip. We did see a few bicycles, but a car was an event.

High View was the suitable name for their home, at the top of a narrow path, up about twelve steps, past a cottage at the bottom where Mr Tuckwell lived and always came out for a chat. Our first job, having unloaded the pram and had a drink, was to fetch several buckets of water from a field across the road and down a few steps. The walk home after tea was a bit slower. We saw Edna's grandparents, aunts, uncles, cousins, besides many folk that we knew.

There were four horses, Colonel, Prince, Flower and Blossom as well as the pony Kitty, who went daily to Burford with the milk-float. Here she was well known, having friends who would give her an apple or biscuit. The brass-topped churn was fastened with irons to a shelf in the float, which was high enough for the brass tap at the bottom to run the milk into the delivery can, which would hold two gallons and had two measures with handles, for one pint or half pint. My sister and I would help before school, with enamel cans, taking a pint or half pint into the houses and pouring milk into their jug or basin. If they were out, they left a covered jug outside. We were quite favourites with the customers, especially the older folk, who would call us "little maid" or "missy". The float had no cover so we got very wet and cold and welcomed a warm by the fireside.

The first bell rang at five to nine, when we had to run to school and line up for nine o'clock. School hours were from nine to twelve, and two to four-thirty, when we had the long, lonely walk home. In the winter it was dark, and we would vary our steps, running and skipping between telegraph poles, and sometimes the telegraph boy saw us and said, "Your mother's coming to meet you with a stick" – she never did! When we got home there were jobs to do: collect the eggs, feed and close the hen-houses, as Reynard often lurked about. Sometimes there were calves and lambs to feed. They were lovely jobs; the piglets always seemed to manage to help themselves. Several of the cows had flower names: Daisy, Buttercup, Tulip, Cowslip, Primrose, also Mary, Queenie, Jubilee. All had great character and were our friends.

There were pigs too, who would produce litters that were soon sold off, which caused great sorrow and days of not speaking to Dad.

We had an old Ford car, which had a hood and side-curtains at the back, but the wind blew in from the front, making us very cold in the back seat. A very powerful car with 23 horsepower, though sometimes Prince had to tow it to get it to start. When staying with Uncle Will on his farm, we had rides in his car, a Studebaker, very posh, with windscreens to both back and front seats.

Our home was a place where visitors were always welcome, and having been the home of our grandparents, relatives often came to stay. The quietness and beauty, the walk over to the little church in the field and up through the park was a joy to them all.'

I'VE LIVED HERE ALL MY LIFE

'I have lived in Shiplake all my life. My father had a nursery in the village. I started school in Henley when I was about six and used to go by train with my older brothers, dressed in my white dress, white shoes and socks and white frilly knickers. We kept hens and on days when "Jimmy Swift" was driving the train I would collect a few eggs in my panama hat; then we would go by the packing sheds and collect some tomatoes. The engine was called *Swift* – hence the name of the driver who was a great friend of ours. When we got to Henley he would cook breakfast with our eggs and tomatoes and his own bacon. This was done on a shovel over the engine fire and very good it tasted. On the way back from school he would let us ride in the cab. One day I fell back in the coal and Jimmy lifted me out. I arrived home with dirty knickers and two handprints in black on my dress and broken elastic in my panama hat. The cat was out of the bag. Mother was very cross and berated Jimmy, saying the boys could ride sometimes but the girls never.

We used to earn pennies at the level crossing by opening and shutting the gates.

Most of our shopping was done in the village where Gooch's store sold almost everything. The Home and Colonial and Pithers (famous for their sausages) used to deliver once a week. A butcher came round with a horse and cart. He was most helpful. Once, when mother was in hospital, he showed us how to set the salt beef cooking with some onions and carrots, and he came back later to check we had everything under control. I remember him teaching us to make toad in the hole. I can see him now beating up the batter. Our grandmother was most impressed and thought us very accomplished cooks but we never let on that it was the butcher who should have had the credit.

During the rail strike (1926) the postman struggled out on his bike delivering the mail and on the way back he collected up three little girls in his enormous basket and delivered them to school in Henley – two miles away.

Doctors were wonderful in those days. They were the carers in the community. I remember my brother came home with a pain which seemed to go down his leg. The doctor came the following morning and diagnosed appendicitis. By the afternoon when I visited him he was sitting up in bed having had his operation, helping the doctors by polishing their instruments. He was very proud and said, "They bring them all to me." My brothers at various times broke their collarbones and it was always the doctor who brought them home in his car. There used to be fights at school between the water rats (boys from Lower Shiplake) and the furze croppers (those from Binfield Heath) and one of my brothers got a stick in his eye. In no time at all a specialist was brought out from Reading to try to save the eye – alas, he was not successful in spite of the quick action.

I remember during the war we made our own butter. My mother would put a pint of milk in a kilner jar and seal it and we would roll the jar backwards and forwards the length of the kitchen floor until the butter was churned. The younger ones thought this the greatest fun.'

IT WAS HARD TO GROW UP

'I was born in 1920 and lived and went to school in the village of Shutford. I had a wonderful home and parents, two sisters and a brother. Our pleasure, when coming home from school, was to play skipping, top spinning, ball games and go for long walks in the fields. When I was seven my father made me some small garden tools which I used to help him with his allotment all summer.

On a Sunday we would all dress up in our best clothes and go to Sunday school twice a day, and sing in the choir with Dad (which was well attended). After the service our parents took us for long walks; Dad used to cut twigs from the ash and hazel and make whistles for us, which I can still make today.

When I was eleven years old I went to work every weekend in the pub, washing and scrubbing stone floors. It was very hard work. Sometimes if the woman didn't hear the scrubbing brush, she would shout, "I can't hear you scrubbing, my dear" – all this for two shillings, which I saved and bought my own clothes. I fetched their milk on a Sunday morning, for which I was given one penny bar of chocolate, of which I gave a square each to my family, as there were just five squares.

In the winter nights we always had a roasting fire, with flitches of bacon and hams drying in the chimney corners. My Dad would tell us tales of the antics he got up to when he was a lad, which were very funny. Then my sister and I used to put on a concert for Mum and Dad. We'd stand on a chair and sing and recite, then they'd clap, which was great. Then it was bedtime, but first of all we had to go in the dark along the garden path to the loo. The worst night to go along would be a Monday night, as there would be a lot of washing on the line. When it was a windy night you'd put your hand round the candle you were carrying and forget the line prop was across the path, so over you went, the candle went out, and you didn't want the loo after that!

When I was 14, on the same day I left school my case was packed, then a big chauffeur-driven car arrived, more like a glass hearse. I was sent to work for three shillings a week as a scullery maid at the Park House in Swalcliffe. It was terribly hard as I was washing up all the time for cook and kitchen maid and eight servants. We had half a day out every week and one Sunday afternoon in a fortnight.'

NEVER GIVE ANYTHING GOOD AWAY

'I was born in 1910 in one of the farm cottages, belonging to St John's College, which used to be down Gravel Lane and went on to live in various homes in Warborough. When living at the north end of the village, on cold days I remember my mother used to give us hot potatoes to put in our pockets, both for warmth and nourishment. Also, in one of the houses along Thame Road, there was a brick missing from the outside chimney breast, and we used to stop there to pop our hands inside to warm them.

One of the most memorable features of my childhood in Warborough was the ditches which bordered most of the main road and were full of water. The one running from the Greet Hall to the shop used to afford us youngsters hours of enjoyment. We used to catch our tadpoles from the pond outside Church View, and swing on the willow and hang from the railings over the grating by the shop. I have vivid memories of the row of poplars that used to stand along the bank from Quakers' Cottage to Gravel Lane. The fire engine used to fill up from the ditch near the draper's, Quakers' Cottage, and cows used to graze on the verges and I was pitched by one, which was, thankfully, nearly empty.

On Saturday many of us youngsters would take our little carts and walk to the wharf, where the coal barges would stop, at Benson (now the cruiser station) to collect the coal for the week. In this way we could earn money to put towards the three pence that we would take to the vicarage kitchen each week to be entered on our shoe card. The vicar would act as "banker" and in this way we could buy a new pair of shoes or boots each year. I remember the vicar, Mr Caldicott used to give us half a crown at Christmas, with which my mother would always buy a jar of Horlicks and some lump sugar. Mrs Greet would give all the children in the village school a shilling and an egg each Easter.

I used to pick up droppings from the sheep grazing on the green and take them to my grandmother, who soaked them in water and used the mixture to water her plants.

The Warborough Feast, which was always the first Sunday after 21st August, was a great highlight of the year. I recall having free rides because my father used to give marrows and beans from his allotment to the showmen.

On Sundays my father would clean the shoes, and then, on his way down to bellringing, he would hand our baking dish of meat and potatoes, and a plum-duff pudding (which would last us a week), to Mr Bullock at the Old Bake House, where it would be cooked. Later on Mr Bond would ring the "pudding bell" and we, along with many other families, would run along to collect our Sunday dinner. I remember going to collect loaves of bread from there, and Mr Bullock used to give us a handful of currants.

At the age of thirteen and a half I was allowed to leave school because Mrs Bousfield had been able to secure me a job at the Red House to train as parlour-maid, as Doris Grant was promoted to nursery maid to Ferry House. I was paid five shillings a month and I left home to live in. I used to sleep at the top of the house with the cook and, in the course of working there for ten years, travelled with the family to Dulwich and Kent. I remember bridge parties in the drawing room and Sunday tennis parties in the summer, when I had to make delicate cucumber sandwiches. I used to be up at 6 am every morning to clean the kitchen range, and once a month we had to go to the 7 am Sunday service in order to have breakfast ready for the family returning from the 8 am service. One of my duties was to wrap the flat irons in paper to warm the cook's bed and, in trying to carry two at once, one turned and burned me badly on my arm. I did not dare to say anything to anyone as the cook was out having a drink at The Nag's Head, which was not allowed. We had one Sunday afternoon a fortnight off – however, we could not leave until the luncheon had been cleared away and everything was ready for tea. We were still expected to be at evensong at 6 pm, and we had to be "in" by 9 pm. But afternoons off were still special and, as I became older, they were put to good use.

In "courting" days lads and lasses used to meet of a Sunday afternoon to go for a walk. I remember asking my father if I could go, but he said not until I had washed my face. Protesting that I had done that already, he insisted that I still had to wash my face – it was the first time I had tried a little face powder! Often we would all walk through the village and the boys would buy a few sweets at the shop in Shillingford. We would wander down to Shillingford Bridge or pay a penny to cross on the ferry. Whatever the route, we usually came back down Watery Lane and made sure we went through the "kissing gate". I met my husband, who had been born locally at Rush Court, and we were married in St Laurence's church. On the day, my mistress, Mrs Hayes gave me away, because my dear father said he "would never give anything good away" – and with that he went off to work on his allotment.'

BOYS WILL BE BOYS!

'When my father and his friend Ron were young boys they went up into Charlton church tower to ring the 8 pm curfew bell for the old churchwarden, Mr Will Shepherd. They forgot the flashlight but fumbled around and found a candle and matches. Will followed them up to wind up the clock.

As Ron was about to start ringing the bell, the rope got twisted round his wrist, so the rope took him up three times. He hit his head on the ceiling and his foot kicked over the candle – his shoe flew off, hitting Tommy's head as he tried to grab his mate.

Ron (who lived down Church lane with his Gran) said, "Tommy, don't tell our ol' Gran." He went home trying to whistle and pretend nothing was wrong; but she knew he had been up to something so gave him a jolly good hiding and came out looking for Tommy. She said "Tommy, what's our Ron bin up to?" "Nothing," said Tommy. She chased him, waving her stick, but he ran like a hare!'

TREATS AND GAMES

Our games came round with the seasons, and we all knew when to stop playing one and start another. We had our chores to do and pocket money was scarce then, but we enjoyed other treats and outings.

NO POCKET MONEY

'Although I was the only child I never had any pocket money until I was nearly 14. My mum used to buy me two pennyworth of sweets a week – that was four things at a ha'penny each. A special treat was Spetterning's ice-cream. It was out of this world, especially his raspberry dishes – two scoops of ice-cream with raspberry sauce. They were threepence each.

We did not have much money in those days and if we didn't like the food that was cooked we had to do without. At one time they were making the pavements down Newland and there was a nightwatchman with his brazier and we took potatoes to be roasted in it. He used to say, "Ain't you got no taters, then?" if we didn't bring any.'

'Even when they were very young, children were expected to help with the household chores. They did the washing up, fetched the water from the pump, and the milk and butter from the farm. They went wooding, especially for kindling wood for the range and the copper. They chopped wood, brought the coal in, planted and picked potatoes on the allotments. They took the accumulators for the radio to be charged. From the age of about eight, the girls were expected to take babies out in their prams, either their own brothers and sisters or the children of neighbours. Nobody was ever paid for doing these chores; you just had to do it.'

WE COULD GO OUT SAFELY

'Although there were no street lights in those days, we could always go out quite safely, finding our way with a torch. Even as children there were no problems for us to go to choir practice, Bible class and anything else we belonged to.

114

Miss Wallis from Elvendon Priory started a Brownie pack when I was nine years old and we were fetched each week to the Priory for our meeting. We had great fun there and she gave us picnics in the summertime. Miss Whittington from Flint House (a big house near Crays Pond) started a Cub pack and Scout troop for the boys and had a Scout hut built for them. Mrs Walker from Wayside at Woodcote took the Sunday school and Bible class and gave prizes each year for attendance and also a Sunday school treat each summer with games and a bumper tea. The "gentry" from the "big houses" were generally very good to the village people.

We had a wonderful Christmas party annually for the Woodcote children, which was financed by a whist drive held in the village hall. Then a number of mothers organised it all, going into Reading to purchase presents which were hung on a huge tree, providing games and Father Christmas distributing presents. It was one of the highlights of the year.'

PARTIES AND BEECHWOODS

'My childhood was spent at Highmoor in the 1920s and 1930s. The beechwoods surrounding the village were our playground; we spent many happy hours playing "houses" or hide and seek, or just wandering in the leafy glades.

Every Christmas all the village children were invited to a party in the village hall, given by Mr Denham, a village benefactor. We had a lovely tea and played the usual games, my favourite being Nuts in May. The schoolchildren gave a display of country dancing, which we had practised for weeks. To round off the celebration, each child was given a present from the tree, and an orange and sweets.

The same benefactor arranged a super bonfire on Guy Fawkes night on the school common; we children had to collect as much brushwood as we could in the preceding weeks, to help to make the bonfire. On the night, each child was given a packet of fireworks – Sparklers, Golden Rain etc. There was a handsome guy and rockets, and we all had a grand time.

In spring, we searched for primroses and violets, and then bluebells. Our summers were spent in the woods, or playing cricket on the common. Later, we went mushrooming and blackberrying, and collected acorns. We sold the acorns to a lady who kept pigs; she gave us one penny for a gallon (a gallon of acorns was an awful lot!). The money we made (which wasn't much) we used to spend at Nettlebed Fair in October, which was one of the highlights of the year. In winter we went wooding, collecting all the old dry wood to help the fuel at home.

A choir outing from Bucknell in 1934. We all looked forward to such treats.

There was no television; we had to make our own entertainment. Every week we had a Family Social club, which cost threepence. On arrival we would draw for a partner, the children separately from the adults. The first half of the evening we played games like darts, rings, shove-ha'penny and whist, one pair against another, recording our scores on a card; the highest score at the end of the evening gained a prize. We had refreshments, tea and cakes, then the second half was dancing and games, musical chairs etc. We all enjoyed our evening out.

Other forms of entertainment were concerts – sketches, songs, recitations, performed by local people, and also travelling concert parties, which were always well attended.

Henley was our nearest town, and we would often cycle there. There was also a bus, run by a man from Stoke Row; I think his name was Jackman. After a Saturday evening at the cinema, the bus would be crowded coming home – but Mr Jackman would always say, "There's plenty of room at the back," although we were packed like sardines! Subsequently, when we came to Grey's Hill, we had to get out and walk to the top. Another time on the bus, in a very thick fog, Mr Jackman asked, "Does anyone know where we are?" – to which some village wag replied, "You be in the b . . . ditch!" We eventually arrived home safely.

These are just a few of my memories of a happy childhood spent in a close-knit village community, when villages were inhabited by real old-fashioned villagers.'

GAMES WE PLAYED

'We played What's the time Mr Wolf? hopscotch, whips and tops, hoops, scooters, skipping, ball games and ring games – all joining hands and singing a rhyme such as "Rosy apple, lemon or a pear", "The wind, the wind, the wind blows high", "In and out the dusty windows", "I sent a letter to my love" etc.'

CONKERS AND TOPS

'At the bottom of the garden was a large horse-chestnut tree and there used to be a scramble to find the toughest conker and to thread it with string. In the game of conkers we would beat all the other kids and to our delight describe it as our "oncer".

Another pastime was "ditch jumping", which was quite good, because the ditches were rather wide. We had a long pole and used to run and vault over to the other side. The inexperienced jumpers very often landed in the ditch, and many a soaking pair of shoes and socks were worn home, I can tell you!

When the pig was killed the kids would shout for the bladder because this was used as a balloon. Many a one had been part of the Morris dancers' gimmicks. One man would carry one while joining in the dance, playfully hitting everyone on the head with it.

I think my favourite game was the wooden top. We used to chalk the top with different colours, it looked quite pretty as it spun round and round, and the stick we used to keep it spinning was made out of a willow branch, with a piece of string tied on the end. One day I remember the stick flew out of my hand whilst making a strike and went through someone's window. I ran away as fast as my legs could carry me, but the man of the house could run faster and caught up with me, and oh dear, that cost my mother something for the replacement of the pane of glass.

Hopscotch was a favourite, too, and skipping into a long skipping rope. We took it in turns to "jump in", as it was called. When I wasn't doing that I had a swing down the bottom of the garden and I would swing and swing for hours. We couldn't afford hoops, we just had old bicycle tyres which we enjoyed just as well.'

IN SEASON

'Children loved to play their games as the season came round, no one remembered why one pastime suddenly stopped and another started – these included hopscotch, skipping, whip and top, hoops, marbles, conkers (which of course had its ordained season), and rhyming games in the playground. Hopscotch squares would be drawn with a stone scratching the surface of the ground, never chalk as this cost money and nobody would buy it.

Boys liked birdnesting and luring birds with a trail of crumbs into a propped-up garden sieve. Holding a piece of string tied to the stick holding up the sieve, they would give it a jerk when the bird was in the danger area and trap it just for a few moments and gloat over their cleverness. One little boy broke his heart when he pulled the string too soon and broke the robin's neck.

Indoor games included snakes and ladders, draughts, ludo, monopoly, consequences and of course, a pack of cards.

Combe is a village with real cricketing history and the game was very popular with most of the young men in the village. Albert Collier at Alma Grove Farm used to take a pigeon with him to away matches and send home the score at tea time by pigeon post.

Girls could join the Girls Friendly Society, Guides or Brownies which met in the local school. The reading room in Combe was for men only where newspapers could be read and billiards and table tennis played; no drink was allowed on the premises and women were barred entry.

Children saved farthings all year which they took to church on Whit Sunday for the collection, but no one seems to remember now where these went. The rest of the year children usually took two halfpennies for the collection on Sunday.

Indoor pastimes included making rag rugs on winter evenings, cutting up old clothing into strips and working them into an old piece of sacking with a ratchet hook. An alternative method was to plait the strips and coil them round, stitching into place to form a circular rug.

Waxed milk bottle tops would be cleaned and saved. Wool would be wound round this base from central hole to outside until there was no more room to fit another thread of wool. Then they were cut on the perimeter, and the card removed to form a fluffy ball for children to play with or to adorn children's clothes.'

THE BEST YEARS OF OUR LIVES?

Schooldays in the first two decades of the 20th century still had a Victorian feel to them, with the children wearing boots and pinafores, the slates and the strict discipline.

MY MOTHER WAS A SCHOOLMISTRESS

'My mother was the schoolmistress of a school in the small village of Waterperry at the turn of the century. The school was one large room – infants at one end and boys and girls of all ages up to 14 years in the rest of the classroom, the elder girls helping with the infant class.

Once a year a clergyman came to test our religious knowledge – and awarded a prize called "The Bishop's Prize". This prize was a lovely prayer book.

I remember being in the infant class using frames with coloured balls and learning to count on them. I learnt to write with crayon and slates. When I moved into the next class we had to answer the register first and then have a scripture lesson – for about an hour, I think, and learn the collect for the coming Sunday. When there were pauses between school lessons, we always had to say, and sometimes sing, our tables.

My mother was very keen on sewing and we were taught to make buttonholes, smocking, samplers, etc. The best of the garments were sent to Oxford to be judged. There was great excitement when the results came back – it meant we were to go to Oxford as a class to receive our awards in Oxford town hall. This, on the day, meant a ride on a waggon to Wheatley station, a train ride to Oxford and a walk to a school called (I think) St Barnabas. There we had ham sandwiches and cold drinks of lemonade or milk, we then walked back to the town hall to receive our prizes (I think it was money in a small packet). It was a wonderful day to be among so many other schools. We returned again by train – then home in the waggon, singing as we neared the village!'

A RELIC OF VICTORIAN DAYS

'In 1921 at the age of five my education began in Wantage at Alton House school, which was virtually a dame school and a relic of Victorian days.

119

Miss Caroline Bayley was headmistress and the school, with about 24 boys and girls, was held in her home, a handsome double-fronted house in our own street and on the same side of the road. Very convenient, even in those quiet days of sparse traffic. Judging by old school photographs, Miss Bayley was quite elderly, but she was a born teacher and dedicated to "her" children.

The five years old were taught by her in the large room on the right of the front door, all seated round a large dining table, probably eight or ten of us. We all learned the alphabet and to spell short words and although I don't remember being taught to read, we could all read. We practised writing, numbers and simple sums on wood-rimmed slates with squeaky slate pencils and also started to learn by heart multiplication tables which we chanted in chorus. As we gradually improved we used pencils and paper instead of slates and practice work was done on the insides of used envelopes, neatly clipped together as "rough pads". We sang simple songs and hymns and carols at Christmas and learned little poems, only one of which I half remember about "cold east winds and poor little robin".

In the second form the assistant teacher taught us in another room, still around a dining table. We gradually progressed to joined-up writing and when reasonably proficient were allowed to use pen and ink – steel nibs in wooden penholders, of course. I always managed to have more blots than anyone else. We started history by reciting, or chanting all together the Kings and Queens of England from printed "King Cards". Real throw-backs from Victorian times. I still remember "William the First 1066, Matilda of Flanders, William the Second 1087, never married", and there my memory fails me! The only punishment I remember was to stand in the corner, a great disgrace! At playtime we played in the quite spacious hall which had a mosaic tiled floor.

The pupils were mostly children of local tradesmen and lived reasonably near the school. Some were children of farmers in nearby villages, so rode bicycles there, and two or three were weekly boarders. I loved it and always ran there early to play with the other children and during the summer often went there in the evenings to play in the garden with the "boarders".

We had a good basic grounding in the three Rs and when about seven or eight moved to the senior school in the Market Place run by the Misses Adkin. But that is another story – equally happy.'

VILLAGE SCHOOLS IN THE 1920s

'Studley boasted a small school of two rooms built near the church, which catered for all the children from the village aged from five to 14, with one teacher in charge. It had two playgrounds, one for boys and one for girls, with an outside toilet in each. These were earth closets with long wooden bench seats accommodating three children at a time – two large and one small! The facilities for washing included one large enamel jug, one tin basin on a three-legged metal stand, one small piece of Lifebuoy soap and a roller towel, clean on Mondays.

Despite the lack of facilities, the teacher was excellent and I enjoyed going to school. On cold mornings she would build up a huge fire and we would all sit as close as possible to it while she told us scripture stories. We all loved scripture (probably for this reason) and would gladly have listened to it all day. There was no school uniform but prior to 1925 the girls wore white pinafores, which were elaborate affairs and seem almost like a uniform in old photographs.'

'At Enstone most of us started when we were three years old to go to the little school, now turned into a dwelling. We went to the big school at five years. Our schoolmaster was Mr Glover, assisted by his wife, and we sometimes had a third teacher to help. I think numbers averaged about 80 children. They came from Fulwell, Clevely, Radford, Lidstone and Gaginwell; no transport then, they all had to walk. There were few cars and most parents were unable to afford bicycles. In the winter those children were sent home early before it was dark.

Our heating was a round black stove which seemed to eat coke. A bucket of water was placed on top for the steam to keep down the fumes and to moisten the air.

During my time at school I only remember two children winning scholarships to Burford school. We had no homework to do from school, though sometimes we might have to collect a specimen for nature study, such as a branch of blackberries or a spray of oak leaves with an acorn.'

'In 1922 I commenced my school days at Ascott Church of England school, which was run by Mr Kinvig and his wife. Mr Kinvig had also taught my father.

The room was heated by a tortoise stove, close to which was a harmonium. The children sat at long wooden desks and had slates on which to write. Each day began with a scripture lesson; the only thing I remember about them was learning the catechism, which I remember to this day.

After the scripture lesson the teacher sat down behind the harmonium and read the daily paper, while we took out our hand-

A class at SS Mary & John school, Oxford in the 1920s. Schools did not change a great deal for successive generations between the wars.

kerchiefs and made rabbits with them. Some of those handkerchiefs cannot have been very clean by the end of the week.

One other lesson I remember was sewing. We were given a piece of white material about six inches by two inches, with a hem tacked on each side. We had to learn to hem these with red cotton. The highlight afterwards was to be chosen to stay in at playtime to unpick the hemming, so that it would be ready to be hemmed again in the next sewing lesson. I wonder what today's children would make of that sort of routine!'

'I was born in 1916 at Kennington. School playtime then was segregated. We boys used to play football in the winter with a tennis ball and we often broke a window. Miss Mundy said, "I'm not stopping the boys playing football" and she had wire netting put up at the windows instead.

We used to wear boots then, never shoes. The place was filthy inside because of the mud. Old Mrs Gibbons was the caretaker. She lived in the village, a very old fashioned lady who wore her skirts right down to her ankles and rode an upright bike. She used to clean the school and light the fire, which was an old tortoise stove. You couldn't get warm. Those who were near the fire were lucky, but as you rose in seniority you went to the back and it was cold.

We had no electric, no running water, and no sanitation. The bucket lavatories smelled very badly in the hot weather. In fact, we used to run all the way home if we could – if we couldn't we'd use the hedge on the way. We used to take our sandwiches and the only drink we could have was either a bottle of cocoa or tea, whatever the case might be. Miss Mundy often stayed for lunch and she would put a big saucepan on top of the stove with water in it. The bottles of tea or cocoa went in it and by twelve o'clock they were warm. Water had to be carried up to the school in a can, or got from the water butt. There was no other water at all.

We had no lights so when it got dark we went home. We had pens to write with, wooden pens. By the time you were seven or eight you were allowed one nib per term and one small piece of blotting paper, about six by four or maybe smaller. That was to last you a whole term. We learnt to uncross our nibs on the desk top. You kept your blotter as clean as long as you could but by the end of term there wasn't much blot in it.'

DISCIPLINE AND ILLNESS

'My memories go back to the 1920s when I started at the village school of The Bartons in North Oxfordshire. It was quite usual to be admitted, as I was, at the age of three plus. We children walked to school, walked home for lunch and back again to school in the afternoon. The heating was by open coal fires and coke stoves and although the school house had a water pump, water used for school was fetched by two pupils from the mill stream in tall white enamel jugs. The school house was where the headmaster and his wife, who also taught at the school, lived. The discipline was very strict and the cane was used. Sometimes even such things as mistakes in writing were corrected by knuckles being rapped hard with thick blue marking pencils. Even now I well remember the pain. Green, coarse knitting wool was used by girls and when the lesson was over the "wool" was rewound and used over and over again.

Games were played in season, top spinning, followed by skipping, bowling of hoops, hopscotch, and how welcome in the twenties were the yo-yo and the biff-bat! My favourite was top spinning and I loved going to the village shop to choose a top. We played in the road and in those days I could spin my top for a quarter of an hour or longer without having to stop because of traffic. Now, just to cross the road, I may have to wait for several cars to go by.

There was, however, a lot of illness – the dreaded consumption, diphtheria, scarlet fever, headlice and ringworm were very prevalent. I remember boys wearing skull caps to hide the gentian blue on their

123

heads after being treated for ringworm. I remember, too, that when children died, it was usual for the coffin to be carried by children at the funeral. We girls wore white when we carried a baby's coffin, and I believe that this, as well as the event itself, used to move bystanders to tears.'

AWARD FOR GOOD ATTENDANCE

'My father attended Deddington primary school and in 1923 was awarded one of the last silver pocket watches given to Oxfordshire schoolchildren for good attendance and never being late. It is inscribed: "Presented to Leslie Percival Harper for seven years attendance. Never absent, never late and good behaviour. 1923."'

GARTERS FOR MARBLES

'My mother was slim and wore lovely costumes – long skirts and tight fitting jackets. I remember the skirts being cut up to make my brothers short trousers, and my Dad's old shirts being cut up to line them; I had the job of sewing three or four pearly buttons at the sides. My brothers wore knee length grey socks for school and I was always making elastic garters for them. One brother was forever needing a new pair as he used to swap his garters for marbles. The boy who got the garters used the elastic to make catapults – then there was more swapping going on.'

OUR TEACHER WAS REMARKABLE

'Our school teacher at North Leigh was remarkable. Somehow she managed to teach two separate classes of nine to ten years olds in one large room.

If we arrived at school with wet clothes, she would drape them on the huge guard around the tortoise stove to dry. My sister says that in the 1920s the teacher used to buy bones and vegetables and cook soup for the children on the stove. It cost a halfpenny a bowl. When my sister started school she wore starched aprons and button-up boots. My old aunt, now aged 96, says she wore starched aprons too, and lace-up boots that cost three shillings and elevenpence from Freeman Hardy & Willis.'

SCHOOLS IN THE 1930s and 1940s

The next generation found things in the classroom much the same, though changes were to begin now and accelerate after the war. Many of us are grateful for the education we received in those days of shortages and overcrowding.

SOUTH MORETON IN THE 1930s

'The school building consisted of one large room divided into two classrooms by a wood and glass partition. On special occasions this could be folded back to make more room for the festivities.

One such occasion was the annual Christmas party. During the morning the glass of the partition was covered over with sugar paper and much guessing went on as to what lay beyond it. Generous benefactors donated the annual Christmas tree and it was this, duly decorated with a gift for each child, that was erected in secrecy behind the partition.

At the party we tucked into jelly, sandwiches and cakes, and played such games as pass the parcel and musical chairs. At the end of the day children danced Sir Roger de Coverley and were each given a bag of sweets and an orange on leaving for home.

The partition was also folded away when the school held a concert, such as on Empire Day (24th May). The flag was flown from a pole in the playground. During the dinner-hour children hurried to the railway embankment and picked moon-daisies to decorate the school. The concert itself was held in the evening and was based on events that had happened in the Empire.

Another special event was Ascension Day. The whole school gathered in the playground before marching in twos to the church for morning service. After this we trooped back to the school and, much to everyone's delight, were given the rest of the day off.

Armistice Day is another time I remember. We stood in the school playground by the open window of the school house to hear the Cenotaph service on the wireless, and observed the two minutes' silence, which always seemed like an age.

The end of the spring term also had its own special ritual. We broke up for the Easter holiday at midday on Maundy Thursday, but had to gather in the playground the following morning before walking to the church for the Good Friday service.

The school curriculum comprised arithmetic, composition, poetry, silent reading, needlework, geography and history. As an eight year old able to turn heels, I was allowed to knit socks for our governess's husband, thus avoiding needlework.

At mid-morning playtime we would drink Horlicks in the winter and goats' milk in the summer. Hoops, whips and tops, marbles, conkers, leapfrog and snowballing all took turns as the playtime favourite.

If children were away from school for more than a week the School Attendance Officer would be sent to discover the reason. The usual children's complaints, such as measles and chicken-pox, would need a visit from the doctor. My favourite illness was a bad cold, when I was allowed a small amount of home-made elderberry wine mixed with hot water and sugar as a medicinal toddy.'

WE ALL WALKED

'I started school at the Old Blake School, Cogges, next to the church, when I was three and a half. The teachers let us go to sleep after dinner in some little wooden beds. We all went home to dinner at twelve o'clock and had to get back for half past one. I think my auntie took me to school at that time as she was still at school.

For nature study we used to go for walks along the lane which was the way to Stanton Harcourt and High Cogges and South Leigh. When we got older we went out to play at nights, in the park and all.

Our houses backed onto a field, where a man who was a second-hand dealer kept a lot of farm implements and old trucks and carriages. There was even an old stagecoach and a steamroller there. We used to slide down the trucks and play in the vehicles, although we had to make sure Mr Calcutt didn't see us. He had to get rid of it all in 1935 as the council made it into a playing field, as it still is now.

When we were at Cogges school, several years we had to dance country dances at the church fête. We loved that as we were able to be out practising on the vicarage lawn. One of our school doors opened into the vicarage garden. When Mr Spence was vicar he sometimes brought strawberries and apples in for us children to eat.

We never had time off school because of bad weather; if it was deep snow we still went to school and we all walked, no one had cars in those days. Not even the teachers; one came on the bus from Eynsham, one rode her bike from Witney and Miss Smith walked as she only lived in Newland. They were all quite strict and we did not talk in school in those days.

My mother and I used to go to Oxford once a year to visit some cousins and aunties of hers, and once a year they came down to visit my grandparents. My friend Carol and I used to go for long bike rides and during the war we used to go to Stanton Harcourt and see the bombers taking off on Sunday mornings.

We played all the usual games, skipping with a big rope to "keep the pot boiling", and hopscotch, bowling hoops and tops. We never played tennis as we had no white clothes to play in, we were only working folk.'

WE WERE BROUGHT UP TOUGHER

'The cane was frequently used at Thame school, and you often had to stand in the corner for being naughty. One teacher was good at catching you out. If you were in the top class, there was a partition between that and the next class and he would go out and then you would start acting about and he would look through the partition, walk in and say, "You, you and you." "I haven't done a thing," was protested but he insisted. "You were out of your seat. Turn round, bend over and touch your toes." Then bang, a cricket bat across the behind.

We always had to sit up straight. One teacher used to make you sit with arms behind your back and twelve inches away from your writing.

One winter at John Hampden school it was so very cold and we got a slide from one end of the school, out through the gate over to the middle of Park Street. The teacher thought it was dangerous so we had to stop using it, but we got buckets of water and threw them across the top playground to make the slide bigger inside the school. You were allowed on the slide only if you wore certain shoes. You were definitely not allowed on it if you wore hobnailed boots as they made candles on the slide. It was even known for the inkwells to freeze.

You were definitely not collected from school otherwise you were called a cissy. We were brought up tougher, but then, there was nothing to be afraid of. Walking to and from school was considered fun as you played games along the way, such as leapfrog, and you would also get to school in time to play games in the playground. One was called flicks, and another well known game was ten/twenty. You would put a tin lid on the ground and you had your ball and if you threw this onto the lid and hit it and then onto the wall and caught it again you gained ten. When you stopped doing it correctly you were out and it was someone else's turn. Marbles was another favourite, together with hopscotch, skipping, handstands against the wall and five-stones. There was a tops season, a hoop season, etc and you always had to be playing the right thing in the right season. We always used to go to the corner shop bowling the hoop with a skimmer. This was instead of a stick, and was a hooked piece of steel which gave the hoop a better speed.'

OUR VILLAGE SCHOOL

'The village school at Appleton was, and is still, a Church of England school. The original 1837 Victorian building in the centre of the village at the top of Church Road, was used until the 1960s, when a new school was built in the playground next to the churchyard. The old school was demolished, although a portion of its exterior walls form a boundary wall for the new house built on its site.

There were three classrooms in the old school. The large one held the children of eleven to 14 years (the then school leaving age). The middle room adjoining the top room and separated by sliding doors, held the nine to ten year olds, and the infants school the smallest room, the small children of five to seven years. This had its own little room for hanging outdoor clothes. A large porch attached to the main school held the coats of the other children, with a bench with enamel bowls for washing hands; water (cold) being fetched from a neighbouring cottage. After 1938, the older children went to a secondary modern school.

The "top" room was dominated by a large black coke-burning tortoise stove, with two smaller ones in the other rooms. They didn't draw very well and were temperamental. Often in the winter the rooms would be cold in the morning and only warm by the afternoon.

The "yard" was approached by a longer passage at the back of the building and consisted of three or four bucket lavatories under wooden seats. They were separate from the main building and icy cold in winter and very smelly in summer. The boys' yard was approached directly off the Church Road.

The three Rs were very thoroughly taught as well as history, geography, poetry, singing and PT. The girls were taught needle-work and knitting. They could purchase, at a very reasonable rate, the pillowcases, nightdresses, underwear, little frocks, socks and gloves they made. The boys had gardening lessons; an allotment in the plots beyond the church was rented for them. In the 1930s the boys went to Abingdon for woodwork and metalwork and the girls for cookery and housewifery. In the 1920s the lady living at the

128

manor gave half an orchard in Church Lane, "Gullivers Orchard", to the school as a playground, the other half for an extension to the churchyard. Up to then the children had to play in the Church Road or on the road opposite the school. This was no hazard then as traffic was negligible. When the shallow pond in the manor farmyard by the school was frozen over, sliding on the ice was a popular sport.

Being a Church of England school the children were well versed in the Bible and Prayer Book, and nearly all could say the creed and catechism as a matter of course. A Sunday school was held in the school and afterwards many children went on to the morning service.

A Christmas party was held for the children, the money for this being raised by a series of whist drives held in the school in the autumn. A tea of sandwiches and cakes, baked by the village baker, was consumed. There was generally an entertainment of some kind and each child went home with a little present, an orange and a bag of sweets. The headmaster's wife had a book with all the children's names and ages. She would descend on the Oxford toy shops and buy appropriate presents for each child. A school concert was held from time to time. For some years before secondary school education was available, a night school was held for boys who had left school. This taught advanced mathematics etc.

Immediately after the Second World War the school was quite crowded as there were still some evacuee children in the village and some families had returned to live with grandparents, either because of lack of housing or safety reasons.

The old double desks with folding seats and inkwell in the corner were still in use. Ink was made up in large containers as required. School dinners were cooked in a cottage nearby and brought to the school in large cauldron-type containers. These were eaten at the desks. The same grace was always said:

> Thank you for the world so sweet
> Thank you for the food we eat
> Thank you for the birds that sing
> Thank you Lord for everything.

The school sports day was the highlight of the summer. The children walked to Upwood Park at Bessels Leigh, where on a magnificent mown lawn, and in lovely surroundings all the usual sports day events were held; egg and spoon, obstacle and other races and perhaps folk dancing. A lovely tea was then enjoyed.

After the war a canteen was built in the playground and school dinners were cooked and served there. Asphalt was laid on part of the playground about this time.

The boys played football matches against other villages on the football pitch at the back of The Three Horseshoes pub.

A scholar remembers that when the news of the death of George VI was received everyone at school stood in silence and then the National Anthem was sung. When one of their friends was killed in a road accident near the school the children stood in the Church Road as his coffin was taken into church.

On leaving the village school at the age of 14, before it became a primary school, boys and girls were given a clothing grant to purchase clothes and boots to set them up for their new life. This came from the Sir Richard Fettiplace Charity, which was an educational charity. As well as the clothing grants, it also provided night school fees and apprentice grants. The Appleton Trust continues this policy with a £10 book token to 16 year olds, and books to all pupils leaving the primary school, and assistance where necessary for school projects.'

WHAT WE WORE

'In winter we girls wore Chilprufe vests and liberty bodices with rubber buttons on the bottom – suspenders were buttoned to these to hold up those horrible fawn lisle stockings. Navy knickers and a navy serge gymslip with a braid "sash" over a jumper or blouse. Brown lace-up shoes, or wellingtons when it was wet. In summer cotton vests and cotton dresses made by my mother, or remade from my cousin's outgrown ones, white socks, brown sandals and home knitted cardigans. When I passed the eleven-plus in the late 1940s and went to grammar school I remember my mother was horrified at the uniform list – *two* pairs of shoes (outdoor and indoor) *and* gym shoes!'

AT THE GRAMMAR SCHOOL

'This was co-educational but boys and girls were expected to keep to their part of the school and playing fields during breaks. Talking to each other outside lessons was frowned upon and so was walking home together. The Senior Mistress was very strict about uniform. We were expected to keep our hats on in the school bus until we were outside the town boundary. If we wore hair ribbon, it had to be black or dark green. One girl wore yellow one day and was told by the Senior Mistress that she had not come to a party and must remove it. We changed into house shoes on arrival at school but this practice was dropped during the war because we had not the clothing coupons for two pairs of shoes for school.

Our uniform knickers were of thick, dark green fleecy-lined material with a pocket in them and elastic at the legs. We rolled them up and they must have bulged under our gymslips.

School Certificate needlework with wartime restrictions demanded that we made a renovation in addition to a new garment. I made a pinafore dress, cutting it out of a woollen dress that had worn out under the arms. The bib was lined with some cotton nightdress material. The cookery was very restricted because of rationing and we only produced the plainest of fare – stew, apple pies, egg and bacon tart, etc. We did make and ice a Christmas cake which must have been a help to our families at the festive season.'

KEEPING WARM

'One of my earliest memories is of the cold mornings in the early 1940s. We lived about two and a half miles from school, which was in Abingdon, and were not entitled to a free school bike because you had to live three miles from the school to qualify.

We had no central heating at home, just a coal fire in the living room, which had to be lit each morning. The house was cold with only lino and rugs each side of the bed on the floor to step out onto. The window panes had frost on the inside of the windows making beautiful patterns on the glass. It was so cold we took our clothes into our beds and dressed in bed.

On rising, we had a nice hot breakfast and were wrapped up warm to go to school. We had our big thick coats on, which were usually too big so that they would last, our scarves were wrapped around our chests to keep the cold out, our gloves were attached to tape threaded through the sleeves so that we didn't lose them and our heads were covered with a pixie bonnet made by our mother, the point of which seemed to stand up so high our heads looked huge! We would pull our socks above our knees as high as they would go. (There was no such thing as girls wearing trousers to school – in fact, my mother didn't think girls should wear trousers at all.)

We would run and skip to school in order to keep warm. On arrival at school we were allowed to keep our coats on if it was really cold.

The room was heated by a large stove, usually to one side of the room, which only seemed to heat the area around it. Our milk for morning break (third of a pint in small bottles) was placed near to the stove to thaw out before we were expected to drink it at playtime (it was always *so* cold).

We always welcomed spring time. On Good Friday morning we would walk from home near Abingdon to Radley College Woods as, according to my mother, the woods were open to everyone on

Good Friday, although they were normally private grounds. On the way there we would stop off at the bakery in Thrupp Lane and buy some freshly baked hot cross buns. These would be gratefully consumed sitting on a fallen tree somewhere in the woods. We would return home later in the afternoon, tired out, with our arms laden with bluebells which were then placed into every available jam jar and placed everywhere in the house, including the garden shed. Somehow the bluebells always seemed to be out in flower on Good Fridays, or is my memory playing tricks on me?'

INTO THE 1950s

'We all worked towards the eleven-plus and hoped to go to one of the grammar schools: Oxford Central Girls School was one end of New Inn Hall Street and the Boys High School was the other end in George Street. At the start and end of the school day the city centre was full of the boys in their brown blazers and the girls in navy trimmed with green. Also in Church Street, now the back of the Westgate, was the co-educational Technical School with the boys and girls in their green uniforms.

Going to school with girls from all over the city we made friends in the various areas, which meant we gained a knowledge of a wider area than our own home districts.

Discipline was very much a part of school life and we all had a respect and a little healthy fear of our teachers. We had 30 pupils in each form, two forms per year. Overcrowding was taken for granted; some lessons were in the hall, which was divided by curtains.

PE took place in the Wesley Memorial Church Hall the other end of New Inn Hall Street. Our sports field was in Manor Road, now the site of St Catherine's college, quite a walk before we even started to play hockey; a walk that took even longer as we progressed up the school and were allowed to make our own way and not stay in crocodile.

We went to school in regulation navy gymslips, white shirts and ties, awful felt hats or berets and webbing sashes in our house colour around our waists. All covering those terrible navy knickers! School dinners were taken in the hall of the New Road Baptist church which was next door to the school.

Despite having very sparse resources compared with today's schools, we felt proud of belonging to the school, and we managed a good standard of schooling. Over 40 years later, many friendships started in school are still going strong. I've been married to one of those boys in the brown blazers for 37 years!'

THE WORLD OF WORK

ON THE LAND

Farms and smallholdings have long been the backbone of Oxfordshire's working life, though how times have changed on the farm, with mechanisation taking the place of the horse and the farm labourer. Harvest was always a special time for the whole village.

STATION FARM

'The Brown family moved to Station Farm, South Leigh in 1928 and found most people employed on the six or seven mixed dairy and arable farms in the village or in running smallholdings.

Horses were still in use until after the war, some ploughs and the threshing machine being powered by steam. Farming then was a sociable affair with many of the villagers called in to help at haymaking and harvest. Mr Mawle, Church End Farm, would fix a "sweep" on the front of his old car to collect the rows of hay and the children enjoyed being allowed to ride in it.

At harvest time when the fields of wheat were ready for harvesting, the reaper and binder went round and round the field cutting the corn and then dropping off the sheaves neatly tied. The men followed it and stood the sheaves in stooks of six or eight where they were left for a few days to dry out. All around the edge of the field men stood with guns ready to shoot the rabbits as they ran out – rabbit pie made a delicious addition to the menu. I remember seeing a rabbit trying frantically to get into a burrow at the end of one such day and being unable to as it was already packed tight with rabbits – there were 36 rabbits pulled out of that one burrow! At harvest time there might be as many as a hundred dead rabbits, after the shooters had each taken a couple; the rest were "paunched" – their entrails removed – and hung in the cellars at Station Farm until they could be taken to Witney to be sold at the local butcher's.

Once the corn had been harvested, small mobile chicken houses would be moved into the fields nearest the house so that the chickens could feed on the fallen grain. Some of the women went out gleaning in the fields to collect fallen ears of corn for their own chickens. Women, in spite of working hard at home with their big families and helping with the domestic work in the farmhouses, also helped out on the farms with casual, seasonal work at planting times, helping to harvest potatoes and root crop vegetables and plucking turkeys at Christmas.

Pigeons were a great pest at planting time – the seed was broadcast then (sown by hand), consequently, even after harrowing, more grain remained visible near the surface, providing easy eating for the pigeons. Men who enjoyed shooting would often erect hides in the fields in the spring and shoot the pigeons – which again made good pies and casseroles. Other bird pests were the magpies and crows which were often shot by local farmers and gamekeepers who hung the dead bodies on the hedges and poles.

My mother-in-law, Mrs Ethel Brown, born in 1887, like many women in the village was skilled at using and preserving all the produce of the farm and garden. She made good use of every bit of the pig, had incubators for hatching chickens in Station Farm's cellars, preserved their eggs in water-glass, salted runner beans, dried apple rings, made jellies and jams of all the fruit and had a large cool larder stocked with foods in the days before fridges. To her the four-burner Valor paraffin stove which replaced the old coal burning range was a great luxury.

Workers were often known by the jobs they did. Shepherd Hicks and Carter Lee worked at College Farm – the carters were the men who worked with the horses.'

WE ALL HELPED

'My first memories of Oxfordshire date from 1931 when my father moved us from a farm in North Buckinghamshire. I was eight years old and with my sister, who is a little older, and an elderly farmhand, we walked the eight miles, pushed our bicycles and drove eight cows. The first mile or so was open common land with bushes on which the cows seemed to enjoy leading us on a "wild goose chase". Then along country roads into Bicester, one person went ahead to stop them going into gateways or taking wrong turnings. There were very few cars on the roads, so traffic was not a problem, and apart from one cow slipping up on cobblestones in London Road in Bicester, we made our journey without mishaps.

We children helped on the farm, with feeding chickens, looking up the eggs which were scattered around the buildings because the chickens were all free-range, and in the summer helping with the haymaking and harvest. When we came home from school we took tea in the field for the workmen. There was always a basket prepared with piles of sandwiches and usually a large fruit cake. The tea was in a big stone jar with a large stopper. It had a small handle and was very heavy and awkward to carry, but it kept the tea very hot.

We also helped by leading the horses and waggons into the fields to collect the hay or corn. We were allowed to ride the horses into the field with empty waggons, but had to walk and lead them home with their heavy loads. The hay was pitched from the waggons onto an elevator to carry it onto the rick, where usually two men were building the hayrick.

The corn was cut by a horse-drawn binder which automatically tied it into sheafs. These were then stacked in sixes, called stooks, in the fields and left to dry. Oats had to hear the church bells ring three times before they could be brought down to the farmyard and put into ricks. The ricks stood until the corn was needed – usually the spring when the price had risen, too. Then the big thresher came in. This was a big machine, owned by an individual or a small firm, who went to the farms when needed. It was a terribly dusty job and the ricks were always full of rats and mice – a haven for them in the winter. The men used to tie string round the bottoms of their trouser legs to stop the mice running up!

On ·the farm milking was done by hand, several men sitting on little milking stools very close to the cows. The milk was then cooled through an elaborate machine and run into the milk churns. In the

Haymaking at Bucknell, when everyone gave a hand at one of the most important times in the farming year.

136

summer months the milk churns were stood in a big pond by the house to keep the milk cool until it was collected by milk lorry every morning.

Hens roamed free in the farmyard and we collected eggs from the hay mangers, barns and straw stacks, quite a time consuming job. The ducks were fed in their hut at bedtime – the only way to get them off the pond and safe from foxes.

I can remember my sister and I being in trouble for making a fire in a cart shed and cooking eggs for the farm cats – the smoke gave us away.

Horses did all the work that tractors do now. The carter went to plough (only two-furrowed ploughs then) very early in the morning and returned at three o'clock in the afternoon to feed and groom the horses. He took his food to the field with him, large slices of bread spread with home-cured lard and often a good slice of fat bacon.

Cattle markets were held in local towns and cattle and sheep walked to market from the farm, the farmer travelling by horse and cart. My father told the tale of a neighbour who often had too much to drink on market day; his friends pointed his horse and cart towards home and the horse knew the way. There were gated roads and so it probably took quite a while to get home.'

'Schools at Combe would close for two weeks in September so that the children could assist in the potato harvest. Potato picking by hand was a bit backbreaking but a popular way of getting extra money for all the family.

Village women would go "rogueing" in season, which was removing the rogue wild oats from a standing crop of corn (this would ensure the farmer getting a better price for his seed crop). The women enjoyed this work and there was much chatter and laughter to be heard about the fields on summer days when rogueing was in progress.'

HORSES AND COWS

'There are not so many farms in Long Wittenham as there used to be. At one time there were ten herds of milking cows in the village and all the farmers used to take their milk to Didcot station but now there is only one farm with a milking herd and their milk goes off in a bulk tanker.

I used to bring the cows down the village street morning and evening to come in for milking and when we first started all the milking was done by hand. We had the first milking machine in the village, that was in 1948.

137

When we took the young ones down the road to the fields it was a bit of a job because you had to have someone to stand in all the gateways to stop them going in.

One time we had a lady vet come out to a cow that was having trouble and one of the men saw her there and said, "I never known a cow have a midwife before."

Of course there were no tractors then, it was all horses. We didn't have our own horses, someone came in with all the horses and equipment to do the ploughing etc.'

CHARACTERS

'Father was born at Begbroke Hill Farm at Cassington in 1894, and as a small boy (probably about six) he was sent on an old boneshaker bicycle to Woodstock to call the vet. On his way he met his first car and got in the ditch to let it pass. When he arrived at the vet's he could not reach the bell and had to get someone to pull it for him.

He remembered when he was about twelve they were threshing with the steam engine driving the threshing box. A little aeroplane went over and old Henry Horne who was driving the steam engine said, "Hubert, how do he get his coal and water up there?" Steam was the only thing he knew.

Two of the "steam" families were the Thornes and the Beckets. Bert Becket used to say his mother was Methodist and his dad was Steam Plough.

Grampy Partridge was always in the farmyard to see the men in first thing in the morning. Jimmy Green was one of the real old farmhands and he smoked a very smelly pipe. Gramp said, "Bless us well, Jimmy, that tobacco should be a sovereign an ounce!" Jimmy replied, "That's what I reckon too, Master, and every ounce should be as big as a hayrick."

In those days the farm hands were expected to go to church. One Monday morning when Jimmy came to work, Grampy said, "I didn't see you at church yesterday, Jimmy?" "No, Master," said Jimmy, "I had a bad dream Saturday night; I dreamt I went to Hell." "What was it like?" asked Gramp. "I don't know," said Jimmy, "I didn't get in. There were 42 ricks of parsons thatched with churchwardens, so I came away." Gramp was the churchwarden.

The character who was acknowledged as the finest poacher in the village was also a hay cutter. With the large hay knife the rick was cut into blocks which were put into a press and tied; the trusses had to be cut to a uniform size for pressing and tying.'

A FARM STUDENT

'We met on the steps of the cinema in Banbury – a nervous 18 year old from the industrial Midlands and a farmer's wife, who was to become my mentor and second mother and change the direction of my future life completely.

I was the first (and only) female student on an isolated 400-acre mixed farm in the heart of the Cotswolds. There was no electricity, just log fires and Aladdin lamps, whose wicks were trimmed before being lit each night, a larder with a cold slab and meat safe and an Aga cooker in the kitchen, also used for drying and airing clothes and reviving ailing lambs and goslings. Water was pumped by motor from a well, somewhat intermittently. It was more than a year before electricity was brought in across the fields from the neighbouring village and welcomed by all.

On the farm, we had two dairy herds – dairy shorthorns and Jerseys, from the wife's native country and her pride and joy. Unfortunately, these tough little cows are somewhat spiteful and derived great pleasure from waiting by the gate and using their

No. 43A (Shepherd). DOGS. No. 572

CERTIFICATE OF EXEMPTION FROM DUTY.
41 & 42 Vict., cap. 15.

I hereby certify that Mr. *Levi Hathaway*, of *Chalford Oaks*, in the Parish of *Enstone*, in the County of *Oxford*, has delivered a Declaration under the above-mentioned Act, stating that he is a **Shepherd**, and that *two* Dog*s* are kept by him solely for use in the exercise of his calling or occupation as a Shepherd, and I hereby further certify that he is exempt from Licence Duty in respect of such Dog*s* while so kept and used until the 31st day of December next inclusive.

Dated this *22* day of *January*, 190*1*.

J. W. Lindley, Supervisor of Inland Revenue.

NOTE.—This Certificate will become void and must be exchanged for a Licence if the dog ceases to be used for the purpose stated, or is used in taking rabbits or game, or, in the trade of a butcher or drover. A Declaration must be delivered and a fresh Certificate obtained in the month of January next, if required.

This Certificate must be produced, when required, to any Officer of Inland Revenue or Police, under a penalty of £5.

M & S Ltd 6752 8222—60m 5/900 [37]

Shepherds could claim exemption from the dog licence we all had to pay.

139

horns on the much larger shorthorns, as they passed through. One day, the farmer stormed into the kitchen and proclaimed, "Either those Jerseys go, or I do! What's it going to be?" No more Jerseys.

In the dairy, milk was lifted by bucket into the top of the cooler above one's head, from whence it trickled slowly through zig-zag metal pipes, which enclosed a flow of cold water, into the replaceable filter and the milk churn below, which was replaced when full. These were then rolled out to the churn-stand for daily collection; some milk was kept for calf-rearing. We kept our own bulls in the yard.

We had sows and piglets in sties nearby, a flock of about 100 ewes, which lambed each spring, and up to 2,000 head of poultry; laying hens in fold-units, which were moved daily, lifted on to a wheeled frame at one end – a very heavy job indeed. Eggs were collected in huge baskets and I recall only too well the day when I was carrying a full basket in each hand and my feet slipped on the mud, with which the farm was well endowed, and sat down heavily. As the egg trickled slowly down from the baskets beside me, our two tractor drivers came round the corner – I was in despair, as they became increasingly hysterical on the spot!

Breeding hens were kept free-range in hen-houses with a cockerel. Occasionally, these splendid giants were very territorial and fights ensued. One magnificent specimen took to tearing round the corner of the hen-house and attacking the unsuspecting egg collector, which was most alarming. One day, this so enraged the farmer's wife that she armed herself with a thick plank and as he approached, brought it crashing down on top of him – he never moved again! Point-of-lay pullets also lived in hen-houses with slatted floors and one day, we found 19 of them dead, mostly headless, which had been attacked by the fox from under the slatted floor. In the yard, we had Indian gamecocks and hens, the former much given to sparring.

I had no form of transport until I learned to ride a bike, which enabled me to go to the local "hop" on Saturday nights in the next village school. One very frosty night, having come out from a hot room, I was found lying in the road nearby with my bike on top of me. I must have passed out on my bike and was carried into a nearby cottage, until the ambulance came, and I knew nothing until I awoke in hospital next day. Sometimes, a party of us would share the local taxi and visit the cinema in Chipping Norton.

Nowadays, when I visit the farm, we talk with nostalgia about the old days, when every building was filled with livestock and every barn full of hay, straw and corn. Now, there is only a house cow and a couple of calves and a few hens, but recently, the pigs have returned in large numbers, all out on free-range. Most of the fields are under the plough, where mushrooms used to grow on old grassland, some are "set-aside" and everything relates to economics. How things have changed!'

THE POTATO HARVEST

'There have been many changes on the farm in the way the work has been carried out, but one of the greatest I think is the way we now harvest, and I begin by going back to the late 1950s and the potato harvest. This comes after the harvesting of the corn, and usually at the beginning of October.

Many preparations had to be carried out before we could start and the most important was making sure we had enough labour. Women from the village who did not normally go to work came to help as the money was useful with Christmas looming ahead, and children after school finished for the day came for the last hour and on Saturdays, anxious to have money to spend at the annual fair in the town.

A loaded trailer with sacks and buckets set off down the field, sticks were inserted into the ground to mark off the rows for each picker to work on, then they each had a bucket to fill. Sacks were put along the rows ready to be filled with potatoes from the buckets. At the end of the day the sacks stood in haphazard rows, fat and

Shocking up oats at Foxhole Farm, Combe.

141

bulging. Some not quite steady toppled over and the potatoes had to be picked up again.

Work usually began at nine o'clock and before this the workers arrived on foot or bicycle and took up their positions in readiness for the digger to come along the row. As it came potatoes flew in all directions as they were dug up. Then it was bending over to pick them up and fill the bucket as quickly as possible and empty it into the nearest sack. At eleven o'clock energy was beginning to flag and a break was called, and if there were empty sacks near, the workers sat on them to rest while having a snack. Dinner was at 12.30 and an hour's rest, then work began again, finishing about four o'clock before the daylight failed. The farm workers carried on picking up the filled sacks and loading them into the trailer to be emptied into the barn or put into a "burrow" on a prepared piece of ground; this was then covered with a layer of straw about eight inches thick and then on top of this another thick covering of soil to protect the potatoes from frost. It was all very good fun.

Nowadays the farm gateway has to be widened to let the massive digger through. This not only digs up the potatoes but throws the haulms (tops) and most of the lumps of soil, so only two or three workers are needed up on the top. They stand on a platform and are protected by a canvas covering from wind and rain. They make sure only the potatoes go up on the elevator and into the trailer travelling alongside. No need to leave off work at four o'clock, this can go on quite late as strip lights are fitted over the sorter and a cord can be pulled to stop the tractor should anything get stuck in the machinery like a large stone. It also digs up two rows at a time. So where it used to take ten days or so to do a field, the work is completed in a quarter the time.

We still get tired after a long day, we still have a laugh together, but no, no back-ache!'

OWNED BY THE DUKE OF MARLBOROUGH

'My father rented about 80 acres of land at Combe from the Duke of Marlborough – known as Foxhole Farm. He kept a few cattle in the field during the summer months and during the winter months in the farmyard. He also kept a few pigs and hens and two cart-horses. The farmyard was cleaned out once a year.

He grew barley and oats and I can remember standing at the side of the field watching it being cut with the binder and seeing the rabbits come out of it. They were lucky if they got away as my father and brother both had a gun. They would either be our dinner or sold to someone else!

The next job would be to shock up the sheaves of corn, then after a few days when it was considered dry enough it would be time for carrying. All the sheaves would be carried on a horse and cart and made into a rick. Later in the year a thresher would be hired to come. The bags (sack bags) of corn would be sold or oats kept to feed the animals in the winter. My father also grew a lot of vegetables and sold some to other people in the village.

Most of the land and many cottages were owned by the Duke of Marlborough. At least eight farms at Combe were rented from the Duke. One farmer had a lot of milking cows and delivered milk around the village with a pony and trap – pouring milk into customers' jugs. The cows would wander from the field to the farm once the gate was opened – no need for human guidance though Cruso the farm dog would help if necessary, as they liked to taste the grass on the village green on their way. When farmers moved cattle (not milking cows) from one field on one side of the village to a field on the other side of the village one or more workmen would have to go in front of them to close gates, otherwise the cattle would soon be in the gardens eating cabbages!'

IN SERVICE

For many girls, going into service was the only work available when they left school. It could mean working on a farm or for a small middle class family, or for a house where their Majesties came to tea!

A COUNTRY GIRL

'Domestic service was the job open to most country girls 60 years ago, who went to the nearest town or city and lived in with a family. I went into such a job in the residential suburb of Oxford. I met the "lady" at an arranged venue in the city where the interview took place. I was only 14 years old, newly left school and never away from home before. I had taken references from the school-master and local vicar. I was engaged for the situation as a between maid, which meant that I had some of nearly all the duties to do. The wage was to be £1 a month and full board – this turned out to be wonderful, to me who had come from a poor home with nine brothers and sisters. I had never seen such food before. There were two other maids in the house and also a resident nanny who cared for a three year old girl. The other members of the household were Mr and Mrs, and two adult daughters. Two other daughters were at boarding school.

We had to be up at 7 am to start off getting morning tea. Cook made the tea while I prepared trays and the parlourmaid took the trays to the bedrooms. Breakfast was at eight o'clock, and when the dining room was served the three staff had theirs in the kitchen. I got all the washing up to do and when this was done had to help with the beds and clean bathrooms. While we were doing this the lady would be with Cook arranging lunch and dinner menus. Orders were given to the gardener to bring the necessary vegetables for the day; these I had to prepare. Lunch was a light meal at one o'clock and I had to take the nursery meal to the day nursery for the nanny and small girl. If we had cleared the lunch and no more jobs were involved we could have an hour's rest before changing from the morning frock of blue, over which we had a white apron and mob cap, into a black dress with a "nippy" apron and cap.

Dinner at seven o'clock was usually three courses but when there were guests it was usually five, and coffee in the drawing room. This had to be tidied while the family were having dinner, cushions shaken and straightened, ash trays emptied and fire made up. Then upstairs to turn down the beds and lay out night wear. Dinner finished, I now had all the washing up again, while the parlour-maid washed up all the glasses and silver in the maids' pantry. We could then have our supper, and when this was finished it was bedtime. I had a small room for myself. There was no reading lamp so I contrived with a length of string tied to the light switch, which was a small brass knob in those days which went up and down, passed over a coat hook on the back of the door to the bed so that a quick jerk put the light off.

We had one afternoon off during the week and alternate Sunday afternoons up until ten o'clock. This usually meant going in to Oxford to the pictures.'

THEIR MAJESTIES TOOK TEA

'I was in service to the Marquise d'Hautpoul at Turville Grange. My salary as parlour-maid was £24 a year. I worked from 7 am to 10 pm with one half day off a fortnight. When George V and Queen Mary were at Windsor their butler would ring to say, "Their Majesties will take tea today." King George liked a boiled egg. His sisters, Queen

Maud of Norway and Princess Victoria often came for lunch or tea, and Princess Marina and Prince George also came.

I later became lady's maid at £36 a year, and with the Marquise went twice to the Royal yacht at Cowes. The King and Queen were on board and many other eminent people.'

THE LOCAL GENTRY

'On the last day at Goring school the local gentry came round and offered jobs. My first job was as a between maid. The lady bought me a bike to get there, which cost £1 12s 6d. I earned seven shillings and sixpence and had to pay her two shillings and sixpence a week. When I'd paid for the bike, I left. I hated the job.'

VILLAGE TRADES AND CRAFTS

Villages were almost self-sufficient in the past, with all kinds of jobs and trades from blacksmiths, carpenters and wheelwrights to shopkeepers and postmen.

AN INDUSTRIOUS VILLAGE

'Most of the men at Appleton and Eaton worked on the land, either on farms or in gardens. Some also worked on the building trade or other local trades. The men walked to work, as usually their work was within walking distance, and later when bicycles were available they cycled. After the establishment of the Morris car company and the Pressed Steel company at Oxford, and the MG car factory at Abingdon, many worked there. A good number were working at these factories when the Second World War started.

The men would also trap moles around the fields and woods, and sell the skins for about sixpence each. This provided a little extra money for the households.

The women mainly stayed at home, but at the turn of the century, piece work from a local trouser factory was carried on in the homes. This was known in the village as "trousering" and consisted of finishing off the trousers with buttons etc. The trousers were brought to the women and the finished goods collected, by an agent of the trouser factory. Gloving was also another cottage industry. The cut-out gloves were brought from Woodstock and collected by an agent of the gloving works. Again these cottage industries provided a welcome addition to the family budget.

The craft of bell-hanging and repairing was carried on by one family, which is still in existence. The work took place at the blacksmith's forge in the centre of the village. The blacksmith was also a farrier and wheelwright. The forge is no longer working but the site is now occupied by a photocopy business.

There was a "wood yard", owned by one family whose work involved tree felling and work in the woods as well as timber in general. Within living memory the tree trunks were pulled along by two carthorses, whose stable was in the yard. A seasonal trade in pea and bean sticks was a little side-line. Another family was employed in agricultural engineering and repairing local farm machinery. After harvest time they were busy travelling round the farms in the area threshing the corn. This was before the combine harvester became king. When the motor car came they had two petrol pumps to keep up with the times. This business closed in the 1960s and housing now occupies the site.

There was also a village glazier, plumber, odd job man and decorator and a village cobbler, "snobber". The village was kept tidy by the village roadman, who swept the roads and paths and cleared out the drains, ditches and gutters.

At one time there were about five medium to small farms in the village, including the Manor Farm, and two large farms at Eaton. We still have the two large farms at Eaton, now with a much reduced labour force, and two farms in the village. By the early 1920s two of the farms were dairy farms, and daily deliveries of milk, morning and evening, were made by the farmers on foot, or later by bicycle, the milk cans being slung on the handlebars of the bicycle. This was before the larger dairies from Oxford and Abingdon started a service in the village. Milk was supplied to people in Eaton from one of the two farms.

We had a general store with a bakery attached. Bread was delivered daily until the 1950s. At the end of the Second World War, before most houses had a kitchen range, the baker would roast the meat for Sunday and at twelve o'clock a bell was rung to tell people their meat was ready for collection. He would also bake dough for families if they wished. This store and baker has now gone, and again housing has replaced the site.

We still have a village shop and post office combined, but before this the post office was a wooden building attached to a house and in addition to the postal services, various groceries and goods were sold. Later the post office was run from a private house in Badswell Lane with our own village postman taking round the letters on his bicycle. This is no longer the case, but the present village shop and post office has reverted back to its original site, now a modern building. The wheel has come full circle.

The village had no butcher's shop, though we are fortunate to have one now. Occasionally pig meat was sold by a man as and when he killed pigs. From the late 1920s butchers from Oxford and Abingdon visited the village, sometimes twice a week.

In the late 1930s a German fleeing from Nazi Germany started a horticultural business specialising in roses. This employed a good few village men and women, some on a part time basis. This is still worked but with a reduced labour force. Another nursery business started in the village in the 1960s but is no longer operating, although we have another recent market garden and produce centre which does good trade in the village. This is run as a family business.

A grocer came from Standlake and made a round of the village on Tuesdays, the goods being delivered on Fridays. The International Stores came out for orders as well.'

'Some men at Combe worked for the Duke of Marlborough at Combe Mill as woodmen. There were builders in the village, who were also the local undertakers. There were at least two gamekeepers; one cobbler who was also the village postman; three pubs; two carriers taking things to and from Oxford on two days of each week (one of the vans was known as "Tin Lizzie"); a post office that was also a shop, and two more shops; and two bakers.'

SAWMILLS AND MOLES

'In the hamlet of Middle Assendon life centred around the Froud Sawmills, founded in 1870. The business passed down through successive generations of the Froud family and at one time employed 100 men. It finally closed in the 1930s and now an estate of houses occupies the site.

In addition to the timber business, brush backs were made and supplied to brush firms throughout the country and to HM Prisons at Wandsworth and Wormwood Scrubs. Shives (beer barrel bungs) and spiles (pegs) were also made, and for about 30 years Froud traction engines were used for cultivating and ploughing fields within a wide radius of Henley.

Lew Froud used to catch rabbits and moles when he was a youngster and sell the skins for a penny halfpenny each. Moleskins were pegged to a board and when dry were sent to London to be made into moleskin waistcoats.'

WORK ON THE ESTATES

'We left school at 14 years and there was very little choice of work. The farmers employed many more men and boys then, who used all horses before the tractor became popular. The Heythrop and Ditchley estates not only employed people on their farms. There were several gardeners, foresters, and grooms who kept the horses in good condition ready for taking people out in horse and trap, riding round the estates and, hunting. Where cars are used now, horses were used then.

Some people cycled to Chipping Norton to work, then used to go on the bus when they started to run more frequently. Girls at 14 usually left home to go into domestic service.

The early 1920s brought much unemployment, when the Heythrop estate was sold up and the Ditchley estate cut down their staff, mostly men.

When Morris Motors became established at Cowley it helped with employment. Men started to go there, also women, and that has continued ever since. I think that was when the workman's bus was started.'

ALMOST SELF SUPPORTING

'Finstock in the 1920s was almost self supporting. There was a resident policeman, a nurse who was also a midwife, two carpenters, a scissors grinder, two dressmakers, a blacksmith, a postman and post office, a cobbler, a wheelwright, an undertaker, a baker, two or three smallholders who kept cows and delivered milk to the door, and a pig butcher. Mr Pratley kept a supply of coal at The Bretch and sold it in small quantities. Mr Holifield in The Bottom kept pig meal, barley meal and topping, and sold it to the cottagers who kept pigs. Mrs Edwards was a weekly carrier to Woodstock and Witney. There were two shops: Mrs Oliver who lived at Waterloo Cottages and sold almost everything as well as paraffin in pints or quarts (enough to fill the bowl of a lamp), and Mrs Dore who also kept a stock of everything, especially bacon and all the other eatables from the pig, including the hams she cured herself.'

'I lived on a farm at Studley and here I learned to care for horses and to drive three in hand. This meant having one horse in the shafts of a waggon and two horses in the front of that one, to help with

148

pulling when the load was heavy. The waggons were made of wood and were brightly painted with the farmer's name written in large letters on the front. A wheelwright lived in the village and was kept continually in work.

Next to the farm was the blacksmith's shop, or forge, where the horses were taken to be shod. Many a time I helped the old blacksmith by pumping his bellows to get a red hot fire, in order to shape the shoes. He held them on his anvil with long tongs and beat them with a metallic rhythm. I watched with interest the paring of the hoof, but shrank from the final fitting of the hot shoes, from which emanated a special and unforgettable smell.'

'The carrier used to do a lot of business in Oxford for people living in Stanton. There was a village shop which sold all groceries and sweets, a baker who cooked joints for households on Sunday, a joiner, a blacksmith, a bootmaker, and an estate carpenter who always pointed out to us the elm boards that were being kept for my grandfather's coffin – many years before it was required!'

'After leaving the army between the wars, my father opened a tobacconist, confectioner and newsagent's in Bridge Street, Bampton. We made our own ice cream and had a pit in the garden for the ice. On Sundays during summer we served teas in the garden. On the day of Bampton Fair visitors could leave a bicycle for sixpence to prevent it being stolen. The garden was usually full of bicycles! My father also built a very large shed at the end of the garden in which there was a large round coal-fired stove. There he set up a business making and repairing shoes.

A man called Oliver Collett, who was a mechanic, had a workshop in Cheapside, which is now Yates the newsagent's. It was here he built a car about the same time as William Morris built his at Cowley.'

HEAD LAD

'My father was head lad at Billy Higgs' stables in Blewbury. Home was a converted hen-house – bitterly cold in winter. Mother cooked for the stable lads. She was given an extra large piece of beef by Mr Higgs at Christmas.

When I left school at 14, I was given £5 by the school to spend at Petits in Wallingford. As I was going into service at Wargrave the money had to be spent on a morning apron, an afternoon apron, a cap and material for my mother to make me a dress.'

A STRONG MAN

'My father, Mr Mark Gibbs, was born in Fewcott in 1872. The family moved to Fritwell when he was a year old. His father was a blacksmith, and Mark and his brother Dela-Mark took over the business at a very early age. Mark shod his first horse when he was eleven years old and the last when he was 82. He was always a hard working man, but people were very slow in paying their bills so eventually Dela-Mark left to find other employment, as there was not enough money for both of them to make a living. Mark was very proud to have shod a Grand National winner in 1908 whose name was Rubio. Rubio was bred and trained locally. One of Mark's ambitions was to attend the Grand National but sadly he was never able to. He was a very strong man and once stopped a runaway stallion at Banbury market. He often spoke about people driving flocks of geese to market; it must have been quite a job.

In the 1950s the forge house which my parents rented was in a bad state of disrepair and it was sold along with the land to the council, where we now have 40 houses and bungalows. The small housing estate was named Forge Place.'

Mark Gibbs at work at Fritwell smithy, a scene that would have been familiar in every village between the wars.

THE CARPENTER'S SHOP

'My mother's family business was that of carpenters and wheel-wrights and my first interpretation of the word "shop" was the carpenter's shop at right angles to the house. This was a super place to while away some time, whether or not Uncle Tom was there. One was enveloped in the aroma of cut timber, the walls were hung with the tools of their trade and the benches were scarred and marked with generations of use. But best of all in my young eyes was the fact that the floor was deep in the ashen shavings from the wood as it was planed. These fell in ringlet-like fronds and I delighted to commandeer them and pin them to my dark straight locks and pretend my hair was blonde and curly. Auntie Louie and Uncle Tom were amused by my imaginings but Mum was rather shocked by my vanity, especially if I went home down the village street so bedecked.

If Uncle Tom was not too busy he could often be persuaded to take down from the wall the old implements our forebears had used when they also used to practice barbering and toothpulling as part of their trade. I would hold the pincers, imagining them clawing at a tooth in my mouth and listening to his tales of how, even in his boyhood, splints had been fashioned in the shop to support broken limbs.

Keeping farm waggons and carts in good condition was an important part of their work, although by the 1930s the building of new waggons was a rarity. Each farmer stuck to one colour scheme for his equipment and in addition his name would be painted in neat lettering on the side panel. Making and fitting the axles and spokes to form the wheels, and then heating and fixing into place the metal rims was an extremely skilled task and we knew by instinct to keep quiet while it was progressing.

In those days, carpentry also involved undertaking, and for several generations this also had been one of their services. We accepted quite naturally the coffins taking shape within the shop – we knew for whom they were intended, and when they would be required – hadn't Uncle Tom himself tolled the church bell to inform the village of a death. A different number of knells for a man, woman or even child. Death seemed to be accepted more passively then, even when it struck at an early age, but combined with this acceptance was an involvement by the whole community in the loss. On the day of the funeral all the blinds in the windows fronting on to the route from the home of the deceased to the church would be closed, no children would play outside as the hand-pushed bier made its journey in silence. When the funeral party left the churchyard all the windows

151

would be unshrouded as though to say "we all mourn your loss but now life goes on".'

THE VILLAGE POST OFFICE

'I lived at Filkins and was fortunate to be offered the post of assistant in the local post office. This was a great opportunity as jobs locally were difficult to come by as it was wartime.

The secrets that lay behind the wire grille were about to be revealed as, at 9 am prompt on a September day in 1940 I was welcomed by a short, severe-looking lady who held the post of the highly respected postmistress for a great many years.

I was led through the kitchen where the local postman was sorting the mail brought in by van from the head office. He would then deliver to the village, outlying houses and farms. In the corner of the sitting room stood a formidable-looking object. This, I was told, was the switchboard for the telephone exchange, manned for a full 24 hours. (The postmistress had her bed alongside during the night.) I hadn't bargained to be dealing with such a complicated piece of equipment. The bell on the board seemed to continually ring so I had just a brief introduction to the actual office. Quite a small room and, believe it or not, the telephone kiosk for public use stood in one corner so the outer door was opened after hours to admit anyone wishing to make a call.

After completing the secrecy form which all employees have to sign, we returned to the mass of cords, switches and the constant requests from subscribers. I was promptly seated in front of the board, instructions issued: this for incoming calls, that for outgoing, file in dockets, don't forget to time each one and dial O for Trunks (as long distance was called), telegrams in and out; goodness, this I would never be able to cope with, my superior seemed to deal with it all so easily.

How would I deal with irate subscribers when lines were engaged, for from nine till ten was really busy. I tried so hard to listen to all that was expected of me but after much thought by noon decided that perhaps that wasn't the position for me. However, my mother had different ideas and promptly at one o'clock I was back once again.

During early afternoon that wretched bell seemed to remain reasonably silent (one must never forget to make sure it had been turned on, for often when dictating a telegram it needed to be silenced). I had the opportunity to learn a little more about the actual office. Larger offices had separate counters, but village offices dealt with all aspects, much more interesting. This one especially, for it was a telegraph and money order office so was responsible for receipt and delivery of same.

Finding someone to deliver the telegrams was no problem as there was always some young person who wanted to earn a few pence, especially when on Thursday afternoons fees paid amounted to one shilling and threepence because other offices had a half-day; a distance of two or three miles didn't seem to matter for money was important.

Strict rules were to be obeyed: stamps to be torn across the page, never up and down (for accounting purposes), date stamp to be changed immediately after morning collection, for all letters were cleared from the box and stamped within the office. 'A' stamp for morning, 'B' for afternoons. One was not fully qualified until one's own thumb had been stamped, very painful!

Allowances, army payments, and ever-increasing evacuee demands as gradually the villagers filled their spare rooms with families having to leave the towns. Licences of all descriptions, Savings Bank, certificates, bonds, and so it went on. Later the issue of clothing coupons became our responsibility.

How pleased I was when I was able to deal with the complications of the telephone exchange. I felt that I had really achieved something! Often when talking to subscribers I would wonder what they looked like.

Half-day closing took place at 1 pm on Thursday, not one minute before, and then cashing up entries in the account book had to be done after locking the door. A very quick dash to grab one's bicycle to catch the 2.20 train from the station one and a half miles away (failing that a cycle ride to Witney, eight miles) – one couldn't afford train fare *and* pictures. Often standing on the platform a voice could be heard that was strangely familiar and so that voice could be associated with a number on the exchange.

Although wartime, the village enjoyed very many activities raising money to help the war effort during Warship and War Weapons Weeks. A very popular evening was when an auction sale enabled the public to invest their cash and also procure an object of their choice. Postal staff gave their services voluntarily and were seen struggling home, safely I add, with a vast amount of money which had been deposited. What outsiders didn't realise was that the withdrawals made the previous week probably equalled the deposits, but everyone enjoyed themselves!

There was the funny side even to a job which had to be taken seriously; like the elderly gent who, when withdrawing some cash, was extremely indignant when the notes given to him did not correspond with the ones deposited some years before! And the one who, wishing to send a telegram (a wire it was sometimes called) promptly went outside to see if he could see it passing along the telegraph wires!

The excellent teaching which I had been given put me in good stead for my time in the HFS, progressing to larger switchboards and control room work. However, sadly the postmistress became ill and so I was asked to return if that was possible. This I did, helping to repay her kindness to me. On her retirement I was offered the post. Unfortunately I had not got suitable premises and February 1945 saw a move into suitable accommodation, a major operation. Such was the efficiency over a great many years, I found not a single halfpenny in the corners.

So I transferred with the stock and the switchboard to work alongside the new postmistress with the feeling that I had been so very lucky in doing a job that I was able to enjoy, and in having a wonderful tutor.

The telephone exchange went automatic in 1952. I kept in touch doing holiday relief in the office after my marriage, but somehow one missed that formidable-looking object!'

THE POSTMAN

'My earliest memories of my father going to work are of the uniform he wore as a postman, the rough navy cloth with red piping and the boat-shaped hat. (This made a lovely cradle for my doll when dad was not wearing it!)

He was a postman, number 13, at Abingdon post office which was at that time in the High Street. His duties were delivering letters and parcels to the villages of Garford, Fyfield, Bessels Leigh, Appleton and Cumnor.

There was no motorised transport, only a pedal cycle with a metal carrier for the parcels and a canvas satchel for the letters. As well as delivering to the houses, he called at all the village post offices and post boxes to collect mail and bring it back to the main office at Abingdon.

His day started at 4.30 am with hand-sorting the mail, loading the bike and commencing the journey by 5.30 am. In winter this meant a dark venture as there was no street lighting in the villages and the means of lights for the cycle were carbide lamps, which was dry carbide in the base of the lamp upon which dripped water to produce a gas lit with a match; a flame was produced which gave the light. After use it was necessary for all parts of the lamp to be cleaned and fresh carbide and water put in. Failure to do this meant no light! It was a messy job, which as a child I yearned to do, but

I was only allowed to clean the hole with a pin to allow the flame to burn.

In 1933 my father was one of the first postmen at Abingdon to learn to drive a postal van. What a difference for him to be able to do deliveries and collections in the dry!

By the time he retired in 1960, all but the town deliveries were done with the assistance of vans, some sorting was by machine and mail was taken to Reading, Didcot and Oxford by motor as well as rail.'

THE VILLAGE BUTCHERY

'My father moved to Upper Heyford, when he was six years old in 1913 and his father bought the village butchery. They had a shop and slaughterhouses and killed all their own meat – cows, pigs and sheep. When Gramp died early, my father and mother took over the business. I remember Mum killing sheep!

In the slaughterhouse at the end of the garden was a pulley and tackle to pull the beast's head down so it could be killed. Pigs were killed outside in the field, then burned to remove hair, then gutted and hung till the next day when they were cut up. We were often given the bladder for a balloon, and I remember Granny cleaning and plaiting the chitterlings, which were then salted and cooked. To this day I still love them!

My mother used to drive the van and go all round Bicester, Hethe, Ardley, Fringford etc, on deliveries, usually on a Saturday and it took all day. We made our own sausages and in an outside room was kept a barrel of PAB, rather like breadcrumbs, which formed a large part of the sausage. I remember twisting the links whenever I had the chance to help.

Before Gramp died, when Dad was about twelve or 14 years old, he used to team up with Reg Moores, the butcher's son from Somerton and they would walk to Banbury market, a distance of about twelve miles and then walk back driving a herd of cows or sheep which their fathers had bought to slaughter. All across open fields. Quite a feat!'

'The oldest shop in Steeple Aston is the butcher's in South Side. It has been owned by the Walton family since 1790 and is still renowned for the excellent quality of its meat.

Until after the Second World War, animals were brought to the slaughterhouse behind the shop, where a rope was tied round the beast's head. This was through a block set in the ground and the local lads pulled on the rope until the beast was brought down. The butchers were ready then with gun and knife. As "payment" the lads were given a pig's bladder to dry and blow up for use as a football. They could also claim the horny outer coat of the pig's trotters, which was used for a game similar to five-stones.'

OTHER WAYS WE MADE A LIVING

There were, of course, dozens of other ways we made a living, from shopwork to factory work, foundries to glovemaking. Here are just a few.

WORKING AT CAPES

'I always said that when I was 14 and grown up, I would work at Capes, and so in January 1929 my friend Chris and I walked into the shop, did a sum, got it right and we were in. We had to look smart, so a new black dress had to be bought, which set our Mums back to the tune of twelve shillings and elevenpence.

We started on the Wednesday, so the first week we had two shillings and sixpence. After that it went up to four shillings, increasing every six months. We were apprenticed for two years, then we were fully fledged assistants. We used to walk from Wolvercote to St Ebbes, winter and summer, going along the Wood-stock Road or the canal. Capes provided our tea, not very elaborate: a cake on Wednesdays and Saturdays.

Sale time was very busy, as Capes' Sale was well known for its bargains. Busiest of all was clothing cards. Customers paid in all the year round and had the chance to spend the money from 1st November, with an added interest of one shilling and eightpence in the pound.

Assistants had to serve "right through" which meant you had to serve everything. The piles used to be so big (and I was no packer) and of course we had to say "May we send this for you, Madam?" (Capes had about 2,000 cards).

I got married, but went back to help out at busy times, and was there when the door was shut for the last time. Dear old Capes!'

WEBBERS DEPARTMENT STORE

'I was at Webbers, the Oxford department store in the High Street, from 1952 to 1969. I mostly cycled, six miles each way; there were no buses through our village. Webbers had a bike shed in Alfred Street where we left our bikes.

Our hours were 8.30 to 5.30 Monday to Saturday, with a half-day on Thursday when the shop closed at 1 pm. Of course, if you were serving a customer at closing time, you carried on until the customer had made her purchase, however long that took.

There was a rest room for customers, beautifully done out, daily paper for them, etc; they didn't see the staff facilities upstairs, though. We had a gas ring, but we sat in the cloakroom to eat our sandwiches at lunch times. In the late 1950s a staff rest room was provided. We used to go two at a time for our coffee to Lyons round the corner, or Browns or Hunts in the Covered Market.

Webbers had a hostel in Oxford for their staff (so did Elliston & Cavell and Badcocks) but that was closed before I started there. When Mr Webber was there, all the girls wore hats to go to work. We were treated very well, otherwise I wouldn't have been there so long. Every year, they held a Christmas party at the Randolph Hotel for the staff.

Of course we were expected to be very polite to customers and always to ask them if we could help them as soon as they came into the department. We must always say "Yes, Madam" — one of my friends was told off for saying "Yes, dear" to a customer!

There was no central buying for the store: each department had its own buyer. I worked in Rainwear and Coats: Miss Judd was the buyer for dresses, coats, suits, skirts, rainwear, but not Furs – Mrs Montagu was the fur buyer. Miss Watts was the under-buyer and Miss Paul the First Sales.

We had regular customers who we got to know – often they would tell us all their troubles while they were being served. Customers would sometimes be in the shop for ages before they made up their minds, but you could tell within ten minutes whether they were going to buy anything or not.

When I first started, there were codes on the labels so that you knew how much you would get in "perks" if you made a sale. Later that became three ha'pence in the pound. We had lectures from a detective about shoplifting: sometimes a woman would have a bag fixed to the waistband of her skirt on the inside and a garment would be quickly pushed down into it. We had lectures about serving customers, too, and how to treat them properly.

Webbers had separate workrooms for alterations: a dressmaking one and a tailoring one. They made a small charge for this service. At one time they also made hats on the premises, but that was before I went there.'

GLOUCESTER GREEN BUS STATION

'My interest in the Gloucester Green bus station in Oxford dates from 1937–38. It had opened on the site of the old cattle market in 1935, replacing an earlier one on a congested and difficult of access plot of land between Castle Street and Church Street, St Ebbes. The latter had opened towards the end of 1929, in an effort to remove the country bus departure points from the immediate vicinity of Carfax, where the ensuing congestion was attracting adverse criticism from police and public via the local press.

The new one in Gloucester Green was a great improvement. The western end was entirely given over to the country services of the major operator, City of Oxford motor services, while the centre section took the coach departures and those of the smaller local operators, who were the natural successors to the country carriers, who still operated to outlying villages for the carriage of goods.

Incoming services entered from the south side, where four parallel arrival bays made of wooden planking ran from south to north, each long enough to take two buses while they set down their passengers.

If the bus was to go out on a departure soon, it then pulled forward to the departure platforms which continued in a south to north direction with a gap between, allowing buses not required for early departure to pull onto the extreme western part of the site, where they could be parked facing Worcester Street, until required for further service.

The departure platforms would each take four buses, and services at first pulled right forward, so that they were facing the bus offices in what had been the Boys Central School. There were bench seats on the departure platforms, supplementing waiting rooms inside the building, and boards at the northern end of each platform displayed the main destinations served.

Wednesday and Saturday afternoons were the busiest times, with buses coming in from the surrounding country districts for the cattle market on Wednesday (by this time removed to Oxpens Road). Saturdays were naturally busy everywhere, as although most people worked five and a half days, Saturday afternoon was free.

While the buses waited for the return journeys, they were parked facing Worcester Street, but on Wednesdays and Saturdays this was inadequate and they were double-banked in a north-south direction across the radiators of the others, thus making a lot of shunting necessary to get a particular vehicle out for departure. Many duplicate vehicles operated on these peak time return journeys, accompanying the service bus as far as necessary.

The carrying of parcels was a large part of bus operations at that time, and did not cease completely until conductors became rare. At its height, buses were stacked with trolleys full of newspapers and parcels. While single deck buses had roof racks, reached by pull-out steps at the back, all the goods carried by double-deckers had to be stacked under the staircase, which must have been difficult for the conductor. The Witney buses in particular, often smelled of fish.

The wooden arrival and departure platforms deteriorated with time, and early in the Second World War were replaced with concrete, with tubular steel pipes set in to form queue rails, tending to make the bus station resemble the cattle market it had replaced some six or seven years earlier. The queue rails allowed the partition of each of the four departure platforms into four separate bays, with clearly defined services departing from each. This must have caused scheduling problems, as there was insufficient width between each platform to allow more than one bus, and those towards the back of the platform were dependent on the ones in front leaving.

Later, the departure platforms had rudimentary roofs fitted, but the sides remained open. By this time, the British public had accepted queueing as a natural way of life, and stood in the "cattle pens" without breaking war-time regulations, but who knows with what thoughts! After the war, the bus industry did well as far as intending passengers were concerned, but struggled with inadequate staff and vehicle shortages, and later, towards the end of the 1950s, with competition from the private car (and television).

Gradually, one-person operated buses and reduced services saw a shrinking of the once substantial country network and Gloucester Green became too large for the services operated. It has now been re-developed and only caters for a few express services. The remaining country services, now almost indistinguishable from the city services, are now back on the central streets of Oxford, causing the congestion complained of in 1929. Which is where we started.'

NOT ENOUGH FOR THE BUS FARE

'The same week I left school I went into Oxford on my own. I went to the Labour Exchange and got a job as an apprentice shoe shop assistant. I enjoyed the job and made lots of friends and I stayed in that job for ten years.

When we first started we didn't make enough to pay the bus fare from Eynsham, which in 1943 was a shilling return, so four of us used to cycle into Oxford and back every day. We had such fun singing as we went along four abreast. My wage was a guinea a week.'

MAKING COPIES

'My first job was in an architect's office and this had coal fires and the drawing boards were covered over at night with old blackout curtains.

Specifications and bills of quantities were all cut onto stencils and rolled off by hand on the Gestetner. The used stencils were carefully saved in case further copies were needed and it was a messy business. There were no photocopiers, so any copies required had to be typed out and details of forms etc noted before despatch. Correcting fluid was available for stencils only and it was pink so one's mistakes were plain for all to see!'

RUSH WEAVING

'My father worked for Mr Pratley the baker at Burford. We used to gather rushes from the Windrush using a special pole and hook to supply my mother's craft of making articles such as mats, baskets, cots and chair seating. She was a little woman, under five foot tall, who attended school at what we now know as Warwick Hall.

Her rushwork was exhibited in Canada. The Lamb at Burford was furnished with her rush mats, as was a castle in the far north of Scotland. In the 1930s a documentary film was made about her craft by a Mr Brian Mill of London, who offered to take my mother to London by taxi to see the film, but she was not well enough to travel and so never saw it. An article on her also appeared in *The Lady* magazine, and a lady going to Spain once asked her to make some rush sandals!'

WE CAME FOR THE WORK

'A lot of people came to Oxford after the war. There was a boom at the car factories. One Littlemore resident recalls coming in 1949, when Morris Motors paid for their move from Bournemouth, they needed workers so badly. Others came from London, or from Wales. Morris Motors is demolished now, but I can remember how the Spitfires practised their manoeuvres by flying between their two chimneys.'

GLOVEMAKING

'In the past there were four or five glove factories in Woodstock, and also tanneries where the skins were cut and dyed and hung out to dry. One factory in Old Woodstock specialized in sports gloves, for boxing and cricket etc, and a pair of cricket gloves was made for Jack Hobbs. When Queen Elizabeth II visited the town she was presented with a pair of gloves as near as possible identical to the gloves that had been made for Queen Elizabeth I.

Both men and women glove workers cycled in to their factories in Woodstock from all the surrounding villages. The men cut the skins into tranks, pressed them, and then cut them into the pattern of the gloves. The pointing on the backs was done and the ends of the stitching tied. Then workers fitted thumbs and fourchettes in place.

The gloves were taken in dozens round to the out-workers to stitch and complete in their own homes. These were collected at the end of the week and a fresh batch left for stitching. The out-workers were mainly women who had married and started a family. Some did hand stitching and others stitched on machines, either their own or machines provided by the glove factory.'

'I did several jobs for a glovemaking factory in Woodstock. I did pointing on a special machine, welting or finishing the tops, and I made gloves as well. We worked from eight o'clock to one and then from two o'clock to half past five, every day except Saturday, which was a half day. We were paid four shillings and one penny for making one dozen pairs, ie 24 gloves. There is still one glovemaking factory in Woodstock, in Harrisons Lane.

In winter I travelled in on the workman's bus. That left at seven o'clock but the local stationmaster was very kind and allowed us to sit in the waiting room until eight o'clock, where there was a good fire. In summer I bicycled in. There were eight glovemakers in our factory, then in a larger factory that expanded, there were twelve. The factories I remember were Dents, Clothiers, Pulmans, Webleys and one other.

We did not supply local shops, as all our gloves were sent to Worcester where the firm and our boss was.'

'My neighbour, now in her eighties, did some work for Hunts in Old Woodstock. She went in to Woodstock for a few days to learn what to do and then did work at home. She made wicket-keeping gloves, and she also did pads for airmen's helmets during the war with chamois leather. The factory supplied the sewing machines. Other people in Combe worked at Atherton & Clothiers and Pullmans, both in

Woodstock. Many of them walked through the park (Blenheim Park) to Woodstock each day, about four miles each way.'

FOUNDRIES AND TRAMS

'The Wantage foundry, in Ormond Road, employed a good number of men in the town. They had a hooter which could be heard quite a distance to warn men of the time – 7.25 am warning and 7.30 to begin work, again at noon for knocking off and 1 pm to restart, then again in the evening when they finished. I was told they sounded the hooter as a lot of the workmen couldn't afford watches – but that may not be true!

There was another foundry about a mile and a half away at East Challow, where more local men were employed.

The Tramway Company also employed quite a few, including engine drivers, as the goods tram brought lots of freight to the town from Wantage Road station, as well as outgoing freight handled and the passenger tram.'

CHURCH BELLHANGERS

'Our company was founded in 1824 by my great great grandfather, Alfred White. He was innkeeper at The Greyhound, Bessels Leigh, a small village, on the A420 Oxford-Swindon road, next to Appleton. It was here that the first work on bells was done by him and many oak bellframes were constructed in the yard at the rear of the pub.

Alfred was born in 1800 and died in 1875. He started trading as A. White, Bellhanger and eventually took his sons into the business and traded as A. White & Sons. Even in these early days he was doing work all over the country including work at Hereford cathedral.

His son, Frederick took over the running of the business in 1875 and eventually took his sons into the business. During his time he installed new oak bellframes at Christ Church cathedral and Merton and Magdalen colleges in Oxford. He moved from The Greyhound at Besselsleigh to The Three Horse Shoes at Appleton around 1880 and from here built and moved to a new workshop in the village.

He was succeeded by my grandfather, Richard White who in turn took one of his sons, Francis White into the business. Francis, or Frank as he is known, is a bachelor and I, his brother's eldest son, joined him in the company in 1958 when we changed the name of the company to "Whites of Appleton". Although Frank "retired" five years ago at the age of 69, he still works full time and is renowned for the quality of his carpentry work.

We do everything to church bells that needs to be done, except retuning and casting of bells. This we subcontract to the Whitechapel Bell Foundry whom we have traded with since our company's inception.

At the present time, we are responsible for the maintenance and upkeep of the bells at St Paul's cathedral in London and a few weeks ago, because we still run a forge and are able to repair wrought-iron clappers, we re-forged the broken eleventh bell clapper and annealed the other clappers at York Minster.'

WAR & PEACE

THE GREAT WAR 1914–1918

Though the fighting took place far away, the realities of war soon came home to the people of Oxfordshire, with hardships and shortages to be suffered at home, and the distress of seeing their young men shell-shocked and maimed. Armistice Days between the war were strictly, and sadly, observed.

PREPARING FOR WAR

'In 1913 the great excitement of the summer was the army manoeuvres which went on all over Oxfordshire and Buckinghamshire. One day a regiment of Dragoon Guards rode up through Spelsbury on beautiful dark brown horses, a lovely sight. People used to follow the sham battles, going on bicycles or sometimes by train, to where they could see what was going on. There was a large camp in Shotover Park, and we all went to a church parade on the Sunday, a most stirring service with hundreds of men singing. Not many of them survived the war.'

'In 1910 the parish magazine for Ipsden reported that: "On April 5th a most interesting lecture was given on 'The First Line of Defence: the British Navy' by Mrs Everett-Green, one of the officers of the Navy League. It is good for our younger generation to grow up with some knowledge of the great Empire to which they belong and be taught some of the duties and responsibilities of citizenship." Even in our little village, thoughts were already turning to "defence".

I was born in Ipsden early in the century and remember the war, although still a child. There was a Baptist chapel in the village (which later became the village hall) and many soldiers were billeted there. A field kitchen was set up outside and army balloons. If an aeroplane landed, as one did occasionally, the whole village flocked to see it.

My father, who owned Cross Farm, would give eggs to the cook and one day received a tin of corned beef in exchange. It was tucked well out of sight up his jersey! Times were hard and in 1916 there was no food in the village and people were existing on rabbits and produce from the garden. Rook pie was made when the boys could shoot them – the meat was very rich and only the breast was usable.

During both wars, the Red Cross and St John's Ambulance had a depot at Hailey House for sewing, knitting and rolling bandages – as many times as needed each week. "Workers that could be trusted" were allowed to take work home!

My father woke me one night and wrapped me in a blanket. He pointed to the sky and there was a German Zeppelin. This was the one that had bombed London and was eventually shot down over the South Coast.'

KEEPING GOING

'I can remember Dad coming home from France – we would buy scented cachous in many colours and shaped in letters and numbers and with these we proudly showed Dad the words and sums we had been taught at school. I wanted to hide him in the blanket box to keep him from returning to France.

At this time my oldest brother was working for the pork butcher in Harpsden. He was offered the job of working in the shop but he was a bit shy so he left and joined the army at 16 years old. He was in the Rifle Brigade and became a sniper. He was cutting barbed wire when he got three fingers shot off. So he was home wounded within six months. I can still remember his poor wounded hand and my mother changing the dressings.

My mother kept the allotment going while Dad was in the army, so we always had plenty of vegetables. She would queue up to buy half a pound of margarine. Then she would boil two or three big potatoes and drain them and plonk in the whole half pound and mash it well and we kids loved it spread on toasted bread.'

'I used to be sent to the shops for sugar. Later when I was attending Witney grammar school I was given sixpence to join any queue on my way home from school for lunch – one end of the town to the other. It was usually for lard or butter. By the time my mother was free to go to town it was too late.

At the end of the war the school had a length of sheeting, about four feet wide, with "Pax cum Honore" marked on it and the scholars fastened red, white and blue flowers all over it.'

'I was five years old when the war started and can remember rationing coming in. The rector of Wigginton had all the coal delivered to the rectory and people collected it from there. There were blackouts against Zeppelin raids, when the engine whistled to give warning.'

167

THOSE WHO SERVED

'I remember being told by an old resident of Enstone, how she could vividly recall meeting two young soldiers as they came home on leave during the war. She went to speak to them, and shake their hands, and was shocked by their appearance.

Both had come straight from the trenches in France, and were still wearing the same clothing. The soldiers were dirty and dishevelled; they looked worn out, with grey faces and red-rimmed, hollow eyes. Later one of them told her how his mother had filled a bath in front of the fire for him, and how his underclothes were burnt in the copper fire, because of the fleas.

This young soldier, who later in the war died of wounds, joked that "his vest had crawled out on its own".'

'I was born in Salford in 1912 and can still recollect my uncle, a young man of 18, sobbing at the thought of what was in front of him when he had to return to France from leave. He had come home to recover from shell-shock.

I kicked and screamed when my father went back to France – I had been made a fuss of and did not want it to end. At about the same time there was a flu epidemic and all the village went down with it, including my family, and there was no one to look after us.

My mother at this time was in the Women's Land Army and part of her duties was to pick up prisoners of war from a nearby camp in a pony and trap and bring them to Salford rectory to work.'

'As a small child I lived with my grandparents in South Leigh. I can remember the children in the village school crying as their well loved headmaster, Mr Pratt, went off to the war.

My grandmother had four sons, three of whom went to war too, and thankfully, all came back home. It was the custom then to put a card in your window for a husband or son who was away at war.'

'After the war willow trees were planted behind the houses in Summerside at Buckland, so that those who returned disabled from the war, such as those blinded, could strip the willow and make wicker baskets. They felt useful again and made many fine goods.'

WE REMEMBERED THEM

'My brother and I huddled together in the armchair by the fire and stared wide-eyed at the magnificent being who sat opposite. We had known he was coming of course, but the mere knowledge of this

The Armistice Day parade in Islip in 1919, when the sorrows of the Great War were still alive for so many.

had not prepared us for the reality – the highly polished black boots reaching to the knee; the white trousers topped by the brilliant scarlet tunic; the gold braid. Outside on the hall table lay the helmet and the brass bugle. No, he couldn't be human, this God-like creature. We didn't speak to him of course, just gazed awestruck.

It was late afternoon and time for tea. We couldn't believe it, but this superior being ate bread and butter with Dad's home-grown celery and appeared to enjoy Mum's fruit cake! Surely we should have fed him something other than our usual Sunday winter afternoon tea?

The time drew on. Soon Dad appeared, having hurried through the farm chores. He was wearing his best suit of course, with the medals he'd so carefully polished the previous evening pinned to the breast pocket. His well-brushed bowler hat was ready.

The uniformed being rose – strange, he was hardly any taller than Dad – and prepared to set off. He was to be taken straight to the church where, at the appropriate point in the service, he would sound those haunting bugle calls "Last Post" and then, after two minutes, "Reveille". Dad would march with the rest of the British Legion to the Remembrance Service.

After the ceremony the bugler would return to his barracks in Cowley. He came from the Oxford and Bucks Light Infantry of course. Every year a bugler would be detailed to attend the service and the British Legion members took it in turns to entertain him to tea. This year it had been our privilege.

Off they went. Mum, even after this passage of time, found the service too upsetting. Instead she busied herself with clearing the tea things and putting us to bed. Then, when we were asleep, she sat by the fire by herself thinking of her brothers who now slept so soundly in Flanders.'

'I remember as a child, on Armistice Day, being in the field where my father was working, probably with one or two other men. As the church bell struck 11 am tools were dropped and they all stood to attention for two minutes in silence. Even the horses seemed to know they had to be still and I knew I had to be.'

THE SECOND WORLD WAR
1939–1945
VILLAGES AT WAR

When war came once again, Oxfordshire towns and villages this time found themselves on the front line. Airfields were carved out of the countryside and we became used to the roar of the planes going out and, hopefully, coming back. All of us were touched by this war and life changed, sometimes beyond recognition.

THE HAILEY VILLAGE WAR RECORD

'This record of Hailey was compiled soon after the war and shows how our village faced that difficult time.

"When war comes it brings folk who live in town or city closer together. Those who have lived in the same street, perhaps for years and have never become acquainted with each other beyond a nod or good morning on the way to the bus, now become comrades together while fire watching or sharing the shelter during a blitz. Mr and Mrs Brown who live over the way become real persons in whom an interest can now be taken, and their family who are perhaps serving in the Forces can be kindly enquired after.

In the village however, it is very different. The war is a much closer and more personal thing. We have always known our next door neighbour and indeed everybody else in the village as well. The sons and daughters, husbands, brothers and fathers who went to help win the war were brought up together and had attended the village school together, the same school that probably their parents and maybe grandparents had attended before them.

So in Hailey we know and are proud of the 50 lads and girls who went from our village of about 500 inhabitants and honour the names of two who gave their lives for their country.

One, the husband of one of our girls, lost his life in Normandy soon after D-Day and the other, her brother, fell at Arnhem with the Airborne Division. We are thankful too, that three who were taken prisoner, one at Dunkirk, one at Tobruk and the other at Crete have returned to their families. We are also proud that two others,

171

one in the Army and one in the Navy, received decorations for their distinguished service. Now we are glad to welcome home those who have finished their term of service and once more take their place in the life of the village, which was also busy helping to win the war. This is how it was done.

Official Evacuation: This took place in June 1940 and after keeping kettles boiling, beds aired and waiting for children who did not arrive. After several days of suspense an LCC school unit of about 75 children and four teachers arrived from Hackney. They were billeted in private homes and the Marlborough Hall was requisitioned for a school. A week or two later when they had settled in, the Mayor of Hackney visited them and gave each child sixpence before he returned home. When the bombing of London started still more evacuees arrived, this time the parents and friends of children already billeted in the village, and they filled all the available accommodation. Most of the families returned home when the danger passed but some are with us yet. When the number of evacuee children grew less, as some left school to go to work, the others were taught in the village school and the Marlborough Hall was fitted as a Rest Centre for bombed out mothers and children from London. This was used during one period and the WVS and helpers organised the catering and helped generally. The Borough of Poplar was adopted by Oxfordshire and after a bad blitz when the folk were in great need, a collection of household goods was organised by the Women's Institute and a large number of useful articles was sent to help them. Meat pies for agricultural workers were successfully distributed from the house of a WVS member.

During the early part of the war a branch of the Red Cross supply depot was responsible for making garments. Later when the Red Cross Penny-a-Week Fund was started, collecting was done in all parts of the village and the sum of £221 3s 10d was raised from August 1941 to June 1945.

The Hailey Choral Society was started during the war, with the vicar as the leader, and provided a very interesting recreation for those keen on music. A number of concerts have been given in the school, and sacred works rendered each Eastertide at the parish church or Methodist church. In 1945 Maunder's *Olivet to Calvary* was given at the parish church and repeated at Finstock parish church and the Ramsden Heath American Red Cross hospital. At the latter place the choir was afterwards regaled with large basins full of delicious ice cream and sponge cake with fruit filling, an incident which will always remain in their memory!

Each Christmas the singers have also toured the village for several nights and sung carols and in this way they have raised considerable sums for the Red Cross Prisoner of War Fund, and the Oxford Eye Hospital.

Like all other villages, Hailey had its Home Guard, Observer Corps, Civil Defence Wardens, First Aid Party and Fire Fighters. We are thankful that they were never needed for active service in the village but it was a relief to know that they were always on duty and ready for any emergency in the dark days and indeed at all times when the task of watching and waiting must have been very monotonous.

Hailey had an almost miraculous escape from destruction by fire through the centre of the village. It was estimated that between 500 and 1,000 incendiary bombs were dropped on the west side of the village about 200 yards behind the main street, all falling into fields except one, which slightly damaged the roof of a house and another which burnt out an empty sheep fold. The wardens on duty soon called up their colleagues and were ready for any emergency. Because incendiary bombs do not cause any noise, very few people in the village knew that Hailey had been in the front line until the next day and heard the news with great surprise.

To keep the Civil Defence services ready and on the alert, several combined exercises were arranged. One of these gave them a very busy time when incendiaries were supposed to have fallen on a house in the centre of the village and there were fires to extinguish and casualties to deal with. High explosives were also supposed to have damaged the school and many "casualties" found lying in the debris were successfully dealt with by the first aid party. The incidents were so realistic that they gave the villagers an exciting evening and provided good training for those taking part. The British army also thought Hailey a good place for manoeuvres and for several days every farmyard, lane and open space was the resting place of tanks and soldiers, when they were not clattering through the village or bargaining with farmers' wives for eggs. Another time a small portion of the Canadian army took up their residence in the manor house while they practised putting up and taking down telecommunications. We were pleased to have them here for a Sunday when their padre arranged a church parade service at the Methodist church which he conducted and a good number of the men attended.

In August 1940 a National Savings Group was started in the village and the amount collected from stamps and certificates from then until September 1945 was £8,286 18s 0d. Special Savings Weeks were also held and during Warship Week £5,114 was raised, Wings for Victory Week £4,703 18s, Salute the Soldier Week £4,365 15s and Thanksgiving Week £2,676 5s. This made a total of £16,860.

173

The Village Hall Fund was born at the first of these efforts in 1942. A week's entertainments were arranged and it was decided to use any profits made to start a fund to build a village hall. The two following years the profits from the Savings Week entertainment were also given to this fund and in this way over £200 was invested in National Savings. Whist drives and dances have also been held regularly for raising further funds. This has not only benefited the National Savings movement but has also provided entertainment for the troops stationed in the district. At the dances there have been many British soldiers and airmen and also visitors from overseas forces including men from Canada, Australia, New Zealand, South Africa, USA, Poland and Czechoslovakia.

A church parade was held on the first Sunday of each of the National Savings Weeks when all the members of the Civil Defence, Home Guard, Special Constables, Women's Land Army and any members of HM Forces met at Delly Green and marched for the morning service conducted by the vicar, once led by Witney Town Band. The Hailey Choral Society led the singing. It was a fine procession, the like of which was not seen in any other neighbouring village. It has been said that only the very young, the very old and the mothers were left to watch as everyone else took part.

During the war numerous dances were held to benefit war charities. Among those receiving help were the British Red Cross, Aid to Russia, Aid to China and the WLA Benevolent Fund. In 1943 the sum of £480 was raised: this is typical of other years and although we have no wealthy folk living in Hailey we can say that we have generous folk who are always ready to help those in need.

The Welcome Home Fund was started in 1945 and £250 has been raised by means of a Flower Show at which the exhibits were auctioned, profits from the entertainments of Thanksgiving Week and by proceeds of various dances.

On VE Day a special Thanksgiving Service was held in the parish church. As it happened to coincide with the Women's Institute meeting, members went to the service first and then attended their own meeting afterwards. On VJ Day a programme of festivities was arranged rather hurriedly on account of the short notice, but with great success. There was a children's fancy dress parade through the village, followed by tea, sports and a dance.

Last, but by no means least, we come to the work done by the members of the Women's Institute during the war years. The biggest job they undertook was helping with the Fruit Preservation Scheme for four years. From 1942 to 1945 4,517 lbs of jam were made at the two centres, Barnfield and Swanhall, to save surplus fruit which might otherwise have been wasted. In 1943 Hailey was second in the county for the quantity made and in 1945 came first, having made one third of the total for the whole county. This included 500 lbs made for a special order for the Wingfield Orthopaedic Hospital. Sample jars of plum jam and crab apple jelly were chosen to be included in the County Exhibition of Fruit Preservation Centres at the Land Army Rally held at Blenheim Park in 1943. Later the whole exhibit was on view in London at the request of the Ministry of Food.

Salvage collection was organised by the WI on behalf of the parish council. At the start children did the collecting and salvage was kept in various depots in the village. Later this system of collecting was discontinued and folk brought their own salvage to the depots. This comprised paper, rags, bones, and metal which was sold to and collected by the Witney Rural District Council.

The money raised by this effort was used to purchase wool to knit garments for the Merchant Navy Comforts Fund, four sacks of wool having been knitted altogether by the members of the WI. Socks were also knitted for soldiers in Burma, scarves for a special order for the War Office for D-Day, and over 100 garments knitted for children under the European Relief Scheme. Hussifs and bags for holding handicraft materials were also made for POWs. Foxglove leaves and stinging nettles and raspberry leaves have been gathered for medicinal purposes and schoolchildren have picked rosehips to make rosehip syrup.

Many folk in the village were wearing clothes that have been turned, remodelled or cut down, by advice and instruction given at two series of "Make Do and Mend" classes arranged by the WI. These came at a time of great need when coupons were scarce (and when were they not?) and stocks of clothes were getting exhausted or old fashioned, so folk were truly grateful for the help given to smarten themselves.

The group meetings were the means of a cycling club being started. Owing to a lack of transport due to the petrol shortage there was no way of attending the meetings except by cycling. So great was the enthusiasm that often over 20 members from Hailey attended the Evenlode group meetings when other WIs could only send a few.

Many other cycle runs to different places were arranged and much enjoyed by the members. The annual Christmas party of WI members and their menfolk is always a great success and during the war years invitations were sent to troops stationed in the district. One year a number of American soldiers were the guests and they added to the enjoyment of the party by entertaining the rest of the company.

Each Christmas that the evacuee children were here, the WI also gave a party for them and all the other children in the village, much to their enjoyment.

In addition to all these outside activities there were the gardens to tend, animals to feed and look after, chickens to rear, blackouts to put up and take down, rations to be bought and supplemented by ingenious methods and families to be looked after in the same way that every other villager was doing all over the country.

We may have thought that our efforts were very small at the time we were doing them but by putting them with everybody else's, they formed one great whole which helped to bring Victory to this much loved land of ours." '

THE FINSTOCK VILLAGE WAR RECORD

'The first impact on the life of the village was caused by evacuation from London on Saturday, 2nd September 1939. Forty children were expected but plans went astray and 13 mothers accompanied by 27 children arrived. This necessitated changing all arrangements, but the village rose nobly to the occasion and they were soon designated to different billets. It was very dark when the arrangements were completed so a special constable escorted each party to their new homes.

Difficulties arose the following day owing to the dirty habits and uncouth manners of a small proportion of the evacuees. The people with whom they were staying definitely refused to keep them. They were then accommodated in the village hall. After two days, two mothers with their children went home. The others stayed for about three weeks, then suddenly vanished, taking various articles that had been supplied for their use eg an alarm clock, blankets, hot water bottles etc. By Christmas 1939 all had returned home.

The second evacuation was in June 1940. The next party to arrive was a number of Enfield children and the village school became very full. These children were of a good type and fraternised remarkably well with the other children. Then in September and October 1940 some of the original evacuees returned. This time they settled and joined in the life of the community. Many stayed till after the war ended. One of the latter is still with us.

Our youngest member was a baby three months old and our oldest was 91 years. The people who took her in were asked by "wire" if they could have a "young wench of 91!" She was brought down by car the next day, a wonderful old lady and "young wench" she certainly was. Young in outlook, mentally very alert and a most interesting personality. Her reminiscences would have filled a book. It was a privilege to have known her.

One frail, delicate evacuee died and was buried in the village churchyard. Her hostess still puts flowers on the grave.

Large numbers took first aid lessons and gained their certificates. All kinds of lectures were held for dealing with poisonous gases. The members of the above took part in fire watching each night in turn.

There was a strong Home Guard contingent. They gave up Sundays to some very strenuous training. They had several alarms and turned out most zealously. Once, owing to some misunderstanding, the church bells rang. In this case, one Home Guard became over-zealous and took a shot at a cow, which he mistook for a prowling enemy. A canteen was run by the WVS for the soldiers billeted in the village. Some good friendships were made during this period.

No serious bombing occurred, although one or two alarming incidents arose. About 200 incendiaries fell in a cornfield, lighting up the countryside. A loud explosion another night alarmed the village due to a bomb exploding about a mile away. The bombs dropped at Witney were felt too.

A huge American hospital was built, followed by a big invasion of American soldiers, which livened up the place considerably. The dances were crowded and relations were quite friendly during their stay and they were generally much liked. The WVS had some most interesting experiences. They were asked to visit the patients in hospital. Before taking on the task, they were given a series of lectures on what to do and what *not* to do. Their duties chiefly consisted in writing letters, packing up and sending to their relations the "Purple Heart" replica issued to all wounded men. They also changed their library books and mended their linen etc. One patient was anxious to learn all the names of our wild flowers, a great variety of which grew round the camp.

The first contingent of Americans gave a Christmas party to all children of Finstock men serving in the forces. The children were conveyed in motor trucks and the teachers in jeeps. The soldiers had saved their own rations for the party – delicious tinned fruit, cookies and well sweetened chocolate to drink. A huge Father Christmas dispensed toys and well filled Christmas stockings. This reception was greeted with loud cries of appreciation from some, and different cries from the younger ones, much to the consternation of the American officers who had each adopted a few children and undertook to look after them and it was their task to console and reassure the children, much to the amusement of the teachers present. Still they did their duty well and "a good time was had by all". A Christmas gift was sent to every man and woman in the forces. This involved a great deal of hard work by the Village Hall Committee. The final gesture was the raising of a Welcome Home Fund. Each of the 111 men and women received a substantial present of about £4 10s 0d. The children knitted jumpers, cardigans and socks etc for the many organisations and did marvellous work. Well over 200 garments were made.'

NOT UNTOUCHED BY WAR

'Despite being so rural and remote, Combe was not untouched by the events of the war. Barbed wire barricades were set up at each entrance to the village ready to be placed across the streets should the enemy arrive. Likewise, fields which could provide good landing areas were planted with large poles all over to discourage aircraft. Piles of bombs were stored beside the roads outside the village.

An American fighter plane crashed in the area known as Navvy Pond and the pilot was killed. It made a large hole, and became a popular hunting ground for local boys looking for souvenirs.

A popular pastime for children in those days was to gather up the strings of silver foil dropped by the enemy to interfere with the radar system. Although its purpose was unknown to the children at the time it was apparently a popular thing to collect and there was plenty to be found in the village and surrounding fields.

The WI would meet in an old disused chapel and stir panloads of jam, mostly rhubarb and ginger, which went to the war effort somewhere. One member had a circular knitting machine and knitted hundreds of yards of socks for the troops. Knitted mittens and other comforts were produced by village folk.

Children had to take their gas masks to school every day and were taught to get quickly under their sturdy desks in the event of an air raid, there being no shelters in the village.

Folk remember War Weapons Week and Wings for Victory Week when special events would be organised in the village – dances, whist drives, films, fetes, anything that could raise money towards the war effort.

ENSA entertainment service had a base at Combe House and many famous people stayed there, going out each evening to entertain the troops. Local people were employed by NAAFI to look after these entertainers and recall waiting on Lew Stone and Oscar Rabin and all their musicians, also Cherry Lind the singer and Bill Owen (Compo of *Last of the Summer Wine*). Perhaps there should be a plaque on the wall at Combe House to record who slept there! Young footballers would play soccer with the visiting big bands and then listen to them practising in the afternoons.

Italian prisoners worked on local farms and were to be seen working in the fields around the village.'

'During the Second World War evacuees from East London came to Appleton. When they arrived they filled a double decker bus. They came from Walthamstow and we also had a few from Canterbury. In some cases mothers came with the children. They were billeted among the villagers and as the London children came as a school party, four teachers accompanied them. A school was set up for the evacuees in the village hall, but later on as some children went back home to London, those remaining were absorbed into the village school. One master stayed and eventually became headmaster in a neighbouring village.

There was a small munitions factory in Tubney Woods near to the village and some villagers and young girls went to work there. If you would not have an evacuee it was hoped you would work there.

At that time an egg packing factory was in operation, run by a poultry farmer who lived in the old Manor Farm house. He also owned large orchards and soft fruit trees. The work of the poultry farm, collecting and processing the eggs from a wide area, and in the summer fruit picking, employed a number of village people. This ground has now been built on. Another smallholding also had poultry and this was in business as a poultry farm until quite recently.

We had a pig farmer who would collect swill from RAF Abingdon and Upper Heyford. He also had poultry. If eggs were sold to the general public on a small scale they had to collect ten coupons from the ration books to obtain food for the poultry. This all helped the war effort.

The WI made jam in the village hall, which was sold to local shops. The children collected rose hips to make rose hip syrup as oranges were not easily obtainable for vitamin C.

We had, of course, our own Dad's Army platoon, who guarded us well. Fortunately we escaped any enemy action, the nearest bombs being dropped the other side of the Thames by bombers returning from a mission.

The night Coventry was bombed we all listened to the continuous procession of droning planes, not knowing their destination and what devastation they would cause. When VE Day came a huge bonfire was made on the village green and stories still vie with each other as to what went on that fire! For VJ Day a special fancy dress parade was held for the children.'

179

A GARRISON TOWN

'During the war Thame was a garrison town and tanks were often seen driving down the streets. The planes towing the gliders for D-Day were also seen passing overhead. Oxfordshire seemed to become just one airfield, there were so many dotted around.

A large number of foreign troops were billeted in the area. The Irish were among the first to use Rycotewood. Americans are fondly remembered by those who were children at the time as they seemed to have a never-ending supply of sweets – and when one regiment moved on they left behind their stores for the locals.

Thame Park was used for the training of women, particularly wireless operators. There were some famous women there, including Odette, the French Resistance fighter.

A Bailey bridge was built over the river in the Long Crendon Road and trenches were dug in the recreation ground. Although very few bombs were dropped in this area one made a big splash in a water butt in the centre of town, and a land mine was exploded near the railway station. The ARP and fire wardens were very active and would dash to any incident with a stirrup pump in a bucket. If you had a ladder and a water butt in your house you were expected to display a sign in the window. The wardens often used to do spot checks by knocking on the door of homes to see if they were complying with blackout regulations.

A large number of children were evacuated to Thame. All children, local or evacuee, had their name and address on a label in their knickers, secured with a safety pin, so if they were bombed it would be known who they were.'

GROVE AIRFIELD

'At the beginning of the war when sites for more airfields were urgently needed, there was often a clash of interests between the Air Ministry and the Ministry of Agriculture and Fisheries. Land was needed for farming and food production and the Air Ministry often gave in to valid objections, but although the site at Grove comprised 272 acres of milk-producing land, ie grazing, there seemed no alternative area that could be used. It was decided to build a three-runway spare bomber airfield for 91 Group.

A farmhouse and outbuildings stood in the middle of the area – my mother remembers looking out of her bedroom window and seeing it blown up by the construction workers, who then removed the debris and levelled the area as work proceeded.

Flying first took place about August 1942, by Vickers Wellingtons

180

of No 15 Operational Training Unit based at Royal Air Force Harwell. By October 1942 Horsa gliders of the Heavy Glider Conversion Unit were based here.

At this time the numbers of personnel were very minimal because the accommodation was far from completed. Because of its size, the station was administered by Royal Air Force Andover from March 1943.

The USAAF officially took over the station in September and was formed as No 3 Tactical Air Depot.

During the first four months of 1943 Brize Norton's Whitleys and Horsas used the airfield and in March 1943 Typhoons of 174 and 184 Squadrons were here taking part in Exercise "Spartan".

Calls to Wantage fire station to attend crashed and crash-landed planes occurred regularly. Missing the airfield they came down in all the villages around – Wantage, Letcombe, Ardington, Lockinge, Hendred, Charney and Lyford all received their share of firstly British, then later American crashed planes.

The only enemy bomb that dropped and exploded was the one that just missed the gasworks in Wantage and the same plane dropped two more bombs near Venn Mill (nearer to Oxford). It then crashed somewhere, but I don't know where.

Grove became known as "Muddy Grove" as mud from the USAAF lorries which were continually being driven in and out of the construction area was deposited over all the roads in the village during a very wet winter. Accidents were common.

In March 1944 a dramatic event took place in poor weather when the highly-secret Vickers Armstrong DW506 bomber force-landed here due to engine trouble, and in the crash broke its back and had to be written off as a result.

While the Americans were in Grove they provided their own equipment: furnishings, food, etc, most of it being flown into their camp after being shipped from America. They did not go short and were generous with gifts to their friends in the strange country where they had to live for the duration of the war. Local girls were keen to have American boyfriends, but generally their parents did not approve. Nevertheless, GI brides went back to the States, some never to return. As well as putting up accommodation on the airfield and in the village, a ballroom was also built and it was here that part of the Glenn Miller Band came to play. On a Saturday evening, 12th August 1944, Sergeant Mel Powell and a sextet flew in to Grove for a dance held by the 9th Air Force Service command.

By the end of the war Grove airfield (and village) presented an unconventional appearance with assorted buildings from 1941, 1942 and 1943.

Firemen on parade in 1944 at Islip. Like many others on the home front, they played a vital part in the war effort.

The RAF took control of Grove once again in February 1946. Today very little remains of the former airfield, housing or industrial estates having been built across it.'

ONE OR TWO BOMBS

'Oxford didn't have any bombs, as I recall, though there were one or two dropped in Oxfordshire. We used to say that the Germans were keeping Oxford for themselves.

Littlemore had one air raid, when three bombs were dropped. No one was hurt but there was a large crater in Spring Lane. One did not go off and was found later and the bomb disposal squad took it away. Broadfield was turned into an airfield with Spitfires, Ansons and training planes. There was a dump there where wrecked planes were taken, some of them with swastikas on them.'

'I was lucky that no one in my family was in the services; my father was an air raid warden but we were really outside the danger area.

We would hear planes going over at night, British and German. Being only 30 miles from London we had quite a lot of air raid warnings, but little in the way of bombing. My parents said they could sometimes see the light from the fires in London, though I do not remember that myself. I do remember coming home from school by bus, one day in 1943 I think, when the driver stopped and made us all get out a couple of miles from Reading and we watched a German plane over the town. I later learned that it had dropped a stick of bombs in the town centre, the only real raid we had; the damage was considerable, but luckily it was a Wednesday afternoon, early closing day (which was strictly adhered to in those days) so the casualties were less than they would have been any other day.

I do not remember being much affected by the war. Rationing was strict, and goodness knows how my mother managed, but I do not recall ever feeling deprived and we were never really short of food. We kept chickens and grew as many vegetables as we could; my war effort consisted mainly of collecting scraps for pig food and delivering ARP leaflets.

When we decided to kill a chicken to eat (usually an old hen past laying and fit only for boiling) we arranged with a neighbour to do the same and we exchanged birds so that we did not have to feel that we were eating one of our own.'

'We had evacuees from London in Goring, and anyone with a spare room had to take some in. Soldiers were billeted locally, we had dances twice a week in the parish room, the older men joined the Home Guard and the ARP, and the housewives struggled to make the rations go round.

We only had one lot of bombs fall on the village. A lone raider returning from Coventry dropped his bombs, hitting one house on the river and killing one lady. Fortunately all the other bombs fell in fields and gardens so there were no other casualties.'

TRAGEDY AND HOSPITALITY

'1939 and before long the machinery and workmen arrived in our lovely village of Stanton Harcourt to start building the aerodrome, which became an operational training unit for bomber crews. As a schoolgirl I was in a local field called Pig Pen having a picnic, when we saw a plane coming over very low. We sensed something was wrong and then could see the swastika on it. As it reached the workmen on the edge of the field it machine-gunned them as they ran for cover and six Irishmen were killed. I remember the impact it made on me as I attended the funerals with lots of other villagers.

Winston Churchill went to the Big Three meeting with Roosevelt and Stalin and flew from Stanton Harcourt. Of course, we didn't know until afterwards as "Careless Talk Costs Lives"!

When the RAF arrived in 1940, the village came alive with dances on the camp and in the village hall and it was "open house" for servicemen. My father and mother were Methodist and ran the chapel. All the RAF personnel who came to the services had a great welcome from them. Every Sunday evening, after evening worship, they all came back to our thatched cottage and would sing hymns around the organ. Then my father could always find supper for them. He was well known by the shopkeepers in Oxford's covered market for his efforts to make a good social life for our visitors and they would donate food: ham, fruit and any goodies that were left on a Saturday afternoon. There was always a snack for them on a Sunday evening. My father was a great gardener and grew lots of produce to help out. He would also load them up with vegetables and fruit when they went home on leave.

As well as being Mum and Dad to the RAF, they were asked to take a London family of evacuees who were bombed out. As there was no room in our cottage my dad made our old shepherd's hut, which was in our garden, into a room and George and his family moved in for quite a while until they could return to London.

As a teenager, I suppose I had a much better war than most, meeting people from all over the world and having fun, but I like to think that we village girls were helping the war effort by helping them to enjoy their lives before going off on operations. I will certainly never forget those wartime years and we are still in touch with some of "our" boys! We visit them and enjoy their visits to us and the old war-time song "We'll meet again" still comes true after 50 years.'

ALL CLEAR

'The school bell shrilled, three times – air raid warning. I heaved a sigh of relief: the French test was about to start and I was very shaky on my irregular verbs. We all knew the drill, we moved sharply in an orderly procession to the cloakrooms for coats and gas masks, then round the corridors till we reached the door leading on to the field. Then all order broke down as we raced across to our assigned shelters.

For some reason these were always known as trenches although they were roofed over with several feet of soil. They were dank, dark and cold and smelt of damp earth. A rough wooden bench ran down one side. Near the entrance was a curtained-off space containing a bucket which we were all determined we'd never use.

We could not have been assigned to our shelters by form as I seem to remember a mixed age group. It may have been by houses. Certainly our Trench Mistress was Miss Harrop, who was St George's house mistress. George's for Ever, Andrew's and David's for Never. Which house was I in? Miss Harrop was the biology teacher and an all-round good egg.

Anyway, Miss Harrop always stationed herself at the entrance where it was a little lighter. She brought a torch and a bottle of water with her but I don't remember ever being in the shelters long enough to get hungry or thirsty.

In fact in our corner of the Cotswolds we didn't really have air raids. We had lots of warnings as the Luftwaffe passed over on their way to the industrial centres of the Midlands and then again as they returned. Most of the really long, severe raids though were at night. The night of the Coventry raid still stands out. We lived 50 miles away and we thought the sky was on fire. Dad was an air raid warden and he was out nearly all night. When we went to school the next day, girls whose fathers were in fire fighting teams told of their departure to help in the early hours, and there wasn't a fire engine left in Oxfordshire – not that we knew that then. As the war progressed the raids gradually lessened. After the Normandy invasion in 1944 they ceased. The V1s and V2s never came so far inland.

But to return to the school trenches. Frankly, after the initial excitement of the alarm and the dash to them, we soon got very bored. We would spend a while chatting and joking and then we would sing. Something rousing like *There'll always be an England* or the latest Vera Lynn song. Later on we sang American pop songs like *Don't sit under the apple tree*. Occasionally we'd put on our gas masks and roar at each other through them, trying to guess what people were saying, but not surprisingly, the staff took a dim view of this. Once the Head came round on a tour of inspection, "Don't you realise this is a very stupid way to treat something on which your life may depend?" We were suitably squashed. But all these activities would pall after a time and we would fall silent, stamping our feet to try to keep warm. In very wet weather there would be puddles in the trench. So eventually we would be quiet and miserable, shivering in the damp atmosphere. French would be better than this even if it were a test. We'd look at our watches every few minutes – could so little time really have elapsed since we last checked? All seemed peaceful outside. Why hadn't the all clear gone? Surely they weren't going to keep us here till the bombers made their return journey?

Eventually we would hear the town siren, which would be followed by the school signal – an uninterrupted ringing of the bell. A cheer would go up, the shelters disgorge their young, and we'd emerge thankfully, to mingle with friends and classmates, and return to our interrupted lessons.'

LIFE ON THE FARM

Growing food for the nation became of paramount importance as the war went on and those who worked on the land were urged to ever greater efforts. As men were called up, so women came to take their places, serving in the Women's Land Army.

QUITE A CHALLENGE

'I got married in October 1938 and took over a very large farmhouse at Kiddington. This was quite a challenge. The kitchen was large with stone floors and wooden shutters and window seats, and had a large Eagle range with two huge ovens which never got hot enough to cook anything! The working kitchen had a stone floor and shallow stone sink. In the corner was a large copper, which had to be filled with water and then on hands and knees you poked paper and sticks in the hole below and lit it with a match and hoped it was your lucky day and it would burn and heat the water – but if the wind was in the wrong direction it would go out instead.

This copper did all the washing, but had another use. We had a bathroom but as the kitchen range did not heat the water, the next best thing was to carry six buckets of water from the copper, along the stone passage, down five stone steps, up 15 front stairs, along the passage to the bathroom!

Kiddington was a very different place during the war. At the outbreak of war we were all asked how many evacuees we could take. Having six bedrooms, it was not a problem. I said "four children". We expected school-age children, but when we went to collect them at the school the wrong consignment had been sent and we got a mother, two school-aged girls and a baby boy – quite a different cup of tea.

As they came from the East End of London, Kiddington was the end of the world. They could not believe they had to walk two and a half miles to the nearest pub and the grocer only called once a fortnight, and you got milk from a cow and cooked your own fish and chips.

The husband worked on a coal cargo boat up the east coast so it was a while before he could visit. He came by train to Oxford one Sunday and took a taxi to *Kidlington* and had to walk from there to Kiddington. After he had talked to his wife, he thanked us and said we had been kind and done the best we could for his wife and family but there was no way she would settle in the country, so they went back to London and the bombing.

The next time was better, we got a brother and sister aged about six years and three years. They had an older brother in the village and a mother and baby brother who visited occasionally. They stayed three years. The boy visited us a couple of years ago, having emigrated to Australia and not been back since. His wife said he told her the years he spent with us were the happiest of his life.

At Christmas it always amazed us that Tony and Mavis could unwrap and know everything they had got for Christmas by 5 am in total darkness, as there was no electricity at that time. Electricity came to Kiddington in the mid 1940s. The SEB wrote to say they needed some people to cover the cost of bringing a line through Kiddington, about £1,050, I think. Mr Gaskell would not consider it for the Hall, but when written to gave the tenant farmers permission to put it in his property providing all the fire hazards were covered. In the end we and another farmer paid a share each and the rector and the man who kept the off licence paid a half share each.

At the Hall at this time there were billeted a number of War Office secretaries. Mr Gaskell was a man who moved slowly and quietly, so that when on their first evening while having dinner, the door slowly opened and "something" came in with a flickering candle, they thought it was the ghost of Kiddington Hall.

As our children came from Enfield somebody must have mentioned Home Farm to their butcher. The next request we had was from Joe the butcher to accommodate his wife and two children.

Most weekends Joe came down very late on Saturday night bringing his mother, a real cockney lady of over 80, who stayed in London all week to look after Joe and then took her daughter-in-law's washing back to do in London! Most weekends Joe also brought at least another couple to get a night's sleep, so we were usually about 16. This with only hot water boiled on the fire.

We had one awful weekend when Joe was bringing the father of three young boys who were staying at the Hall with their mother.

They stopped for a rest from blackout driving and no signposts, and as they got out of the van the father was knocked down and killed by a drunken driver leaving his local. We had to break the news to his wife and small boys.

While all this was going on indoors the farm still had to be kept running. This meant I had to drive the tractor which pulled the binder, and lead the horses and carts which brought in the corn. This was loaded by hand – one sheaf at a time and then unloaded in the rickyard to the man building the rick. In peak busy periods we had the help of all sorts of people. We had land girls from Chipping Norton dropped off every morning for potato picking, we had gangs of Irishmen, Coldstream Guards just back from Cyprus (for a rest!) and Italian prisoners of war who brought their own cook. We nearly had a strike one day when my husband said I would cook and the man could work. I got a great cry of "No cooka da macaroni right". So that was the end of that.

We had two German prisoners – the two Walters, Big and Little, for a long time. They worked very well and came in the house for dinner with us. They also spent Christmas with us. We also had a Yugoslav who was the most temperamental person we had ever had to deal with. If by any unfortunate chance we had to keep him working late on a Tuesday – which was picture night at his camp in Over Norton Park – my sister-in-law feared for my safety while taking him back, in the greatest possible haste.

Sheep were evacuated from Romsey Marsh during the war. We had 100, supposedly all male but when they left their number had increased by one lamb.

The next excitement was that a large part of my brother-in-law's farm at Gagingwell was taken over for a wartime aerodrome. One day when I answered the door (which was always left open) there stood a very tall RAF Warrant Officer – 6 feet 6½ inches to be exact. He was being transferred to Enstone from Edgehill. He said he had looked all round the district and thought ours was the only house he could stand upright in. Please could we rent him, his wife and son a sitting room, bedroom and cooking facilities, as they preferred looking after themselves. After some thought we agreed and they moved in. That was the start of a new influx of people, all members of the RAF and similar organisations. We had Canadians, Australians, New Zealanders and Czechs and men from all areas of the UK. One particular Yorkshireman and a Scots sergeant organised parties for haymaking etc followed by a snack, a chat and a drink in the farmhouse kitchen.

Quite a few of them played tennis, so on Saturdays when no work was urgent, we organised tennis tournaments. Kiddington girls had never had so many partners. This was followed by tea in the garden. One large Canadian Flight Sergeant could eat a whole plate of jam tarts, if nobody rescued them in time. Mrs Gaskell used to come and present the prizes.

One morning not too long before D-Day, Kiddington woke up to find the whole of the park was covered with large tents, jeeps and army transport. An American Medical Corps had arrived. That certainly livened up the village. The children were given lots of gum. Women in the village did washing for them. When walking down the road often a voice said, "Say Mam, could you wash the Colonel's shirt?" If you agreed, they would come and collect it and bring a large chunk of "Devil's Cake", which was very dark chocolate cake topped with cream, made from evaporated milk whipped with lemon juice, or a can of fruit or jam, all of which was in short supply. They were friendly and entered into village activities. Herman the bugler played the appropriate calls morning and evening.

One evening several of them called in and brought pairs of boots, shirts, etc, and said they didn't need them. In the morning the park was bare, they had left to join the D-Day landings. We corresponded with several of them over all these years. There is only one left now, living in Florida.

Entertainment to look forward to was the annual St Giles Fair held the first Monday and Tuesday after the first Sunday, after the first of September. There was also the Mop Fair at Chipping Norton and Banbury (Thursday nearest the 13th October) and Kiddington Feast, held in the cricket field, about the first week in July.

On cold, frosty moonlight nights we would walk to whist drives held at Glympton school, or cycle to whist drives and dances at Over Worton village hall and hear the nightingales singing in Worton Woods on our way home. We held whist drives and dances in Kiddington school, one shilling and sixpence including refreshments, which was coffee made in Mrs Gaskell's copper urn and kept hot on the tortoise stove. We also held whist drives in our large sitting room and there was always very brisk bidding for tea and sugar between the RAF and the locals.

We did get extra rations of tea, sugar, margarine and cheese for our workers during corn and potato harvest and there was always someone willing to give a bit of something for the war effort.

Apart from all the extra people, we did not see too much of the war. In the evenings when walking up the field to shut the chickens up, which would not be until nearly 11 pm due to the double summer time introduced to help the war effort, we would see our bombers on their way to Germany.

189

Our WI president at that time wrote a book of poems; included was –

> Like phantom birds the bombers flew –
> Fifty black crosses in the sky –
> Surrounding every gallant crew,
> But – thoughts unbidden, unresolved,
> Tore at my heart; all ill-defined
> My plea – O God – the pain involved –
> What can I pray for but man's mind
> And spirit? Thou, who knowest, dost share
> These desolate years; O hear our cry.

Her youngest son was a prisoner of war.

On the night that Coventry was bombed we could see the red glow in the sky from the higher part of the farm.

We had our own "Dad's Army", the stonemason, Mr Busby was our air raid warden and most of the farm workers were involved. We were all issued with gas masks.

On VE Day we arranged an impromptu party. Everyone who had anything to spare contributed. The lady staying at the rectory came over and said she could not cook but she had been saving two blancmanges for a special occasion – please would we use them that day.'

A SMALL MIXED FARM

'I was born at home in Shrivenham in 1941. My father was a sergeant in the local Home Guard and, using his Riley 9 motor car to go on Home Guard exercise, he missed my christening, much to my mother's annoyance!

My father owned a small mixed farm and he tenanted extra land at Watchfield. The man he employed joined up. In consequence Land Army girls and prisoners of war replaced him. One cow laid down while a land girl was hand-milking her, because she took so long! I could hand-milk a cow before I was four years old.

Milk was cooled and put into ten-gallon churns which were collected by Cadel's lorries and taken to the Express Dairy at Faringdon. My mother used Grannie's butter churn. This was a wooden drum with a hand-turned paddle which produced real butter. People collected their milk in jugs at sixpence a pint. All weights, scales and measures were regularly inspected, usually in the men's institute.

Later we had five prisoners of war: two Italians, Gino and Lesbo,

190

and Germans Fritz, Ada and Zepp. Christmas cards were exchanged with some of them into the 1950s.

Because of the war, new equipment was non-existent. My father waited years for a milking machine. It was never unpacked as the heifers were accustomed to hand-milking. A brand new Fordson Major tractor, EJB 24, came in 1948. This replaced an old Fordson with spiked wheels, forbidden on roads. Our cart horses were Violet and Diamond.

I remember mangolds, grown for fodder, and potatoes clamped in the fields. A clamp is a pit filled with potatoes or mangolds, covered with straw and soil. I remember my father opening one up for the first time and his relief on finding the contents undamaged by frost. Rabbits were an addition to our meat ration. They were caught in nets, when ferrets chased them out of their burrows.

The war had little effect upon me as I had no knowledge of peacetime. Once I was forbidden to walk the 25 yards along the pavement to the farmyard, because an army vehicle had demolished our wall. Previously a lady was crushed by a tank.

VE evening remains in my memory as a large circle of people dancing the Hokey-Cokey and Knees up Mother Brown all over the road outside the Barrington Arms.

A few days after, my father and I went up to the Uffington White Horse to help remove the camouflage. This was soil, foliage and coiled wire to render the horse invisible and not a navigational aid to enemy aircraft.'

BACK TO THE LAND

'After leaving school I did a hairdressing apprenticeship; shop hours were long before the Second World War, but everyone worked long hours then. I had hardly finished my apprenticeship when we heard over the radio that we were at war with Germany again.

As the first few months passed, we were asked to work for the war effort and so it was back to the land for me and even longer working hours.

Grass fields were ploughed and planted with wheat, oats or barley, the corn was all cut with a binder and sheaves of corn dropped every few yards. We followed the binder round the field and stood up the sheaves about eight or ten to a stook. When the corn was dry, which often took weeks in a wet summer, we had to pitch the sheaves up on to a horse-drawn waggon and take the load back to the rickyard to be built into a rick. When all the harvest was gathered in the ricks were thatched to keep them dry until threshing day. Threshing was often done in January or February when a cold east wind was blowing and frost and snow on the ground. I was usually put on the corn rick and had to put the sheaves on to the threshing box – really hard work when the rick was nearly down to ground level. Mice had often nested in the rick and they would be running everywhere.

Haymaking was very different in those days, hay was raked into rows and loose hay loaded onto waggons and then built into a rick and thatched.

Ploughing was done by tractor by then – we had no warm cab to shelter us from the winter wind. I could hardly move when I got very cold and had to get off the tractor and walk around for a little while to warm up a bit.

Sheep shearing was hard work. I usually had to turn the handle on the shearing machine while a man did the shearing, and then the fleece had to be rolled into a neat bundle.

My childhood friend also went back to work on the land. She had to do a daily milk round with a horse and cart, and measured out milk from milk churns, customers bringing out their own jugs.'

I JOINED THE LAND ARMY

'I enrolled in the Women's Land Army some time before the war was declared, at the County Hall in London. I was working at Laings, the builders, in their head office in Mill Hill as a secretary, close to where I lived at home with my parents. Although living in London all my life, I had always preferred the country and loved animals from a very early age and had no fear of them.

When war broke out I was immediately put on the Reserved Occupation list and was held by my firm until 1942 when I was called for an interview and told I was to be conscripted. At this interview I explained to them how I had enrolled in the WLA and that this was still my preference, but they would not say into which service I would be sent. Eventually, I had to go for a medical and was accepted into the Land Army and received the first instalment of my uniform, which, if I can remember correctly, was two short-sleeved shirts, one green pullover, two pairs of socks, one pair of shoes, one grey bib and brace overall, a hat, a pair of rubber boots, and a very long, thin mac which came down to my ankles. This was in November! We had to give up most of our clothing coupons, but always had to supply all our own underclothes. I had the rest of my uniform during the next six months, including a greatcoat and a pair of breeches, and I was able to buy some secondhand uniform over the years from the Oxford WLA office.

On 2nd November 1942 I was sent to Sparsholt training farm near Winchester for four weeks very intensive training in dairy

Land girls did essential work on Oxfordshire's farms during the war.

and general farmwork and given my number – 0101337. I still have my Notification of Training giving the train I had to catch at Waterloo station, with a travel warrant and stating that "board and lodging will be provided free and in addition a personal allowance of ten shillings a week, less National Health and Unemployment Insurance contributions will be paid during training." We were met at Winchester station by an open lorry – there were six of us from London, and the rest from other parts of the country. We were put into a dormitory with, I think, six in each room.

At Sparsholt we were up at 5 am and allowed a cup of cold milk before milking. We were taught how to machine and hand-milk. Most of the milking was under cover in the cowshed, but I had to hand-milk one cow out in an open pen and it was very cold and frosty. We also had to use the bail milker which was out in the middle of a field. We had to clean the cowshed out with some of the largest and heaviest buckets and brooms I have ever used. It was my turn to fetch the cows down from the field, and in the dark early one morning I could just see one which would not come to my call at the top of the hill, so went up to find out what was wrong. I

193

felt so stupid – I had been calling a bush! I never lived that down all the time I was at Sparsholt. Our food rations were a pot of jam to last the month, a small bowl of sugar, and a dish with our ration of butter and margarine to last the week (it never did!). All had labels on with our names. We used to go into Winchester on our one half day and buy Marmite (which was not on points or rationed) and anything else we could "persuade" sympathetic shopkeepers to part with. Our parents sent cakes which we shared amongst our dormitory. We always seemed to be so hungry.

At the end of the four weeks we went home for a day then on to our delegated farms. I was sent to Banbury, a place I had never been to before. I was taken to an excellent private billet and made very welcome and soon felt quite at home, *and* I always had plenty to eat! I started at 6 am and was told I was to do a milk round in and around Banbury in the morning and farmwork in the afternoon. I had a shock when told I was to drive a van (I had never driven anything other than a bumper car at the fair!), but the farmer said they would soon teach me. My first experience of driving would have shocked the law today. The van had no brakes and no hooter, and I had to drive through Banbury Market Place on a Thursday, market day! I became known as the Yellow Peril. One day I had a very heated argument with a policeman. I had to deliver milk in the town and leave the van while I went to several customers with two large crates of milk. When I returned to the van a very large officer told me I couldn't leave the van there, so I told him that if he would carry my crates I would leave the van wherever he wanted. He eventually turned away and told me not to stay there any longer than necessary!

If our money was short on a Saturday it was taken out of our meagre wages, but if it was over we never had that. I was ten shillings short one week and could never find out how, but had to lose it in my wages, at five shillings a week. We paid our own lodgings out of our wages.

I was in Banbury for just over a year, then was sent to a farm about seven miles away owned by an old and very eccentric lady. I did not know it until later, but I was to be her 26th land girl and I stayed with her the longest – one year. She had two enormous sows – Luscious Lucy and Gracious Grace – though I had very different names for them! When I went to feed them one morning, they got out of their sty which was at the top of a large gorse field. It took me over an hour to get both of them back into the sty after running them up and down the hill and dodging in and out of the large gorse bushes. One dark night at about 10 pm when I was having my night drink, my employer called for me to help get Lucy and about ten of

194

her small piglets back into the sty as they had forced themselves out and were loose in a field. She told me to pick up one of the little pigs which was still in the sty and she would find the sow and the others and drive them towards me. Knowing what Lucy was like when she had her young, I said, "She will go for me if she hears this one squealing." "No, she won't," was the reply so I did as I was told. The small pig was squealing blue murder and as the old sow came thundering towards the noise, I dropped the little one as the sow grabbed my leg, and cleared a five foot six inch fence as I'd never done before – nor since. My wellingtons bore the teethmarks until the end of their days!

I had to drive this elderly lady into Banbury each week in a large old Austin 16 car, and this after driving a small Austin van. I always had to dress in my best full uniform for this duty. I soon realised why she couldn't keep her land girls and after an unforgettable year, I was transferred to another farm in the nearby village. This was completely different. I used to work with three horses, Prince, Bluebird and The Colt. My first job was to fetch these huge farm horses from the field each morning. All went well until one morning I had the halters on Prince and The Colt, but Bluebird wouldn't come, and as I stood there holding a horse each side of me, ears back he suddenly charged straight at me. He could only have been about twelve yards from me when I threw up my arms and shouted the first thing that came into my head – "Scram". The enormous animal was so surprised that he skidded to a halt and as I walked the other two down into the village, the rebel followed. When I told the farmer what had happened, he said, "Oh, has he started that with you – a pity." I asked him why he hadn't told me what he was like and he said, "If I had told you before, you wouldn't have fetched him would you?"

One afternoon I found the bull had got out of his pen at the end of the cowshed. He was a nasty animal and had a long chain fastened to the ring in his nose. I managed to shut the doors to prevent him getting out into the village, and got behind the stalls where the cows were to be milked and managed to lean over and grab the chain. I pulled him back into his own pen into which I had climbed, then got out and shut the gate. It wasn't until a few minutes later that I realised what a stupid thing I had done – pulled the bull in by his chain with my back to the wall of his pen! It was some time before I stopped shaking.

I used to carry two and a quarter cwt bags of meal and corn on my back, and have suffered with severe back problems ever since. I worked with two Italian prisoners of war, Toto and Antonio. I taught them quite a lot of English and they taught me some Italian words.

On the whole they were good workers. As they couldn't buy lighter flints at their camp, they used to bring me cakes and I bought them lighter flints from Banbury in exchange. We were unloading hay from a trailer on to a rick one day, I was on the rick with Antonio and Toto was on the load of hay. Suddenly the horse bolted. I shall never forget the sight of Toto first jumping up then disappearing in the load of hay, then up again, shouting in Italian. Luckily the field gate was shut and the horse just stopped there, but it was one of the funniest sights I have ever seen, just like a Jack in the Box.

One of the fields we had to cross with the loads of hay was in "lands" and the farmer told Antonio to go straight across the "lands" and not slantways as he was on top of the load and didn't want to be tipped off. He forgot, of course. I was following behind and the next thing I saw was the whole load tipping over with the farmer underneath. We had to dig him out quickly as he suffered from asthma. What he called Antonio when he surfaced I couldn't repeat.

Coming from London, I had never had anything to do with hurricane lamps, and one morning when I went into the cowshed the farmer had left one alight. Thinking of saving paraffin, I turned the wick down until it went out. The air was blue the next morning when I went into work. The farmer had spent nearly half an hour trying to get the wick back up with a safety pin at 5 am in the dark cowshed – his only means of lighting! I was not very popular for a few days.

Once I harrowed up a dead hen that a fox had killed and buried, and when I took it to the farmer's wife, she said I could have it for ten shillings. As meat was so precious, I took it back to my billet.

There were no combines then, just stationary threshing machines, and how dusty they were. I've also fed hay into a stationary baler. I worked non-stop until 11 pm week after week during haymaking and almost had a breakdown and the WLA headquarters sent me for a week to one of their rest homes at St Elmo in Torquay. This break made a great difference and I went back to the farm feeling much better.

It was while working on this farm that I was to meet my future husband, who farmed the adjoining farm with his widowed mother. We used to cycle the seven miles to Banbury to go to the cinema in completely blacked-out lanes and roads. Eventually we married and I carried on in the Land Army for a few years working on my husband's farm.

Although girls were called up into the Land Army as in the other services during the war, they had no benefits like other services. They were allowed into places of entertainment etc at reduced prices, but not the Land Army. I can remember going to the zoo with my friend who was in the ATS; she was allowed in at a cheaper rate, but not me even though we were both in uniform. This made the land girls very bitter, and we had nothing when we left like the services did.

Among my Land Army years there were happy days, sad days, exciting days, wet days, hot days, icy cold days, and *all* very hard working days, but I wouldn't have missed any of it for anything, even though I have been paying for it ever since with no compensation.'

LIFE GOES ON

There were rations to be stretched to feed the family, make do and mend classes to attend, evacuees to shelter, and even some fun to be had – life had to go on, just the same.

MUSIC WHILE YOU WORK

'During the war and for many years following, in factories and homes for half an hour each morning and afternoon of each working day, the BBC put out a programme of *Music while you work*, playing popular music with the big bands.

In factories where people were often employed on monotonous jobs, such as in the car factories, this half hour of music would suddenly seem to lift people's spirits and the workers would either sing along or whistle, and for a time their jobs were more bearable.'

EVACUEES AND AIR RAIDS

'We came to live at Grove, near Wantage, in 1936. From the upstairs window of our house we could see out across the airfield that was built on farmland between Grove and Challow. This was used first by the RAF, then by the USAAF, then after the war it was used again by RAF National Service men. There were also prisoner of war camps in Grove for both Italian and German prisoners.

We had evacuees staying at our house – a family from Canterbury who were later joined by their grandparents after they had been bombed out of their wool shop. They brought all the rescued wool with them and took over three rooms in our house.

My own family actually slept in the air raid shelter while these evacuees were with us, but it was rather a posh one, specially designed by my father and friends. All the produce yielded by "Digging for Victory" was also stored in this shelter and the aroma of apples was very strong, mixed with wood smoke from the stove built at the opposite end.'

'We came down to Long Wittenham from London during the First World War because of the Zeppelin raids.

During this war we had a family of evacuees, a mother and four children. They fitted in very well but after a while the mother found she couldn't live in the country so she went back home with her two youngest children. She left the two eldest with us though, and used to come down to see them. We taught them to swim in the river.

There was an air raid shelter on the lawn. If we had to go down there my mother and I used to try to amuse the children with games, but this worried my father who felt we ought to keep silent so we would be able to hear the all clear. He found it difficult to appreciate that it was totally different to the First World War.

In the village we had lessons in home canning and there was a team of women who were trained to use the fire engine. We used to practise twice a week. All the water had to come from the river.

Later on in the war a packing station was opened just outside the village. Tools were sent from the ordnance depot together with packing instructions and these were packed and then collected. This was good for many of the women who wanted to go to work but couldn't go out of the village.

Gleaning went on in the fields and if people could get enough they would take their gleanings to be ground into flour, which was a great help with rationing.'

WE MOVED IN

'In 1941 I was living with my father in Essex as my husband was in France in the army. When France capitulated in the June, my father thought I ought to take my baby sister and brothers, then 15 years and six years, to the country, so we were off to Launton in Oxfordshire. We moved into a thatched cottage with stone floors, no water, no light, with a grate in a very large chimney place.

My first try at frying breakfast was ruined as soot fell down into the pan. I was told I hadn't let the chimney get warm enough before cooking, and in any case it was safer to put lids on. Once some RAF

198

from Bicester 'drome came round to ask me to keep my fire down at night as they could see it through the chimney, it was so big when they flew over.

For two shillings and sixpence a week a man of the village brought me two buckets of water a day, and this I had to manage with for everything. There was a large paraffin lamp hanging on the ceiling which was very low. We had to walk round it. I often forgot and set it swinging madly.

Our loo was up the lane we lived in, next door to two other loos belonging to my neighbours. Mine was a two-holer, one for adults, one small one with a step in front for children. My neighbour, Uncle Billy we called him, would empty my buckets for me so that he had fertilizer for his garden. Believe it or not, I had six lovely new-laid eggs a week in payment, also some gooseberries, blackcurrants, peas, beans and loads of root vegetables.

Only some of the big houses had pump water of their own. My aunty had a pump. The well water wasn't very nice, so they used to fill a large tank up which was put in the roof of a proper toilet outside the back door. This tank had to be filled up once a week, no more, so that for a treat we could pull the chain. The village pump was owned by a farmer and he used to shut that off if he thought it might run dry.

We used to get all our milk from the farm. We would go with our billy-can and most times we helped ourselves and put our penny down at the side of the churn. Sometimes the farmer would serve you but this wasn't too good as his hands were not too clean after being in the cowshed.

The village had twin ladies living down a little lane. One would always do the paying, while the other followed behind, carrying the shopping. They wore buttoned shoes and when the heels wore down one side they changed over and put the right shoe on the left foot and the left shoe on the right foot. It looked most odd. Goodness knows how they managed, they were very poor.

There is a small railway bridge just before you approach the village on the Bicester side. My uncle was a butcher and had to go in to the meat market once a week in his horse and trap. His friend, also in a horse and trap, used to race him home in the early hours of the morning just to see who could get over the little bridge first as it was very narrow. On one occasion they had had just a little too much ale at market and had gone to sleep. The horses, thinking that racing to the bridge to get over first was the thing to do, did just that and when they were found by a road-sweep both carriages were locked together and the men still asleep, the horses wondering what had happened. My uncle was unable to live that down.'

RATIONS AND MAKE DO AND MEND

'During the war we had to "make do and mend". This meant mending our clothes and using our coupons carefully. I could buy soft check dusters without coupons and three made a child's dress. I sewed by hand. One day a lady in the village had a treadle sewing machine for sale and when she heard that I made all my children's clothes by hand she let me buy it for £2 instead of the £5 she had previously asked.

All married women had to do war work and until my first daughter was born I worked in the canteen at De Havillands where they made parts for Spitfires.

During the war we had a WVS clothing exchange system in Bampton. Good clothes could be taken and points were given. These points would be used towards an exchange garment. I took three smocked dresses my daughters had outgrown and exchanged them for a green corduroy coat. In the pocket there was a note saying "This coat was made by J. Sutcliffe of the Lady Galwey Guild from New Plymouth, New Zealand." I wrote to Miss Sutcliffe and we corresponded for 36 years. She worked in a large store and could sometimes get pieces of material which she made up.'

'During the war I lived in Kidlington. Regularly every Saturday morning my mother would send me, with my younger brother and our evacuee, Sheila who was three years older than me, to Summertown on the No 93 Kidlington to Oxford bus. We got off at South Parade and walked down to Middle Way and queued outside Oliver & Gurden's cake factory.

There was a nice shop where I think we were allowed to spend two shillings. This meant that as many people as possible could have something from the limited supply. Sometimes the queue was 50 yards long and we spent the time worrying that there would be no cakes left. We usually had to queue for over an hour. When we were near the door we would look through the window to see what the choice was. We always chose round shortbreads as that was cheaper and made up our quota. One cake had chocolate, pink and yellow splodges through it and was called a Russian Bar. My favourite was a Madeira cake: I never taste one as good nowadays! It had a round of angelica on it.

My mother was a good cake maker but because fat was rationed there was never enough for home-made cakes and puddings. Biscuits were plain too, so when Sheila had a large parcel from Vancouver in Canada, where her aunt lived, we were very excited to find four packets of biscuits. I still think of them when I buy Maryland Cookies and Treacle Crunchies!'

'In spite of the war we had a lot of fun. The Bartons WI had a preserving centre during the fruit season and we all enjoyed our week working there. A farmer's wife used to bring a bit of butter, a tremendous treat, and we had this with baked potatoes for our lunch. Delicious! At the end of a hot and tiring day in the hall kitchen, all the produce, and it was a lot, had to be carted uphill in the Scouts' trek cart and finally up two awkward flights of stairs to be stored. We were all back the following week, perhaps for lunch, certainly for the good company.'

'At Chadlington the WI met in the afternoons because of the blackout. During the fruit season we used to can plums and make huge pans of jam for the Ministry of Food. It was always difficult to produce exactly the right number of jars of jam filled to exactly the right level, for the quantity of fruit and sugar (supplied by the Ministry) used. We did not find it too difficult to dispose of surplus jars before the Inspector arrived!

We also made camouflage nets in the Methodist schoolroom. I remember doing ones in "desert colours". My brother was serving in North Africa and I used to wonder if he ever used our nets.'

WARTIME FOOD AND COOKERY

'Sugar was allocated to Hardwick and Ducklington WI in 1940 to enable it to organise a preservation centre for making jam and canning fruit. The President lived at Cokethorpe Park. She allowed her kitchens to be used to make jam and to can fruit up to government standards. The WI bought its own canning machine and local fruit – plums, gooseberries, black and red currants, apples, blackberries, crabapples etc were all used; by September 1940, 2,767 cans of fruit and 3,890 jars of jam had been produced.

Clothing coupons restricted the purchase of new clothes hence "make do and mend" classes were very popular. Adult clothes were re-shaped, even joined together or cut down to make children's clothes – pieces of blanket, silk parachutes, tweed coats etc were used to make snug dressing gowns, silk slips, dresses etc. Fathers' uniforms were made into beautifully tailored overcoats, woollies unpicked and re-knitted, curtains used for skirts and tablecloths, shirt tails made into aprons.

Householders, if surroundings were suitable, were allowed to fatten a pig for domestic consumption. Other stock kept was rabbits, ducks, hens etc. They were fed on household scraps. The pig was killed by a licensed slaughterman. Every part of the carcase was used, the meat when fresh, or salted and cured with herbs and spices to bacon or hams. Offal was used to make faggots, meatballs, sausages, hog-puddings and black puddings. The leaf, skin that lined the stomach and encased the intestines, made pure lard when rendered down. Ears, head and trotters made brawn and excellent stock. Brains were cooked – seasoned with salt and pepper and mixed with butter to make sandwiches. Intestines were used to make chitterlings; the intestines were scraped clean of fat, then turned inside out, cleaned scrupulously, steeped in brine and knotted into convenient sizes. They were cooked and eaten hot or cold or fried. Even the tail went into the stock pot.

Electricity was being laid to the village when the war started and fortunately it was completed. Witney Urban District Council was the electricity authority then and also supplied rented cookers and sold suitable saucepans, frying pans, steamers etc (and china lampshades).

Parishioners and pupils at local grammar and secondary schools in Witney had their Christmas cakes cooked by a local baker in his bread oven after the bread had been cooked. Some householders took their cakes and joints to be cooked at the bakery.

Witney grammar school had a just-completed building for domestic science classes. Equipment could only be supplied when a qualified teacher had been appointed. This problem was overcome and the equipment started to arrive. Tables were too high and some too low, saucepans, colanders, basins, spoons etc. were all canteen size. The only cooker was a large solid fuel stove which needed blackleading. Excellent meals were cooked in steamers and baking in one oven, thus instilling in pupils economy of fuel! Experienced members of the village willingly shared their knowledge. An excellent cook made Christmas cakes with customers' own ingredients. She was very fortunate to have a husband who was willing and able to beat the cake mixture and the royal icing which was beaten in a large wash-stand bowl. He just managed to beat it – it was too heavy for a mere woman. No electric mixers!

Foreign fruit that is seen regularly today was almost never seen. Bananas especially were few and far between. Many children objected to the new flavours when bananas came back in the shops.

Special rural pies or puddings were eaten. In the spring and early summer part of the lambs' tails were cut off with hot sharp irons and the end pieces were dipped into boiling water to enable the wool to be pulled off easily. The tails were then used as a pie filling or a steamed suet pudding filling. Pieces of bacon were added to give extra flavour.

Another type of pie was made with young rooks that had been shot just before they were completely ready to leave the nest. The young birds were not plucked and dressed but skinned. The back was never eaten as it had a very bitter flavour and taste.

Other game – in season – was eaten: pheasant, partridge, pigeon, hare, rabbit, trout, eel and crayfish. In late summer and early autumn groups of friends went to the river bank of the Windrush in the evening and into the night to catch crayfish. To catch crayfish an iron ring about twelve to 14 inches was covered with a string net and very highly smelly fish was tied securely in the centre. The net was carefully lowered into the water until it was firmly *flat* on the river bed. A long string plus a piece of rag was left to mark the place. Other nets were lowered downstream at regular intervals. Later nets were raised working upstream and if the crayfish were "running" the brownish olive-green fish were removed from the net and the net replaced. The crayfish were cooked in boiling water for 20 to 30 minutes. Of course, they turned red when they touched the boiling water.

Water meadows were ploughed up for the first time in living memory. An incredible crop of mushrooms grew up under the leaves of the potatoes that had been planted in the fields. People came from Oxford by train to pick them for sale. The strongest flavoured wild mushroom growing on the local fields was the horse-mushroom that would grow to a size larger than a dinner plate in a night.'

JOINING IN THE FUN

'The Canadian forces were camped in tents in a farmer's field at Salford and the local children would visit them and come away with chocolate and pieces of cheese. A luxury when you only had one ounce of cheese a week each!

I helped to run dances, socials, whist drives and concerts at this time to get funds to build the village hall – and to send comforts to our young village men in the forces at Christmas time. It helped to keep our spirits up. Some of the American servicemen stationed locally would come and join in the fun. Some of the younger ones, about 18 years old, would just like to talk to us about their families and friends, obviously missing their home life and not knowing what lay ahead for them. These events took place in the school and we had to light the fires, take our chairs over, put up the blackout curtains and carry the crockery over and back each time, as we were not allowed to store anything in the school.'

'One of the most enjoyable evenings I remember was a Christmas party in Enstone school, during the first year of the war. The Durham Light Infantry were stationed at Enstone, but with many of the soldiers being away on a course, only about 16 of them were left in the village. So the WI thought it would be a good idea to invite them to their party.

They certainly made the evening go with a swing! With everyone joining in the games, there was not a dull moment. One young girl, in order to pay a forfeit, was told to kiss the soldier seated next to her. So she blew him a kiss, but he said, "Hey I want a proper kiss." This led on to the soldiers kissing everyone present.

In that early part of the war, George VI came to Chipping Norton to review his troops. The Durham Light Infantry marched from Enstone to Chipping Norton for the parade. It was a bitterly cold day, but the Durhams were without overcoats, as they had been lost in transit. As the King inspected the troops, a dog, belonging to a local scrap-metal merchant, walked with the King and stood by his side as he took the salute.'

WARTIME OXFORD

Two memories of wartime Oxford from the colleges, one from a woman don, the other from a medical student.

AN OXFORD DON IN A WOMEN'S COLLEGE

'It was a time when the two year shortened course was in operation. Several of the Oxford colleges were taken over for military purposes which involved shifting people to a certain extent. At Lady Margaret Hall we took in about a dozen Somervillians when Somerville was taken over as a hospital for head injuries. One evening it was the duty of one of the Somervillian guests to see that the blackout was complete.

There is a long terrace which runs across the Senior Common Room out into the garden, and below the terrace was a row of cloches which were devoted to the cultivation of tomatoes and looked after sedulously by the splendid person who organised all our digging.

This poor girl stepped back off the terrace and put her leg through one of these cloches, which were very good cloches, and dear to Miss Gardener who looked after the whole project. When in the morning we told her, she showed not an iota of sympathy for the poor victim, who of course had been patched up by then. It was simply that she had to pay for the cloche and I discovered years afterwards, to my great satisfaction, that the JCR had been so horrified that a guest should have had to pay for the broken cloche, not to mention the damage to her leg, that they clubbed together and paid her fine. That was one absurd event in the whole blackout system which was a complete nightmare for all the colleges.

Another exercise we were commanded to carry out was the use of the fire pump, and one of the Dons who was a very severe historian, alas now dead, became an absolute wizard with this pump and she trained pupils in the use of it. One evening she was up in the attic teaching them how to put out a bomb, which was actually a flower pot on a table, and presently in their enthusiasm one of them stepped a little heavily and went straight through the ceiling of the said Don and a leg came through.

Miss Hurnard was a wonderful person who also added to the rare pleasures with her wonderful way with animals. On one occasion one of the wild ducks who nested in the Parks in a little stream which enters the Cherwell near Lady Margaret Hall, had left her nest and it was full of eggs. We rushed over with a tea cosy and rescued the whole clutch. Miss Hurnard reared those ducks by the most patient skill. She had them in her bedroom and she rigged up a kind of ceiling heat for them by swinging a hot water bottle above them, and she got them through. It was a very rare thing to be able to hatch a wild duck. She brought them up and she put them on the Cherwell and the next generation of ducks recognised her. We also had hens on the tennis courts. It was lovely to have the hens, but hopeless for the tennis court.

There were other people who did ambulance work. I remember that we were always very much more afraid of our neighbours and making fools of ourselves than we were of anything Hitler might drop. There was one Sunday when it was ordained that the whole of Oxford – all the services – were to have an exercise. A very shy, very gentle colleague of mine looked up at breakfast and said, "Oh well, I suppose nothing but an air raid will save us now."

The regular discipline of sirens and waiting until the all clear and going into dug-outs was very wearying indeed. I believe that only one bomb fell on Oxford, but the alerts were frequent. I remember the night when the planes flew over and we later learned it was the night they raided Coventry. Another problem was the gas masks.

It was largely a case of knowing where they were and how to put them on, also the tin hats. The peril of a tin hat was if you went out at night when, of course, there were no lights, you could run into a lamp post, which was extremely painful. However there was one wonderful plus in all this. In total blackout, I have never seen anything so beautiful as St Giles in full moonlight – flooded with moonlight. It was a wonderful sight.

We were fed reasonably well – other people were worse off, but we were hungry. We had a change from a very nice, careful Bursar to a new one who was very cheerful and promised very well. We had the most superb soup and were greatly cheered until we discovered that it contained our week's ration. The rest of the days were rather thin. We did not allow ourselves any dessert at the High Table, but sometimes when there were guests we got a cream horn. There were no implements with which to eat them, and I remember sitting at one end of the table and looking along to see how my colleagues tackled a cream horn. It was most instructive. There was no simple way of doing it. You could start at the base and travel upwards and it exploded on you or you started at the top and got the explosion first. Bananas were only available for children with "green" ration books. I remember a notice displayed in the Queen's College – "Gentlemen under 17 are asked to collect their bananas at the lodge."

The Bursar had difficulty in getting adequate staff to do the domestic jobs. We had a small cohort of ladies who were known as "the lady moppers". One of them was a titled lady in disguise. They were not very domesticated but very willing. Towards the end of the war we imported half a dozen Dutch girls who were to learn the language and do domestic service. The irony of it was that we were always being told that there was starvation in the Netherlands, but they were marvellously fit – young, strong and plump. It was also necessary for undergraduates to do their own fires. We were each allowed about two buckets of coal a week. Most of them had no idea how to lay a fire, so that was a part of their education.

Another part of their education, and indeed of ours, was the cultivation of vegetables. Every afternoon Senior and Junior Common Room members worked to a rota digging and double digging the sports pitches and tennis courts, indeed every bit of land we had. We were taught by a geologist, who had also learnt gardening at Waterperry and she supervised all our horticultural operations. We used to eat 40 pounds of cabbages at a meal so that we needed a lot. She used to come in at breakfast and say, "There will be an issue of radishes today." All hearts rose. I have younger friends who tell me how grateful they were for this tuition. They learned something besides writing essays.

Another plus was that there was for undergraduates a University system of fire-watching and if you stayed up after term you were given your keep and you fire-watched on top of the Bodleian or a college. The marvellous thing was that the rest of the day your time was your own and it served for a very good reading purpose. In the old days you had reading parties, but then you could have your reading party at home as it were, and be paid for it. People look back on these sessions quite nostalgically now.

We were cold all the time. I always had a store of rugs that I threw over my pupils' chapped knees, partly because I could not bear to see how red they were and partly in kindness for their comfort. There was one room in the college where people were often to be found sitting along a bed and it was the room directly over the heating system and therefore you got the warmth, rather in the way that people used to go to the National Gallery and look at certain pictures. People wondered why. It was because when you were before that picture you could stand on the grating over the heating. People used to store what little coal they had, sometimes, I am ashamed to say, in their wardrobes, much to the Bursar's fury.

One of the more unpleasant jobs I remember was, not at Oxford, but during the vacation at Beaconsfield. I made munitions for a little while and was also put onto making camouflage netting and that was really hard. The smell of the coarse hessian and threading it with scraps and rags was very dirty and dusty. I also had washing up jobs for hospitals. We had a hospital of Free French in Beaconsfield. They had a Chinese cook whose habits with crockery were barbaric. They had good rations – they also had horsemeat. It was quite a job and I have never had any fears about washing up since those days of doing it for the Free French.

Clothes were rationed. We had a very clever system of "points" by which one had the illusion of choice. Psychologically it was a brilliant move. At one time we had among us an American professor as an academic guest for a term or two. She once overheard some of us saying we did not know if we could get enough points for a mackintosh or a pair of stockings and she was horrified that people might not be able to acquire obvious necessities. She did not say anything at the time, but when she went back to America she summoned her academic friends and she sent us really superb parcels of all but new clothes. Clothes that gave some colour in life, some silk in life, also warmth. We devised a scheme among us of auctioning them. You had them on display in the Principal's guest room for a while, then the Bursar organised an afternoon when people could put in a bid for this garment or that, and if you got it then you did not bid for the next two or three. After we had received one or two of these parcels, if you looked round the room, there was not a single person there who was not wearing an American garment somewhere either above or below the belt. After the war we were able to reimburse her a little for her kindness. These garments really restored our morale in a wonderful way.

I remember that with great gratitude, especially as everything was so depressing. China was thick, like station crockery. It was all so desperately utilitarian. One knitted for ever. I am ashamed to recount one of my memories which does not come from the Second World War, but from the first. I was a child then and was set to knit stockings for seamen – long tubes of oiled wool. I was at school and had got to within the last two inches of finishing. It was a cold night and I put them on and continued to wear them in bed. No seaman ever got them. It was very shaming and I did not dare confess to the authorities, but now in my old age, I confess it to posterity. I cheated the government.

An interesting thing about academic hospitality was that just before the war it had been the practice for senior members to give breakfast parties to younger members and to have open house for hospitality. All that had to go. None of the materials were available but gradually it developed into smaller kinds of entertainment. After the war a kind of sherry party hospitality emerged. Within the college the pleasant amenity of having a cake provided for the Dons once a week for people who dropped in went all together.

There was a much wider type of hospitality for refugees – Viennese and Germans who came over. Oxford and indeed national life was greatly advantaged by these often brilliant people who came and settled down and worked in their own niche. I think it must have been very hard for them sometimes, but overall it was a great success. I remember I had two colleagues who were German and deeply anti-Nazi. One of them was a very fierce lady, very frightened lest anything should overtake her and she asked a colleague of mine, I remember, that if there was a German invasion would she take over and conceal the fact that she possessed a copy of Low's cartoons. She felt that that would have been a dangerous possession. The other, who had family back in Germany, spent all the extra coupons she had left in collecting little parcels for them because they were far worse off than we were. The pain she had particularly was that because of her nationality, she was not allowed to do certain forms of public work. However, we found that she could keep bees so we got her some, only to discover that she was allergic to them. She was terribly stung and somebody else had to take over. There was a sort of ironic pathos in that.

Occasionally we had evacuees who came to Oxford. I remember one time there was a party of East End children delivered to us and none of us knew how to treat them. There was one friend of mine who was not at all used to children, standing in the front hall not knowing what to do with a baby that was inverting itself in the way that children do. No harm was done. Nobody dropped it but we felt our insufficiency.

More seriously, the great difference of that period and now, from the point of view of women, was that women perforce had to take the jobs that men did and were found to be able to do them. This loosened up the whole distribution of responsibility in work for women in the University. It would have taken years to accomplish this, both in teaching and on committees, had it not been for the accident of the necessity of the period. There was a much more even sharing of that kind of work. It was inevitable and mercifully there was no regression afterwards. It helped the opening up of the acceptance of women into University life to a very great degree.'

A WARTIME MEDICAL STUDENT

'I first came to Oxford as a medical student in the spring of 1941. The city was full of people – not students, their numbers were greatly decreased in wartime but people from such bodies as the Intelligence Corps evacuated to Oriel College and Chatham House to Balliol College. St Hugh's was a hospital for head injuries, the Examination Schools were, once again, a military hospital, Ruskin College a maternity home for London evacuees and the Canadians had constructed their military hospital which is now the Churchill – and in 1942 the Americans arrived!

Catering was made more difficult by the increase in the population. Living in college, we were spared these problems, but were forever looking for something to improve our diet. A good curry was obtainable at the Taj Mahal in the Turl – what was curried it was better not to enquire! The best dried egg omelette could be found at the Chinese restaurant in an alleyway off The High, strawberries and cream at the Welsh Pony in Gloucester Green, whale meat at the Randolph and, in desperation, a bag of chips in the Cowley Road! Clothes rationing then started and the gloom descended further.

The first sign of things looking up was on a lovely sunny autumn morning in 1942 when the bells pealed out from all over Oxford. They had been silenced since the outbreak of war and were only to

209

be rung as a signal that the German invasion had begun. At least the danger of that seemed to have passed.

June 1944, of course, brought D-Day and I heard the news of the Normandy landings on the early morning wireless bulletin. I was then aware of a continuous droning overhead and looking up saw wave upon wave of bombers, transport planes and planes pulling gliders, a constant stream that never seemed to end.

By that time I was a clinical student at the Radcliffe Infirmary and when I arrived at the hospital that morning it was to find that all the patients well enough had been moved to outlying hospitals and the wards made ready to receive the expected casualties. They soon came pouring in, first to out-patients hall where there were rows and rows of stretchers, each one having several labels attached giving relevant information – a dark red one giving time and dosage of sulphonamide administration, a bright yellow one for penicillin.

This was the first time that penicillin had been used on a large scale. There had been small clinical trials which proved the efficacy of the drug, but only after the Sicily landings had it been used on a large scale and proved itself as a great step forward in the control of sepsis, which had caused more deaths in the First World War than the actual injuries. Professor Florey and his dedicated team had worked for years to produce enough of the drug for just this event, but even so it was only available for combatant forces. The wards rapidly filled up – not only with the wounded, but with flowers. The ladies of Oxford seemed to have stripped their gardens of every bloom and sent them to the hospital to cheer the sick.

Eventually life returned to "normal" and civilians again filled the wards. Casualties had been fewer than expected and the military hospitals were able to cope.

Then came the harsh winter of 1946–7. Rationing was still strictly in force but far worse than the food shortage was that there was very little coal and electricity, with the resultant frozen pipes and sometimes no cooking facilities. On the plus side was the joy of skating – on the frozen Cherwell in the Parks, on Blenheim Lake, but best of all the huge frozen expanse of Port Meadow in the moonlight.

Then came the spring and the floods throughout the Thames valley. Melting snow and rain inundated Days lock and another mark was made high up on the wall at Shillingford Wharf – "Up to this stone the water ran!" Summer 1947 was glorious non-stop sunshine.

Eights Week returned with its College Balls, then Commem. Balls. Clothes rationing was still in force but was somehow overcome and ingenious ways were used to deck oneself out suitably for the occasion. Soon after that I left Oxford, not to return for many years. Things have inevitably changed, but if you search you can still find things to revive happy memories.'

A CHILD'S WAR

Children soon came to treat the war as normal, finding excitement in the sight of Spitfires fresh from the factory and getting used to sharing their schools and their homes with strangers.

AN INDELIBLE MEMORY

'The sky glowed red. Mr Timms lifted me up and said, "That's London burning." The year was 1940, the London blitz was at its height and I was a six year old evacuee in Minster Lovell. My mother had stayed in London and was doing war work, my father was in the Navy.

I'm not sure what Mr Timms' occupation was, but he and his wife lived next door to the school at the top of the hill out of the village. I was fascinated by the fact that the cottage was built on the edge of a steep drop down to a field, consequently all the garden was in front of the house. If you looked out of the back windows, you could see lots of rabbits running about. I think rabbit stew was often on the menu.

I stayed in Minster Lovell for two years, eventually moving (when Mrs Timms' mother was taken ill) into a cottage in the main street, a few doors up from The Black Swan.

Although such a young child, I have some very clear memories of that time.

– The planes from Brize Norton flying so low over the hedges that the pilots in their flying helmets waved to us children. I was terrified of these planes and I didn't know why until my mother told me years later that on a visit to me, a German plane heading for Brize Norton had strafed us and we had had to dive into a ditch.

211

- The marvellous mashed potatoes with chopped raw onions mixed in served up by the Timms' Irish daughter-in-law who lived in the next cottage, which incidentally was the other way round to ours – cottage up on the road, garden at the back.

- The snow of the winter when I was living down in the village, so deep that the villagers dug tunnels up to our shoulders to get up the hill to school.

- In the summer, fishing for tiddlers in the Windrush in the field where the cricket pitch is, paddling about with our dresses tucked into our knickers.

- But, best of all, the ruins. We took our dolls and spent endless hours playing house. My mother was dragged along to the ruins every time she visited. It seemed an enchanted place to me. Imagine my surprise when, in the late 1950s, I went back to Minster Lovell and found that Lovell House was now part of the National Trust and we had to pay to go in.

Unfortunately I was ill twice when I was there, eventually ending up in the Radcliffe Infirmary so in 1942 my mother took me back to London, but Minster Lovell left an indelible memory.'

A PUZZLE

'It was the end of August 1939. I was seven that year and all the family, mother, father, uncles, grandmother and four children were holidaying in two chalets at Highcliffe, Bournemouth. It had been a lovely hot fortnight and the sea was at the bottom of the cliffs and there were lots of open spaces to fly our kites.

On the Friday evening Uncle Ralph, who had not been on holiday with us as he had the village shop in Wolvercote, where we all lived, came to collect my auntie and grandmother to drive them back home overnight. All the grown-ups seemed very anxious at that time and did not seem able to enjoy their holiday. It was a strange atmosphere but we children were not told anything.

It was decided that I too could travel back with Uncle as I could easily sleep in the back against Granny. It was a very long tedious journey as we were only able to use the minimum of car lights. We arrived back in Wolvercote village in the early hours of the morning and I was popped into bed.

When I awoke that Saturday morning and went out into Godstow Road I remember being extremely puzzled. We children in this small village all knew each other as we attended the same school in Upper

Wolvercote. But what were these strange-looking children doing here? They had unusual eyes and very black hair. The village had received its first London evacuees and these were from the Chinese area of Poplar in the East End. I remember asking over and over again, Who were they? Where had they come from? Why? What for? I had never before seen anyone like this.

We all became friends of these children and many of the families stayed in Wolvercote after the war.'

OUR SCHOOLS WERE BULGING

'There was a feeling of unreality about the summer of 1939; would the Prime Minister bring off another Munich settlement or would there be open conflict with Hitler? We went about our lives fearing yet hoping.

The weather was beautiful that year, school holidays came and the Guides camped on the Isle of Wight (a spectacular display of searchlights each night was not reassuring!) but the girls cooked, swam, collected coloured sands and thoroughly enjoyed themselves.

After camp we returned home and waited. The men on reserve had already been recalled to the armed services. Each day the news was more disquieting – Poland invaded on 1st September, then at 11 am on that first Sunday in September our worst fears were confirmed: Sir Neville Chamberlain announced that we were at war with Germany. All teachers were ordered to return to their schools immediately. Back in Oxfordshire we waited to receive the evacuees.

Emergency plans had long been made: first aid training, setting up of rest centres, possible food and petrol rationing, billeting, blackouts and all aspects of air raid precautions as well as the setting up of the LDV (the original Home Guard) with their armbands or ill-fitting uniforms and sticks for rifles.

Then came the evacuees from the East End of London – to our "safe" village (one surrounded by airfields!). I remember two groups, the children and the adults. Over 100 children came to Dorchester as a school with their headmaster and teachers and slotted into their billets with very little trouble. (We had to hastily change one around – the only young unmarried teacher had been allocated to a bachelor schoolmaster's house!)

Accommodation for the adults was an entirely different situation. At 9 pm the billeting officer knocked on our doors to ask if we would go around to help to find more mattresses or airbeds to put in the village hall. At that time the village was without mains water or drainage and electricity had only been available for about ten years, so many houses still had only the free allocation of three lights and one power plug – and many cooked with a coal-fired range or paraffin stove.

I heard of one woman and her mother being taken to one of our older, bigger houses where the gaunt, elderly owner led them along a creaking passage with a flickering candle; it was more than they could take – they fled back to the village hall! A safe haven in the country? That was one of the saddest sights I have ever seen. Rows of desperate unhappy bodies lying on that floor, the only drinking water in a bucket and an inadequate chemical toilet. We were helpless; there just was no more room.

Many returned to London the next morning; as one woman told me, she even whitened her front door step every morning, country ways weren't for her, she'd go back to her home and the possible bombs.

Our schools were bulging. At first the local primary children went to school in the mornings and had long walks in the afternoons while the London children used their building. Later the Londoners were housed in the Old College so all had full-time schooling.

The senior school was for eleven to 14 year olds from the surrounding villages; these also had evacuees, senior children from another part of London, so that too was bulging. At one time we had a "class" of 72, that was in the biggest room where we could fit in that number of seats; other rooms had up to 60.

Our "air-raid shelter" at first was a deep ditch about 150 yards from the school (later we had a brick-built shelter). The woodwork master and some of his senior boys spent the month protecting the windows of all the surrounding schools. Sticky brown paper strips criss-crossed the glass and wooden frames with wire netting were fixed inside (the corpses of several wasps remained there for the next six years!).

We all had to carry our gas masks in little square boxes and sometimes we would read wearing masks. I had another gas mask duty – showing new mothers how to fit their babies into the special baby hood and how to pump the air through.

By the end of the month the village and school had settled into a routine, helped by the perfect weather; but we wondered what was to come.'

THEY WERE EVERYWHERE

'What do I remember? Summer holiday visits before the war; the poplar trees by the bridge, which (to a child) seemed the very essence of Islip. The steam engines coming down the hill, fearsome and noisy

214

monsters and really frightening to a little girl swinging on a gate. I expect they were only on their way to thresh a farmer's corn. Then I remember coming over from Belgium in 1939, saying goodbye to my toys and saving up a book to read when I went back in the autumn, but of course we never did go back. The lovely hot summer days went by and the realization grew that even one's parents were powerless to stop the coming war. I remember the helpless feeling knowing that nothing and nobody could stop it coming.

We had two waves of evacuees in Islip. The first came in, I suppose, autumn 1939 and was mothers and babies and they only stayed for a very short time. I don't think the children can have all been babies as I'm sure I remember hearing about a small boy climbing over a wall and falling into a cucumber frame.

Our main group of evacuees was a school from Bethnal Green. The local billeting officer, a group of villagers and the Guide company met them at the school, to welcome them and to take them to their hosts. All went well to begin with, but I do remember the terrible feeling of helplessness when there were about twelve children left and no one to take them. I remember going into our house and asking my gran to take one or two, but she wouldn't (well, I suppose she hadn't got room as she already had us living there). Of course, eventually places were found for all of them. There followed a somewhat uneasy time; Islip children were completely outnumbered. Evacuees were everywhere, we couldn't even walk over the bridge without being shouted at, but we settled down together eventually. It can't have been very comfortable for them and some had to go to school in the Swan clubroom. The evacuees joined in with the rest of the village in the special money raising weeks for the war effort. I remember we had a target by the post office with a picture of Hitler on it, and the excitement during the week as we tried to raise the allotted amount.

Wartime; what else do I remember – collecting salvage round the village every Saturday morning for years, herb gathering, picking rose hips, shortages, lying in bed at night and thinking life was wartime and it was going on for ever.'

SETTLING IN

'Many evacuees came to Buckland from East Ham, London. Mr Williams, Buckland's headmaster, in 1940 had the challenge of settling the "lost" children. However, with the help of Miss Rouse, the schoolmistress, and Mrs Wright, the carpenter's wife, who made triangular cakes with delicious icing and sang "Happy Birthday" outside the window of the children's homes on their birthdays, life

215

became more fun in the country. Ned Tanner, the road cleaner, was on the receiving end of the more relaxed and settled children who would call out, "Mr Sixpence!". This more often than not provoked the desired reaction from Ned, who gave chase up the road waving a broom after the youngsters.'

SOLDIERS AND THE KING

'Our air raid warning system was a whistle blown by a farmer's son riding round the village on his bicycle. I am not sure what happened if he was working in the fields and could not be contacted! The all clear was the same man riding round ringing a bell.

Our mothers went to first aid classes and several of us children went along too, for them to practise their bandaging on us. Fortunately, their skills were never put to the test in our village. A van came to the village green for us to test our gas masks with tear gas.

The army had taken over one of the big houses in the village and suddenly there was more activity than usual and more soldiers appeared, many just lying asleep on the village green in the peaceful summer sunshine – they had come from Dunkirk. Children asked them for souvenirs and were rewarded with a few French coins, the like of which we had never seen before – they had holes in the middle!

In January 1940 we walked from Kingham school to the railway station where George VI was to leave the train and travel by car to Chipping Norton to review the troops. We were very excited as the train with a shining brass coat of arms on the front drew into the station. After a few minutes the car came by and we could see the King clearly. He was wearing a Field Marshal's uniform. He waved to us and we waved the little Union Jacks we had been given.'

SAVE THE BEAR!

'I was three years old when war was declared in September 1939. One of my earliest memories is that of coming downstairs and seeing two soldiers in the house. They were to be billeted on us for a while. My mother and father told me that I wanted to know where they had come from and why they were here.

I can remember that when the sirens went off at the beginning of the war I was carried by a soldier into next door's air raid shelter, but I wouldn't go unless my sister's battered teddy bear went as well. Apparently I didn't want the Germans to have him!

When I started school at the age of five years in 1941 after Easter, my father had a disc made with my name and address on which I

216

wore round my neck. I also had to take a Mickey Mouse gas mask with me to school, which was Littlemore junior school.'

SPITFIRES AND SKATES

'The day war broke out, as we listened to the radio my mother started to cry; Father tried to explain that we were at war again, but at seven years old I did not understand the importance. My cousin from Brighton was staying, and there was a great rush to get her home; my aunt arrived the next day to take her back.

During the Battle of Britain one lovely sunny Sunday afternoon my father and I were walking round Marlborough Pool and individual Spitfires flew over, quite low. Father commented to me that they were being flown straight into battle from the factories. He had understood a situation that was not admitted until well after the war. I also discovered later that a great number of the ferry pilots were women.

In the run up to D-Day large convoys of army lorries and tanks came through Cassington and along the Eynsham Road. I can remember getting off my bicycle and getting in the ditch whilst tanks passed, much to the amusement of the soldiers. Frequently we had soldiers sitting on our front lawn making tea whilst waiting to continue their journeys; we had eggs, they had corned beef and our mothers would swap eggs for tins of bully beef – all were very satisfied.

I learnt to skate in the winter of 1940–41 on Marlborough Pool. I was given a pair of skates, and as Mother couldn't get a pair of boots they were put onto shoes (probably not a good idea). With Father holding a broom and me hanging on to the handle I learnt to stand up. I was later given a pair of real boots and skates, and when I grew out of those carefully saved my Christmas and birthday money and bought a second-hand pair. We skated for up to six weeks each winter (January to late February) until the 1960s. It was fun as it began to thaw; the ice sort of rippled and if you told Mother then your skates would be taken away and locked up! The weather pattern has so totally changed that this does not happen any more.

Mother was one of the committee who dealt with the evacuees. We ended up with one unfortunate for whom a room could not be found. I was (unwillingly!) turned out of my room to sleep on a mattress on the floor of my parents' room, so that the girl could have my room. Her parents turned up most weekends to see her, and in fact she only stayed about a month. My best friend of those years was the evacuee who lived with my godmother. It was interesting after the war to be taken to London by my godmother to visit Nancy

– she lived not far from St Paul's and it was my first sight of bomb damage, and also a large block of East End flats.

One night that London was bombed my father stood me on the stone table in the garden and showed me a great glow in the sky and told me that was London burning. We heard the fire engines going by, heading for London to help. It was freezing and the firemen must have had a very cold, uncomfortable, long journey.

I went to Witney grammar school in 1941, and there were eight to ten of us going from Cassington. In the blackout we used to collect together to cycle up to Eynsham, making sure we had at least one front light and one rear light between us and then ride in convoy; we were not popular as anyone passing in a car with shielded lights must have had difficulty in seeing us!'

WARTIME SCHOOLING

'I vividly remember going to the town hall in St Aldates, Oxford with my mother and my brother, to be issued with our identity cards. Looking up at those wide, white marble steps, all you could see were families like us – queueing. We joined the line, gradually worked our way to the top, turned right – still queueing – until we reached the Assembly Rooms and a row of desks or tables. I am sure we were there *all* the afternoon – it was all so apparently leisurely and unhurried!

Many schools arrived in Oxford as the London Blitz started and various church halls were taken over by them and temporary desks set up. One (blissful) time we had half-day school, alternating mornings and afternoons with these Londoners.

I was a Catholic and several Catholic schools, including the Convent of the Sacred Heart from Hammersmith, came. My parents seized the opportunity to send me to a convent and I travelled – on my own – by bus to Norham Gardens and joined a handful of children being taught by (it seemd to me) very elderly nuns. This school also used the old Milham Ford School in Cowley Place and the Holywell Music Room (with its stories of underground passages and visits from Handel!). I have clear pictures of lessons in these buildings, but we seemed to spend an enormous amount of time walking from Norham Gardens to Cowley Place and Holywell. The best thing about Norham Gardens was its access to the University Parks and a wonderful game invented by Mother Lillie (Sacred Heart nuns were always called "Mother" followed by their surnames) which we played every afternoon before the afternoon school session.

Most of the schools returned to London when the Blitz was over, and the convent was one of these, so then I became the first "Oxford" girl to go to St Juliana's Convent at Begbroke, which had been evacuated from Bognor Regis. This school stayed – and so did I! Many of the girls at the convent had fathers, sometimes mothers too, in the Forces, and we heard whispers of "D-Day landings" and Arnhem, and as the school was on the main road from the Midlands to Southampton and the coast, we watched the endless convoys travelling past.

At the end of the war the German POWs were working on the new dual-carriageway. The Italian POWs were around as well but I remember them standing around and smiling – not working!'

GROWING UP

'I was not born or brought up in Oxfordshire but came first to stay in the 1930s with my godfather, then curate to St Mary and St John's church in Cowley; his house was almost opposite the Regal Cinema. That was for two years running, 1932 and 1933, and it was a family holiday and included sightseeing in Oxford city, Christ Church and Merton. I can remember especially, drives to the surrounding countryside which were great treats. After that there was a gap until 1937 when I went up to St Hilda's College for three years of hard work, good friends and exploring the surrounding countryside.

As the summer of 1940, with Dunkirk and the disaster of the fall of France, drew on, the war affected my parents' home in Sussex; they could hear the guns, my father died, the house was taken by the army and my mother and the furniture arrived in a removal van through roads crowded by weary troops marching to rest camps on Port Meadow. I can remember waiting for the removal van at the Plain and the endless marching soldiers, for me the first real lesson of war.

My mother went to join her sister who ran a hostel for home students in Woodstock Road and helped her to run it in the face of rationing shortages until 1943. I had a bedroom across the road and my mother shared with her sister. At various times of year there were "home students" and students from other colleges and "evacuees" from the South Coast resorts (South Coast schools came to Oxford and shared accommodation with Oxford schools, St Bees and Eastbourne College shared with St Edward's).

It was an uncomfortable year but good tempered and friendships were made, more varied than usual. The students who were at loose ends soon found something to do to help the war effort. Five of us joined the Women's Land Army as temporary members; gumboots, dungarees, white shirts, a boiling hot summer and the pattern of

219

our various shoulder straps showed white on our shoulders. One week we picked caterpillars off brussels sprout plants, put them in a jam jar until we reached the end of a row, then tipped them out and stood on them – not nice.

We were billeted at Stanton St John and I cannot remember a thing about the lodging except it was where we all foregathered in the evenings. At the beginning, in September those of us who were going to train for reserved occupations eg teaching, house property management and almoning, scattered. I went to London into a charity organisation office, coming home at weekends.

The Blitz began and it was rather traumatic; my time was divided between doing formal training in London and returning to Oxford and helping to find places for individual evacuees from Islington. Wherever we lived, there we took part in whatever activity was required – shopping; cycling down to the gasworks to collect coke for keeping the home fires and hot water going; getting fruit direct from the market; cycling out to Mount Skippett to pick gooseberries; getting apples or whatever fruit was available; buying apples from Miss Bolton at Finstock Manor.'

DOING OUR BIT

We all did our bit, from joining the Home Guard to working in the factories. Some efforts were more unusual, like the Congregational minister who became a "temporary rabbi".

THE HOME GUARD

'The Cassington headquarters of the Home Guard was at The Chequers pub. Ron thought he would get kitted up so he brought a camp bed there to sleep on. Shifts were 11 pm to 1 am, two at a time, 1 am to 3 am and 3 am to 5 am. Ron used to sit up telling a tale or two until first shift returned, then he would go out on the middle shift, and when he returned to get into his bed someone else was already in it, so he never did get a chance to use it.

Roy remembered when there was the call-out when it was thought the country was being invaded. He was not old enough to be given a rifle, but he was rung up and told to go round and call the Home Guard out.

On an exercise they were supposed to capture Manor Farm: Mr Cashmore was the officer, and Tom Hedges the sergeant, so Mr Cashmore set them off up the river and round the back of the farm whilst he went off home for something. A single round was to be fired at the beginning of the exercise and one at the end. When they got to Manor Farm there was no one there, they could have taken it easily. There was no final shot, and when they reached The Chequers the rest of the group were there and it was time for last orders!

There was a barrier on the bypass and on the night of the great call-out it was manned. Two soldiers walking back off leave were challenged, swore roundly and said they would stop there, for it was about the fifteenth time they had been stopped and they were afraid someone would shoot them, so they waited until daylight.

The Home Guard at one time were responsible for looking after the electricity sub station at Yarnton, and some Canadian soldiers stationed at Blenheim threatened to shoot Mr Cashmore one night when he challenged them. They were considered to be a bit wild. They stole one of the Duke's pigs and roasted it. A bit later they took a young steer and the Duke got a bit upset – there were all of us on coupons and the Canadians living well, so the Law went to see them in the early hours of the morning, only to be told if they had been a bit earlier they could have had a piece!

Ernie Pancott was chief ARP officer. He had the siren, a hand-wound box-like thing, and then he would cycle round the village with a whistle for the all clear. The first air raid warning of the war, a few days after the declaration, he was winding it up with one hand and telling everyone to get under cover, "it's a big gas raid".'

'Tom and Dick, taking their nightly rations, checked on for duty at the Home Guard post and then went up the hill to the observation post overlooking Oxford to be manned that night. It was actually an old cattle shed near the hill top which had been completely blacked out and made quite comfortable by experienced old soldiers with a couple of sagging old armchairs, up-turned boxes and a small stove with a plentiful supply of dry firewood. The night was passing in its usual way with a chat and a doze between the regular patrols and look-outs.

When Tom went out he noticed that the little tin chimney was bravely shooting sparks high into the frosty sky, a veritable hill-top beacon! Then to his horror he heard air raid warnings sounding all round. He rushed back to the hut shouting, "For goodness sake put that fire out – Jerry's overhead!" After much argument and frenzied activity they eventually managed to stuff the stovepipe with old sacking.

As the dawn broke two pairs of red-rimmed eyes gazed out of their blackened faces. "I daren't go home like this," groaned Dick, "my missis will kill me!" Tom took him home where his long-suffering wife provided enough hot water to clean them up and lent Dick a clean shirt! No bombs fell on Cowley on that eventful night.'

'Local men at South Leigh were recruited for the Home Guard and twelve to 14 volunteers, later dwindling to a band of six to eight, patrolled the village and surrounding fields in twos, from approximately 11 pm to 5 am. They were not issued with uniforms but each had a gun. The village air raid alarm was fitted to the station and the Home Guard used this as their meeting place, enjoying many a game of cards if their duties were not too onerous!

An Ack-Ack battery was set up near Church Green and the searchlights and guns fascinated the children, as did the soldiers' cookhouse in the vicar's garage!'

'My brother tells how his platoon in the Home Guard at Chadlington were most fortunate in having both the butcher and the baker amongst them. They supplied most of the ingredients of the good fry-ups they had when manning their post, which was at first our shepherd's hut, towed up the main A361 road where they patrolled.'

'The Home Guard took most of my time later in the war when I was company clerk to the Deddington company. This was not without excitement. We worked hard and became very efficient and won a number of cups and competitions.

A Scottish battalion in our area was on the move and our company commander, who was a hop broker and able to get more in the drinks line than most of us, got our sergeants to invite the departing Scottish ones for a party. It was a good one and during the evening we acquired a couple of mortars and suitable ammunition to be ready for any possible invasion. At the end of the war we had some difficulty explaining where it came from!

As we planned to form a Rifle Club we wrote off a few rounds every time we had a shoot and built up a nice little stock. Imagine our horror when the rifles we were offered were withdrawn and the new ones supplied were a different calibre.'

RAIDS AND GAS

'My first memory of the war was hearing Neville Chamberlain making the announcement on the wireless at eleven o'clock on Sunday morning, 3rd September 1939.

My father was digging in the garden and I called him in to listen to it. His face suddenly went grey and haggard, no doubt it brought back memories of the First World War when he fought and was wounded in France.

Soon afterwards, the air raid siren sounded and we heard the drone of an aircraft overhead. Thinking we were already under attack from the air, I dragged my invalid mother away from the windows and pulled the curtains together. A little while afterwards, the all clear sounded, but next day I went out and bought sticky tape to criss-cross over the windows to stop flying glass.

I remember getting up and going out with my father during the night when he was on air raid duty. Everyone in the street had to do their turn of duty and sometimes we were out two or three times during the night. We had to watch out for incendiary bombs being dropped and everybody was issued with a stirrup pump and a tin helmet as well as a gas mask.

I also remember the evacuees being delivered from Oxford railway station in a furniture van. It stopped at each house and asked the householders how many children they could take.

Huge lorries went by our house loaded with damaged aircraft probably being taken to the pressed steel factory for salvage. The factory was then making munitions.

Men and women of 18 years and over were called up to "do their bit". You were exempt if you worked in the munitions factory or were doing work of equal importance to help the war effort. I was on the staff of a wartime nursery looking after children of 18 months to five years while their mothers did war work.

Standing by the Wingfield roundabout at the junction of Windmill Road, The Slade and Old Road in Headington, we threw cigarettes and magazines to the lorry loads of wounded soldiers and airmen as they were brought to the Churchill Hospital. The hospital was used by the Americans during the war and as a Girls' Training Corps cadet in my spare time, we were asked to visit the wounded and put flowers on their lockers beside their beds. I can remember this huge man with thick black hair on his chest suddenly grabbing me as I stood near his bed. I was 17 and it absolutely terrified me!

We were taught aircraft recognition, first aid, and how to recognize the smell of different gases by their association with other smells, such as onions, geraniums etc, and we had to meet at East Oxford school in Cowley Road to undergo a gas training test. After putting on our gas masks and seeing that they fitted correctly we were led into a "gas chamber". I can remember it being dimly lit and the walls were of white tiles. We had to stay in there for about ten minutes, breathing and making rude noises as the air escaped from the sides of the masks. It was quite frightening as we fully believed that the room was full of poisonous gas. Only recently have I come to the conclusion that that was what we were supposed to have believed!

I met my husband at one of the ATC dances and from then until the time that he was called up into the army, we danced to Reg Crowhurst and his Rhythmic Serenaders at the Holyoake Hall in Headington, Stan Rogers and the Blue Star Players at the Carfax Assembly Rooms and Eddie Turton and his Band at The Forum in High Street. How our present generation have missed out by not sharing our privilege in being able to listen to and dance to their beautiful music!'

THE ALUMINIUM FACTORY

'During the war, Vera and her sister Nancy went to work at the Northern Aluminium factory at Banbury. Neither of them had ever done such heavy work before, and at first they found it very hard, particularly on the arms and shoulders. At times there were complaints that the work of lifting the aluminium sheets was too hard for women. But most of them got used to it in time. For Vera, the worst part of the work was repeating the same jobs over and over again, which she found boring, whilst for Nancy it was the shift work which she disliked. The factory operated continuously, working throughout 24 hours. Women were bussed in from the surrounding countryside in order to keep the production lines rolling. These buses became popular with people from neighbouring villages, as they linked areas which had never had a bus service before.

The aluminium arrived at the factory in ingots, which were melted down into sheets and then stretched into the required length and thickness. Vera worked in the mill where the sheets were stretched. Most of the chargehands were men, but some of the supervisors were women. Vera could only remember one case of discontent amongst the girls she worked with; this was when the woman supervisor, who no one liked, complained that they were lingering too long on their breaks. The girls grumbled that they were being treated like schoolchildren. They were told, "If you behave like schoolchildren, then you will be treated like schoolchildren."

Nancy remembers that she eventually worked on the circle mill where the aluminium was cut into different sized circles, which were then transported to another factory to be manufactured into articles to help the war effort. No finished articles were made at Banbury. In this part of the factory there was a woman chargehand besides two men. Nancy enjoyed the work in the circle mill, as it was much more pleasant work.

Towards the end of the war, Nancy could remember one of the other girls arranging an outing to the theatre in London. This was considered a great adventure, as it was the first time some of them had been to a London theatre. They finished work at six o'clock in the morning, after working on the night shift. They immediately caught an early train to London, and on arrival the group made for Selfridges. Nancy remembers going to a Lyon's Corner House where they had a meal, and then going on to a matinee at the Palladium, where they saw a variety show. They caught an evening train back to Banbury, with Nancy having to walk up to Banbury Cross, where she caught the ten o'clock works bus back to Enstone.

Although Vera ended her war work in 1946, as soon as she was offered her old job back, Nancy was happy to go on working at the "Allie" until 1948, when the bus service was stopped and she therefore had no means of travelling daily to Banbury from Enstone.'

JOINING UP

'The end of 1938 the news from Germany was very bad and we knew war was coming. Leaflets were in various post offices asking women to volunteer for war services. I signed one of these leaflets and posted it to the Headquarters, Officers' Training Centre, Manor Road, Oxford. A few days later I received a letter telling me to report, which I duly did at 7.30 pm the following Thursday. There was quite a gathering of us. The Duchess of Marlborough was in charge. We reported each Thursday and learned about military procedure, hygiene, etc. Then one Thursday we were issued with uniforms: shirt, tie, jacket, skirt, cap, shoulder flash "1st Oxfordshire" and horrible "pea green stockings, thick", and told to wear the uniform to the next meeting. We caused great interest and some amusement walking through Oxford. In February 1939 the Auxiliary Territorial Service was formed (the ATS).

About this time young men were told to register for the army, or the coal mines (these were called the Bevan Boys). As my trade was clerk/shorthand typist I was asked to report to Manor Road HQ to complete the enrolment form for each man joining the army.

In July 1939 we went to Tidworth on Salisbury Plain for a week's training. We camped under canvas and there were ATS from all parts of the country, 1,000 of us. We watched military manoeuvres, cooking in field kitchens, and a demonstration of RADAR (which was very hush-hush at that time). The main thing I remember was rain, and did it rain!

One evening I went to the Ritz cinema in George Street, Oxford. After the main film a message came on the screen asking for people to go to the Oxford town hall after the cinema closed, to pack gas masks. Many of us went to the town hall. In the main hall we sat on the floor, in front of us a pile of gas masks and small square boxes. We packed the mask face down in the box, folded in the straps so the box could be closed, and put them in piles. As we finished one lot another lot was put in front of us. Larry Adler was playing at the New Theatre, George Street, Oxford (now the Apollo). He brought his company with him and they played to us the whole night. I did not get home until well after midnight.

September 1939 war was declared and I was officially called up. I was told to report to a house in South Parks Road, Oxford. I walked up to the front door and was met by a sergeant in the Royal Army Medical Corps, and taken downstairs to the kitchen in the basement. On the kitchen table was a very old typewriter and I used the kitchen range as a filing cabinet. I stayed with the RAMC until the end of October 1939.

The 1st Oxfordshire Platoon was posted to Tidworth at the end of

The mothers of Newman Road, Littlemore got together to give the children a treat in one of the many street parties held in 1946 to celebrate victory.

October 1939. We were billeted in Bhurtpore Barracks, but there was no hot water. Large boilers were put outside and fires lit under them, to heat water for us, but when we went to get hot water for washing the troops in the next block had helped themselves. We were then moved to the other end of Tidworth to old married quarter houses, Mooltan Barracks. They were grim, not dirty but very dowdy. Lord Nuffield heard about this. He sent us ten shillings each to spend how we liked to brighten up our rooms. I bought some pretty curtains to hang inside the thick blackout ones, and cream paint. I painted all the woodwork and cupboards cream.

We stayed here until early 1942 when the Americans came and took over Southern Command. The platoon was posted to Catterick Camp, Yorkshire. I was demobbed June 1945, still with the 1st Oxfordshire ATS.'

A TEMPORARY RABBI

'The war changed our lives and we had to get used to having evacuees in our village and our homes. At the outbreak of war we were living at Peppard where my father, Thomas Wilson, was minister of the Congregational church. Our village received a large number of Jews as evacuees on 3rd September 1939; we had four billeted on us at The Manse.

They were concerned about their worship on the Sabbath and my father offered them the use of our church on a Saturday afternoon. Realising they were without a leader, he said he would conduct the services provided the necessary permission was granted from the Chief Rabbi and service books obtained. For several months he was a temporary rabbi and conducted their services, including the special service on the Day of Atonement. One evacuee is still a very dear friend and on my father's death in 1976 he wrote: "I well remember the occasion when I first met your family so many years ago and all that your parents did to help us along." '

HIGH DAYS & HOLIDAYS

MAKING OUR OWN ENTERTAINMENT

From whist drives to cricket matches, libraries to brass bands, we found our entertainment locally – and what a fund of home-grown talent there was in even the smallest village (not to mention the support given by those essential tea makers!). Those, of course, were the days before television (and before radio), and visits to the cinema were great treats.

ENTERTAINING OURSELVES

'People had to make their own entertainment. Whist drives were very popular, especially towards Christmas when poultry drives were held and it was possible to win your Christmas dinner if you were lucky. Fetes were held in the summer, usually in the gardens of the manor, the old rectory, the Close or in suitable fields. Bowling for the pig was a great attraction, at a time when that useful animal was usually kept. A village feast was held in August in the paddock of the Three Horseshoes pub.

The church is dedicated to St Lawrence whose festival is 10th August. This was regarded as a holiday for the men of Appleton. Another event was the parade of the local order of the Royal and Ancient Order of Buffalo through the village at Whitsun, a peony being obligatory for the top of the banner. This also culminated in a feast at the Three Horseshoes.

At one time there was a village band, and this was revived in the late 1930s by the Boy Scouts. Alas, the band and the Boy Scouts have now gone.

At the Silver Jubilee of George V an oak tree was planted at the war memorial, and has grown into majestic proportions. A tea party for schoolchildren was held in the Church Road for the coronations of George VI and for Elizabeth II.

During the 1930s, the wireless set came into most homes which provided a new source of entertainment.

There was no special bonfire celebration though the letting off of fireworks in the street was a great pastime for the older boys.

Penny hop dances were held in a wooden hut erected after the First World War on a piece of land known as The Pound. However, by the early 1930s a village hall was built on this land. Every villager contributed at least sixpence a week for a brick. In this new village hall the WI, formed in 1926, was able to hold its meetings and folk dance sessions, whist drives, dances, concerts, boys club, Scouts and Guides could now function. It soon became a focal point of village life. The hall has been brought up to date and is a well run and attractive meeting place. Two cricket and football teams were established in the early 1900s and in spite of many vicissitudes, there is still a village football and cricket team.

Although it may not be considered perhaps as an amusing pastime, the men took immense pride in their allotments of which there were about three sites. These allotments were an important part of the village economy, not just for day to day vegetables but for main crop potatoes and root crops to see the family through the winter. The root crops were stored in a clamp, a pit dug out about two spits deep lined with straw and earth mounded on top to make it frost free. It was opened only when the weather was mild. One elderly allotment holder who owned several plots, grew horseradish for Coopers factory at Oxford and would have a big hip bath on wheels in which he collected horse dung from the roads.'

'The villagers of Great Rollright made their own entertainment by whist drives, penny hops and concerts in the village school until the village hall was built on land belonging to the manor and on a long lease at a peppercorn rent. The money was raised by public subscription and the hall built as a labour of love after a hard day's work.

Small boys liked to stand at the door of the Unicorn Inn to watch the men play darts because they were often given a halfpenny for cider, and later they would buy a "puff" of a cigarette from the lady in the off licence!

There was a Boy Scout troop run by the local pheasant farmer, and the village also maintained a cricket team and a football team, both now sadly gone.'

PLAYS, CINEMA AND RADIO

'At the village hall at Bampton there were cinema shows on Saturday evenings. I used to badger my mother to let me spend my sixpence going there. Unfortunately they showed serials, so it meant going each Saturday to follow the sequel! We sat on benches.

Some Saturday evenings there were village hops at the same hall which also cost sixpence. There to the sounds of a piano we danced the Military Two Step, the Palais Glide, the Dashing White Sergeant, the foxtrot and the waltz. I also belonged to a folk dance society run by Mr Francis Shergold, held in the dining hall of the school.

Sometimes a portable theatre set up in Lavendar Square. It was run by a family called Wright, and usually stayed six weeks. I used to play the piano for them at the age of 14 and I received two shillings and sixpence a week. They performed plays such as *Murder in the Red Barn*. They told me they had played at the Queen's Theatre, Dublin.'

'In the days before radio or television our amusement was our gramophone, and a visit to the pictures in Abingdon. The best seats cost ninepence and we could buy three bars of Cadbury's chocolate for sixpence from the shop next door.'

'The local dramatic society entertained in Farmoor village hall with plays, often quite ambitious works such as *The Importance of Being Earnest*. There were also variety shows and occasionally a film show. It was here on an ancient newsreel I saw Neville Chamberlain returning from Munich waving that famous piece of paper. There were two cinemas in Chipping Norton and they had shows six days a week and later seven, usually changing the programme midweek. Going to the pictures was the thing to do on a Saturday.'

Regulars of The Craven Arms at Uffington enjoying their annual outing. The driver also seems determined to enjoy himself!

232

'When I was 13 years old, the headmaster of Wheatley Church of England school, Rees Leyshon, and his daughter Winifred who was a pioneer of X-rays, helped me to make the first wireless set in Wheatley.

All the pieces had to be hand made in school so I missed a lot of lessons. The set comprised 120 leclanche cells all linked together and positioned around the room to provide power to run the wireless.

A cell was a stone jam jar filled with acid and with a lead connector to each. Every day they had to be tested for specific gravity and distilled water added. Aerials and panels were made to house the valves etc. When the loudspeakers were introduced, people came from far and wide to listen in wonderment!

One day, while working on the set, the hounds came into Avery's wood yard so I went with some friends to watch the hunt, not knowing that the headmaster was watching through binoculars. This resulted in a stroke of the cane on Monday morning!'

'The Sterling cinema at Kidlington was popular with Combe folk and buses went every Tuesday, Thursday and Sunday virtually from door to door, though some families never allowed cinema visits on a Sunday. Sometimes films would come to the village and be shown in the schoolroom.

The church choir was well supported and a popular pastime. There was a Combe Concert Party, organised by Wilf Huckins, which entertained round the villages with singing, monologues and music. He would write and produce pantomimes for his travelling group.'

ALL SORTS OF OCCASIONS

'The VC Gallery in Wantage had been the Corn Exchange and was adapted to hold a collection of paintings given to the town by Lord Wantage. They all depicted soldiers winning their VCs in the Crimean War and were displayed on the walls.

A lovely sprung floor was laid for dancing and the VC was used for all sorts of occasions. There was a chrysanthemum show each autumn, a Guides' bazaar in December, and the church had a parish party annually with entertainment provided by local talent. Hospital balls were held to raise money to pay for the new hospital, and lots of other dances. I was allowed to go to them now and then when I was about 16. There was always a crowd of men or youths standing at one end of the hall, looking on, mostly smoking, and a blue haze of smoke drifted over the hall.

As a memorial to those lost in the First World War a local

solicitor, Mr Ormond, presented about ten acres of land to the town as a recreation ground in about 1925. Swings and maypoles were provided for the children, and tennis courts for the adults. As children, we spent hours there playing.'

OPENING A LIBRARY

'An extract from the Ipsden parish magazine in 1910 gives the following information:

> "We are glad to announce that a Lending Library is to be opened at Ipsden chapel on Monday May 9th. By the kindness of Mr Reader and others nearly 70 books have been got together, suited to all classes of readers. Miss Wear has kindly consented to act as Librarian and will be in attendance each Monday from 5.30–6.30. The library will also be open on Monday evenings for men, when Mr Greenaway will be in charge.
>
> All using the Library will pay 1d per month or 1/- per year. The money thus raised will, after paying expenses, be devoted to the purchase of new books. Only one book may be taken at one time by each subscriber, but may be changed every week. Other rules will be put up where the books are kept. We hope the Library will be well used. If it is, no doubt fresh books will be forthcoming." '

SPORTS FOR ALL

'There were football and cricket teams at Wittenham. In summer cricket teams from the Oxford colleges would come down for all-day matches. They would have lunch at The Plough and then afterwards there would be a tea put on by the village team's wives.'

'Between the wars, and even during the Second World War, Weston on the Green had a tennis club which played regular matches against neighbouring towns and villages. Westfield Farm, Oxford House and Manor Cottage had tennis courts, all grass courts but such fun to play on (if one knew the hazards of one's home court it was easier to win points!). A court at Newbridge Farm was revived during the war and when the BBC were at the Manor, villagers were still able to use the hard courts there. Weston also had a flourishing ladies' hockey club, a football club which won a shield, and bowls were also played in the village.'

'In Bix there is a field which is a relic of the old strip cultivation system and is owned in common by the landowners who adjoin it.

Part of this was given over by them as a cricket ground and cricket still flourishes, though it is difficult to get an entire team from the village. Part of the common field was the rector's glebe, and when a new church was built in 1875, it was on this part of the field. The rector in 1912 raised money to build a church hall on part of the field and I was told by an old resident that the children at the village school used to take a penny a week to help pay for it.'

'The village cricket team played on my grandfather's field, using the hay barn as the changing room, and sitting on bales of hay for tea. In those days my mother and I made the tea under difficulties, using an old oil stove. It was a far cry from our modern pavilion at Gallowstree Common – to say nothing of the beautifully mown pitch and surrounding outfield!'

MAKING THE TEAS

'The Islip Cricket Club had asked the Women's Institute if they would be willing to provide the teas at home games in May 1920. This was no mean task as the cricket field was a good walk outside the village, across railway lines and fields, often wet and muddy. A pavilion provided shelter for the tea makers, 22 players, umpires and scorers. Water had to be carried from a spring about 200 yards away. At first this was done by women, but the players did it later, requested by the ladies! The water was heated on primus stoves, the sandwiches were butter and paste mixed together and spread on white bread, made by the local baker, who also provided the seed dough cake and doughnuts, much beloved of the college undergraduates who made up many of the visiting teams. When the tea had been served to the hungry players the washing up had to be done on the table previously used to serve the tea, the water thrown away, the crockery packed away, then the walk home. These teas went on until the cricket pitch was moved into the village, the war came and cricket was abandoned for the duration.

During the period between the wars, other forms of catering took place. Parish teas were held to celebrate the feast of St Nicholas. There was a supper for the grown-ups, with entertainment, followed next day by tea for the children. These were held in the tithe barn in the middle of the village. Tables, benches and crockery were all there, but the heating for the large room had to be imported. Oil heaters had to be collected, filled with paraffin, then stood around to provide background heat. The water collected from the well across the road was heated on an old open grate in large kettles. When the washing up was finished the water was thrown away into the road, choosing the right moment to avoid swilling the passers-by!

The food for the children included jam sandwiches, iced sponge cake, doughnuts and Chelsea buns. The drink served in a large enamel jug was a mixture of milky, sugared tea. The children brought their own mugs and tea was followed by local entertainment. I remember Robert Graves singing a song which ended "if you want any more you must sing it yourself". As a small child I thought it rather rude of him! During the years that he lived in Islip he was writing *Goodbye to all that*.

Another great occasion was the celebration for the coronation of George VI in 1937, when the school playground was used and everyone sat down to a cold meat meal. Again the crockery, tables and chairs, and everything used for a meal of this size had to be taken to the venue by voluntary labour. But at least water was by now laid on, and electricity in the village helped.'

ROYAL OCCASIONS

Jubilees and coronations were celebrated with enthusiasm through-out the county, though the weather has not always been kind. We all did our bit to make the street parties and organised sports and games a memorable occasion.

POURING WITH RAIN

'I have vivid memories of being taken to a firework display at South Park, Headington to mark the occasion of the Silver Jubilee of George V in 1935. It was pouring with rain so we had to sit in the car at the bottom of Headington Hill to watch the fireworks. I was only a small child at the time but remember seeing the figures of the King and Queen lit up in the sky as the fireworks exploded.'

TEAS AND STREET PARTIES

'George V and Queen Mary's Silver Jubilee was celebrated at Dry Leas in Henley when there was a sports day and all the schoolchildren had tea in a big marquee. Much the same kind of thing, as well as street parties took place to celebrate George VI's coronation. To celebrate the present Queen's coronation, the WI planted a chestnut tree near the village hall. It is still there but is very slow growing.

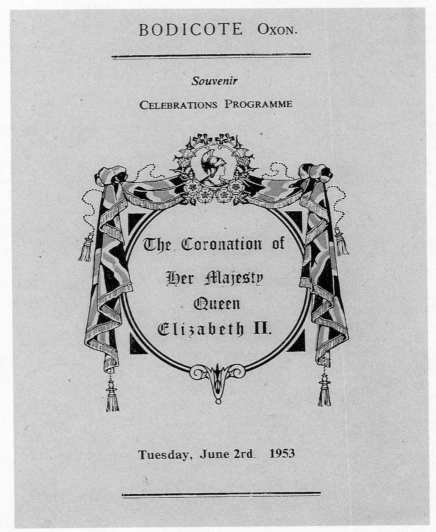

BODICOTE Oxon.

Souvenir

CELEBRATIONS PROGRAMME

The Coronation of

Her Majesty

Queen

Elizabeth II.

Tuesday, June 2rd. 1953

Bodicote's programme of events in 1953, just one of the many celebrations held on Coronation Day across Oxfordshire.

This area has had its share of visits by royalty. Queen Mary was well known as an antiques collector, and used to visit "Teddy" Giles' antiques shop in Henley quite often, as she had a friend, the Marquise d'Hautpoul who lived nearby.

John Piper lived very near the village and he was visited by Queen Elizabeth, the Queen Mother. In addition, the regatta has had many royal prize presenters, including the Queen (as Princess Elizabeth), the Duke of York and Princess Grace of Monaco. Princess Margaret planted the first of an avenue of turkey oaks along the Fairmile in 1953.'

ON THE GREASY POLE

'Bampton celebrated George V's Jubilee in the grounds of the Grange. Captain Gough, the owner, gave a huge party. There was a greasy pole over the river on which the men fought with pillows, a greasy pole to be climbed, and sports for the children. All the food and beer was free and each child was given a Jubilee mug.'

SPORTS AND POTATOES

'To mark the celebrations for the coronation of George VI in 1937, Ducklington held sports in the afternoon – running, high jump, egg and spoon, sack race, tug of war, slow cycle race etc. Needless to say, a great feast followed. I remember peeling mountains of potatoes the day before – and again on the actual day. The peeled potatoes had been stored in water in galvanised baths and each potato touching the metal was discoloured with black patches.

In 1953 the coronation of Queen Elizabeth was celebrated by streets or small areas of people getting together, rather than collections of all the parishioners.'

BOWLING THE FIRST BALL

'Combe recreation ground, set in beautiful surroundings between chapel and cottages and backed by cornfields and a view across the Evenlode valley to the Berkshire Downs, was the setting for a visit by HRH the Duke of Edinburgh in July 1949, when he officially opened the playing field in his capacity as president of the Playing Fields Association. There was a cricket match between a combined Oxford University team and a county players team, the Duke bowling the first ball. The Duke lunched with worthies at the Old Farm House and the party included Combe football and cricket team captains of the day. They were soon put at ease when the Duke helped himself

238

The Empire Day parade at Kingham in 1928.

to a handful of crisps as he arrived at the luncheon table! The Duke also planted a tree at the front of the sports field to mark the occasion of his visit.'

IT WAS WONDERFUL!

'A vivid memory is of Coronation Day in 1953. We lived opposite a large recreation ground and there was a carnival organised. My mother dressed me in red, white and blue crepe paper ruffles, all around me in layers attached to a petticoat, and the same crepe paper layers round a circular piece of cardboard for a hat. I thought it was all wonderful!'

CELEBRATIONS THROUGH THE YEAR

Every year we looked forward to the feasts and festivals that were so much part of our lives, from Easter to Christmas celebrations.

ST VALENTINE'S DAY

'When I first came to live in Chipping Norton in 1932, it was the custom for young schoolchildren to serenade the shopkeepers before going to school on St Valentine's Day.

The shopkeepers heated up a shovel on which was a handful of coppers, mostly halfpennies. The children (all boys) gathered outside and sang,

> "Please to be my Valentine,
> I'll be yours if you'll be mine."

The shopkeeper then stood in the doorway and tossed out the hot coins, for which the boys scrabbled on the ground, often getting blistered fingers in the process. I don't know when the tradition started, but it continued until the 1950s. Perhaps the reason it died out may have been that the shops were no longer individually owned, but were part of larger companies – or maybe the children were more affluent and one or two coppers were insufficient incentive. Both my boys remember taking part and both suffered blisters.'

SPRING DELIGHTS

'My grandmother told me a rhyme for Shrove Tuesday –

> Shrove Tuesday, Shrove Tuesday,
> Poor Jack went to plough,
> His mother made pancakes and didn't know how.
> She tossed them, she turned them, and made them all black,
> She peppered them over and poisoned poor Jack.'

'On Shrove Tuesday and May Day in the 1920s we would go to Gundry's brewery yard in Oxford and be given a penny each. We spent this on sweets!'

'Rumour has it that the people of Finmere were a greedy lot, so Shrove Tuesday was quite a feast, all gorging pancakes. At midday the church bell rang out, "Turn, turn, the pancakes burn"! An inter-Women's Institute pancake race was organised in the 1950s but was abandoned through lack of entries. Was it because we always won?'

'Easter always meant something new to wear to the church service on Easter Sunday (if you didn't the birds would mess on you!) and a chocolate egg in a novelty eggcup.'

'Boat Race Day always used to be celebrated in Thame with children wearing the dark blue favours which were on sale at Castle's to show support for Oxford.'

'On Mothering Sunday all the girls who were in service would go home to their families.'

MAY DAY MEMORIES

'The evening before May Day at Combe, children with their mothers would explore the woods and meadows to pick primroses, bluebells and cowslips, armfuls of them as they were not protected flowers in those days. These would be made up into posies and many hours would be spent transforming the old village invalid carriage into a bower of flowers, covering the carriage with a canopy.

The children would rise early on May Day and set off for school wearing old-fashioned smocks, their posies set upon sticks which they could hold aloft. The May Queen, dressed in white for the occasion and with flowers in her hair, would be drawn around the village in her carriage by the other children. Not a lane or cottage would be missed on their parade through the village, often followed by mothers and babies, to listen to the sweet young voices singing their springtime songs – *Come lasses and lads, Now is the month of May, Amo, amas I love a lass.*

The children would have the afternoon off school and return at teatime for a party, followed by the crowning of the Queen on the village green before a large crowd who were then entertained with dancing around the maypole, intricate weaving in and out to form single plait, double plait, barbers pole etc.'

241

Maypole dancing was a popular part of the May Day celebrations. Here the pupils of SS Mary & John school at Oxford pose for the camera in the 1920s.

'May Day was a big occasion in the year at Great Rollright when a girl was crowned May Queen and with her King (uncrowned) and four attendants, led the maypole dancing on the village green before all the children toured the village on a farm cart carrying garlands of flowers.'

'For May Day at Studley we made garlands of spring flowers by tying on and weaving the stems of flowers into an old bicycle wheel, so that the wheel was completely covered. If we had no wheel we made a star shape with crossed sticks. The flowers were put on at the very last minute to keep the garland fresh looking. We used white bells, bluebells, polyanthus, wallflowers etc. We went round the houses and sang –

> We've come to visit you because
> It is the first of May
> We've come to show our garland
> Because it is May Day.

The money we received was divided between us and was usually spent on sweets. You could buy a lot for a penny then.

The young men of the village often used the local flowers as an excuse to get the girls to go for walks with them at this time of the year. They would say "Have you been bluebelling yet in Blackwaters Woods?" or "Let's go kingcupping down by the brooks?" '

'May Day in Oxford in the late 1920s early 1930s went something like this.

"5.00 am   Got up on a fine cool summer morning and dressed myself in a summer dress and blazer with ginger nuts in my pocket.

5.30 am   Arrived at Magdalen Bridge – noticed a few people strolling back and forth and children collecting for charities such as the Nazareth Homes, Barnados and Sunshine Homes. Huge garlands made of wild flowers were set in each niche of the bridge. Jimmy Dingle, the board man resplendent as ever in his black tailed suit, spotless white shirt, bow tie, spats, gloves and topper exhorted everyone to give generously.

6.00 am   A sudden hush, as above the mist angelic voices floated down from Magdalen Tower. Everyone was spellbound. The May Day hymn was sung.

6.10 am   Morris dancing in Radcliffe Square, then home to breakfast. Undergraduates in punts and rowing boats cruised gently under the bridge eating from their splendid hampers.

7.30 am   After breakfast a stroll through the fields by Iffley Lock to search for snakesheads (fritillaries).

3.30 pm   A ceremonial crowning of the May Queen at a school near St Clements where all the participants were dressed in white and decorated with ribbons and lace. I was quite entranced!" '

'May Day at Thame used to see the crowning of a Queen, garlands being paraded round the streets and the chanting of "Please to see my garland because it's the first of May. Give me a penny then I will go away." Maypole dancing was a great favourite with the children at the local primary school.'

'On May Day at Fritwell we went along to school early to deck the may garland (always with a Crown of Pearls around the top), then to church for a short service and the crowning of the King and Queen. We sang a May song at every house, the King and Queen kissed, and money was collected in a tin. Back to school for a scrumptious tea prepared by the "mum", after which we danced round the maypole. The money was shared by all the children, the King and Queen getting slightly more. Such a happy day.'

FAIRS AND FEAST DAYS

'Combe Feast was related to St Lawrence's day, which is 10th August. On the 10th August or the first Sunday after the 10th there was the usual service at the church and then at 7.30 pm there would be an open air service on the corner of the village green. Many people from neighbouring Stonesfield, Hanborough and North Leigh would walk to Combe for this occasion to meet up with friends and relatives. In the early hours of Combe Feast Sunday morning people would hear the rumbling noise of the fair arriving. As soon as the children were up, and often without stopping for breakfast, they would be at the green to watch the dodgems and swinging boats being put up. Every available space on the green would be taken up with rides, sideshows or their caravans.

On the Monday and Tuesday evenings people would visit Combe again for all the fun of the fair. Two things that seem to have gone with the times are the water squirts and the balls on elastic. Prizes used to include tortoises, budgerigars, canaries and goldfish.

Combe, being well known for playing cricket, always had special matches on the Monday and Tuesday of Combe Feast week. The players arranged their annual holiday for that week so that they could play.'

'From an early age I can remember the excitement of our yearly Hanney Feast, this being the second Sunday in August. Lots of us children gathered at the village green to await Harry Barnard and his fair arriving at about four o'clock. There were swinging boats, roundabouts, coconut shies, roll-a-ball, and stalls selling toffee apples, home-made sweets and penny water pistols. This went on for a week and Saturday night was when families came to the fair and to the pubs.'

'The feast day at Wittenham was a big celebration. There was a procession from the cross to the church for the service. All the showmen would be waiting just outside the village until four o'clock when they were allowed to come and set up. There was a sweet stall where sweets were actually made, swingboats, roundabouts (pulled by a horse) and donkey rides. We used to have two days holiday from school.'

'The Hatwell family were a traditional fairground family, of Cassington. All their equipment was kept in the field alongside the house, where they lived in the winter. One was a skilled painter, decorating the rides. They lived in summer in a superb traditional showman's

244

caravan. It was recognised that they paid all their bills with small change.

Cassington Feast, on St Peter's day on 29th June was fairtime. On the Sunday the showmen would line up on the Yarnton Road and the Eynsham Road, waiting for the two o'clock deadline. While waiting they would come and drop poles where they wanted their pitch, and then someone would come along and move them, and there would be fights over this in The Red Lion, the pub on the green. As well as the rides there were donkeys, and they were trained to go only so far, you could never get a longer ride as they knew just where to turn and come back.

The occupants of Cassington almshouses at Goring were always brought to the feast. They were all issued with a uniform.

The other highlight of the feast was the church fete. In some families it was the tradition that members from neighbouring villages would collect at one house for tea and then enjoy a visit to one of the local pubs and the fair.'

'The village fete used to take place in Sandford Field at Bampton. There was a fancy dress show on ponies in the far field, a greasy pole, and bowling for the pig. George Bishop was very good at keeping his balance on the greasy pole, whacking the village youths and successfully unseating them.

Bampton Fair was a horse fair and dealers used to tie their animals to iron rings in the walls along Bridge Street. They frequented the public house called The Horse and Groom. Opposite the pub the houses had fenced gardens and I would steal away from home, hide behind the laurel bushes in one of these gardens and listen to the drunken dealers swearing at each other. Mother would come looking for me, wearing her old ragged coat, which was a great embarrassment. I managed to do this for four consecutive years, although I nearly gave myself away once or twice by asking, "What does xxxx mean?" "Wherever did you hear that?" my mother would ask.'

'Three fairs, in May, September and October, were (and still are) held in the Market Place at Wantage. There were roundabouts – gallopers and waltzers, chairoplanes (which were rather daring and prone to accidents so later banned), coconut shies, a rifle range, hoop-la and various other amusements. The stall we enjoyed very much was the "Jumbo" stall run by two Wantage women from a "fair" family. They would make the Jumbos on the stall – throw the sugar mixture over a shiny hook above eye level and pull it, looking almost like a skein of wool, then when sufficiently worked, cut it up into large humbugs which we held in a piece of waxed paper and licked for ages, good value for money.'

COWLEY FAIR AND CARNIVAL

'The villagers always looked forward to the fair, which came every year. We saved our pennies in a box so that we could ride on the roundabout horses. Skipping over to this particular ride, I would pull at my mother's skirt to make her hurry along so that I could climb up on one of the horses. Round and round it would go and I would wave to her as it came round to where she was standing. The music came from the centre, a kind of musical box playing organ music. For this ride we would have paid threepence.

At the coconut shies, it was very hard to knock a coconut off; the fair people certainly had a way of sticking them on a cup-stand, ready to be knocked off with wooden balls, six for a shilling. An old man had a stall with prizes and called it "Penny a Pull". It was a lever which when pulled catapulted a ball into a hole which was numbered to a particular prize. He used to shout, "Come on, na! penny a pull, penny a pull!" Then came the time for candy-floss on a stick. It just melted away with each bite and was very sweet tasting. We would purchase a "tiddling stick" and the friend who passed by used to get a tickle around the face, or on the head. It was made of feathers, almost like the feather mops of today.

The fair stayed with us for three days and it seemed so quiet after the fair people had left, but there was always next year to look forward to!

Each year we had a carnival and a Queen was chosen at a dance in the village hall. It was a great day with people taking part on the floats or individually and awarded prizes for the best one. In the beginning the parade was led round the village by a drum and fife band attached to the Scouts of the village. They have been replaced by other musical bands now and one I remember was a Scottish band with their bagpipes. What a grand sight they made, their sporrans swinging as they marched in front of the parade.

There would be a pram race calling at quite a few public houses en route. In each one the competitors had to down a pint of beer then continue to run to the next one, until they reached the last one before the parade started. What a laugh that was, because they were all men who took part and they dressed up in women's clothes and the one being pushed in the pram would have a baby's bonnet on and a dummy in his mouth! By the time they had finished the course some would be pushing their pram so fast, they were coming round corners on two wheels, staggering a little under the influence of the ale they had supped.

Yes, Carnival Day was very colourful. The church held a flower festival which added pleasure to the day.'

CLUB DAYS

'A big day in Oxfordshire villages which everyone looked forward to was the Club Day. It began with the Ancient Order of Foresters going to church. There was usually a band, and the whole village turned out to watch the procession, as the men returned from church and then went off to have lunch. During this time the band played outside the houses.

For the children of the village the day now began in earnest. The day before, they had all gathered at the school playground gates, to watch the fairground people pull into a field in the centre of the village. Now they all made for the field, where the swings and roundabouts had been erected. The children had saved up their money in anticipation, but they only took coppers. Apart from the rides, the main attractions were coconut shies, and hoop-la stalls. But what they seemed to remember best were the stalls where they bought "squibs", small metal tubes which were filled with water. The children chased each other with these squibs and ended up wet through. Although the boys tried to put the "squibs" down the girls' dresses, it was only done for "a bit of fun"!'

'We had Enstone Club the last Thursday in May. A silver band led the procession to church at ten o'clock and we attended the service, after the band had played at various places in the village. We had a fair in Rods Close, and the band played, then it moved into the parish hall for a dance at night.'

'After we moved to Stanton in 1910 the two great days of the year were the village feast which was held the first Monday and Tuesday in July. These days were holidays, and they were run by the two Friendly Societies; one day was for the local organisation and the other the Ancient Order of Foresters. These were clubs that workers belonged to and which paid out sick benefits etc. before the National Health Service.

The Oakley Brass Band was hired on the Monday and began to play outside the pub about 10.30 am and met the club members, who marched to church led by their banner, a very colourful flag carried by one man. Most of the parish went to the service where the hymns were sung with much fervour. Afterwards the members and

247

the band progressed round the village playing at different houses and having refreshments.

There was a dinner in the club room at The Star pub for club members and men guests. In the afternoon everyone went to watch a cricket match and in the evening there was a fair with merry-go-rounds etc. which we were not allowed to go to!

On the Tuesday it was much the same, except a different band, and there were two banners for the Foresters Club. The cricket match was against a college servants side.'

BONFIRE NIGHT AND CHRISTMAS

'After school there would come a time to prepare for Guy Fawkes and no one was left out because over a period of time up to the very night of the bonfire, we collected dried leaves, which were dry and crispy and burned well. When the fire was lit we would put potatoes in their jackets to cook in the red hot cinders, also quite a few chestnuts. Our fireworks were not very elaborate like the ones of today, just Catherine wheels pinned to a piece of wood, which would go spinning round once they were lit, and some bangers which jumped around, but against the glow of the fire we all had sparklers in each hand and it was lovely to watch.

Christmas time we used to go round the village carol singing and it brings to mind the tale my grandfather told of a group of fellows who went carol singing at a house where an old chap lived. No one, not even children, were welcomed around his estate. However, they decided to try out a carol; when halfway through *Away in a manger* they rapped on the door. In answer to this the old fellow opened the bedroom window and called, "How many are there of you?" "Six," was the reply. He disappeared only to return with an old-fashioned chamber pot, known as the "gus-under" and shouted to them, "Well, share this among you and clear off!" With that there was a swoosh of "water" all over them!'

'It was the custom to have a huge bonfire on Guy Fawkes Night in the market place in the centre of Thame before the war. However, this was frowned upon by the local constabulary who tried to prevent the local lads from starting one – one year by hiding in the market house to keep watch, but of course they soon got locked in by the boys. At other times decoy fires were started in neighbouring streets.

The way they overcame building the fire without being detected was to "borrow" a farm cart and pile it with hay, straw and anything that would burn, then drag the cart towards the town centre and when the coast was clear, set fire to it and pull it to the market square where more materials were added. It was essential to keep any burnable items well locked up. However, one year, two local businessmen were watching the activity, shouting encouragement, and saying, "Come on boys, pile it on, keep it going", to which someone replied, "That's good of you, guv, it's your cart!" and when his business friend laughed, he was told, "And those are your wheelbarrows going on now!" (wooden wheelbarrows in those days of course). There were two rather irate gentlemen that night.'

'When Bonfire Night was approaching, most children at Studley would spend their spare time sweeping up leaves and twigs and drying them in a barn, at the farm, ready for the 5th. They would make a guy by stuffing old clothes with straw and, by putting a long pole through his arms, they could carry him around. The alternative method was to sit him in a box, fixed on to discarded pram wheels, and push him round the village. They would knock on doors and ask for a penny for the guy and recite the following –

> Please to remember
> The 5th of November
> The gunpowder, treason and plot,
> We see no reason
> Why gunpowder treason
> Should ever be forgot.'

'Christmas was a very exciting time. Looking back over 60 years to my childhood, the winters seemed much colder then with very sharp frosts. The ice on the ponds at Fritwell would be thick enough for us to slide and skate. In our stockings on Christmas morning would be an apple, tangerine, nuts, sugar mice and a shiny new penny plus a selection of books and toys. Christmas dinner with the goose, silver threepenny bits in the pudding, mince pies, boxes of dates and chocolate novelties – annual treats and how we enjoyed them.'

'As Christmas approached we children sat making paper chains, stuck with flour and water paste. I always thought the most exciting part of Christmas was finding threepenny pieces in the pudding, and lighting the wax candles on the Christmas tree in the dark. The holders never stayed upright and the wax dripped on the carpet.'

MUMMERS AND MORRIS DANCERS

Old traditions were kept alive by dedicated men and women, often holding the secrets of their dances and plays in their heads.

I WAS FRIGHTENED

'At Christmas the Mummers would come to our house in Thame to perform a play. I cannot remember what the story was (I think I was too frightened by these big men shouting and crashing about in our breakfast room), but I do remember they had blackened their faces and that they had fights with staves.'

BAMPTON MORRIS MEN

'Bampton has the longest unbroken celebration of the traditional Morris dancing in the country. A notable musician called Jinky Wells lived in a cottage in Lavendar Square. The renowned Cecil Sharpe came to Bampton and made recordings of his tunes. The dancing always takes place at Whitsun and villagers used to return home to their families during that weekend.'

'My great grandpa was known as Fiddler Butler and he used to run a dancing booth. My great uncle David Edgington was the Fool. At one time all the morris dancers came from the Tanner family. My father and Uncle Reg used to dance a broom dance and a sword dance. My uncles Victor, Will and John were all dancers and they rehearsed at the Elephant and Castle.'

THE ASCOTT DANCERS

'Mr Reginald Tiddy came to live in Ascott and had the Tiddy Hall built for morris and country dancing and all the young folk learned to dance. Mr Cecil Sharpe often came to Ascott collecting old folk songs and dances. My sister had a shilling for singing to him. He borrowed my grandfather's morris bells and William Kimber had them copied for morris teams.

Soon the Ascott dancers were in great demand at fetes and flower shows and we had many lovely times dancing at Bruern Abbey,

Abbotswood, Cornwell manor, Lower Slaughter manor, Shipton Court, Lee Place etc. The women made the dresses – the adults had dresses with a tight bodice and full skirt, white spotted muslin Dutch bonnets and fichus, their hair in long plaits with ribbons. The men had white flannels with coloured baldrics and bells on their legs. The girls wore coloured print dresses and matching sunbonnets and the boys had Holland smocks and red scarves with wide brimmed hats. Mr Furniss from Chestnut Close used to play the fiddle to accompany the morris dancing, although he was blind.'

THE UFFINGTON MUMMERS

'The Uffington mummers performed at fetes and private houses, traditionally on Boxing Day. They enacted life and death. One of the old mummers, when asked to reveal the words of the play, said, " 'Tis in me 'ead and when I dies it goes with I!" '

THE BAMPTON MUMMERS PLAY

'The Bampton mummers performed on Christmas Eve, acting out their play in the large houses early in the evening and ending up

The Bampton mummers are a traditional part of Christmas celebrations.

in the pubs. The stories told were all passed on from generation to generation by word of mouth but I wrote the play down verbatim from Mr Hunt and the first verses of it are given below.

When the Bampton mummers went to dance in Witney they always blacked their faces so they would not be recognised.

In, first of all, came Father Christmas:

In comes I old Father Christmas, welcome, or welcome not.
I hope that Father Christmas will never be forgot.

There's time for work, there's time for play,
Time to be melancholy and for to be gay.
A time to be thrifty, a time to be free,
And sure enough this Christmas we all shall jovial be.

This is the time that Christ is come that we might happy be
So listen all ye gentiles to hear what we shall say.
St George, the Doctor and the Turk are here together tonight,
The Doctor has his physics and the Knights have their sword
    sharp set.

One will kill the other and the Doctor shall raise him up.
Now all we shall happy be with each his Christmas cup.
And Robin Hood and Little John will pass the beer around,
For two nobler chaps on earth there never yet were found.

So ladies and gentlemen, I pray you give good cheer
To Father Christmas, he comes but once a year.'

Index

254

255